OPERATION RALEIGH

Adventure Challenge

By John Blashford-Snell

The Expedition Organiser's Guide
Where the Trails Run Out
In the Steps of Stanley
A Taste for Adventure
In the Wake of Drake
Operation Drake
Mysteries: Encounters with the Unexplained
Operation Raleigh: The Start of an Adventure

Co-authored by Ann Tweedy and John Man
Gold-Dive

OPERATION RALEIGH

Adventure Challenge

John Blashford-Snell and Ann Tweedy

HarperPaperbacks
A Division of HarperCollinsPublishers

HarperPaperbacks *A Division of* HarperCollins*Publishers*
10 East 53rd Street, New York, N.Y. 10022

This book was originally published in 1988 in
Great Britain by William Collins Sons & Co. Ltd.

HarperPaperbacks edition: November 1990

Printed in the United States of America

HarperPaperbacks and colophon are trademarks of
HarperCollins*Publishers*

10 9 8 7 6 5 4 3 2 1

This book is dedicated to
His Royal Highness
THE PRINCE OF WALES KG KT GCB
Patron of Operation Raleigh, whose support has
enabled so many to share these adventures

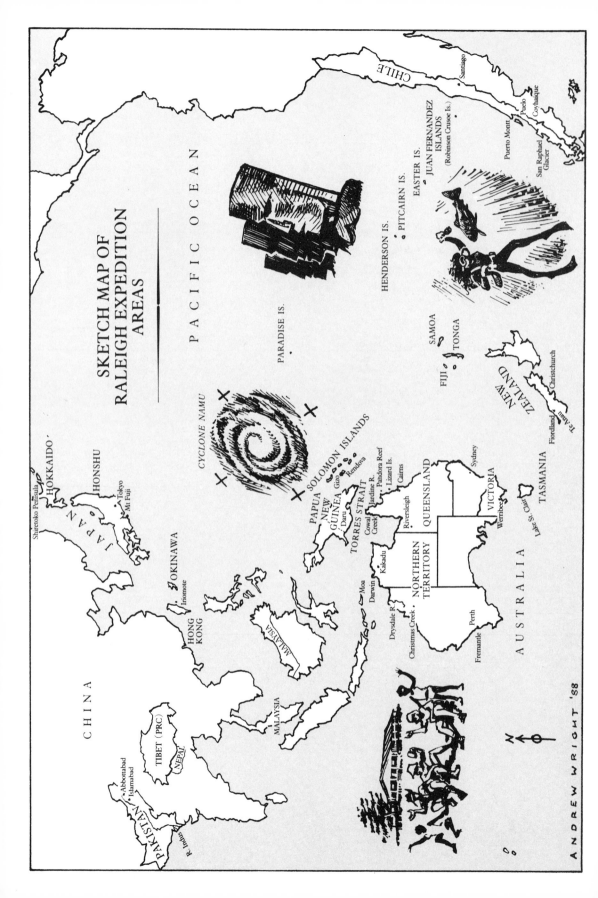

SKETCH MAP OF
RALEIGH EXPEDITION
AREAS

PACIFIC OCEAN

CHINA

PAKISTAN

Abbottabad
Islamabad
R. Indus

TIBET (PRC)
NEPAL

HONG KONG

MALAYSIA

MALAYSIA

JAPAN

HOKKAIDO
Shiretoko Peninsula
HONSHU
Tokyo
Mt Fuji
OKINAWA
Iriomote

PAPUA NEW GUINEA
Daru

SOLOMON ISLANDS
Gizo
Rendova

CYCLONE NAMU

PARADISE IS.

HENDERSON IS.
PITCAIRN IS.
EASTER IS.
JUAN FERNANDEZ ISLANDS
(Robinson Crusoe Is.)

CHILE
Santiago

Puerto Montt
Puelo
Coyhaique
San Raphael Glacier

SAMOA
FIJI
TONGA

NEW ZEALAND
Fiordland
Te Anau
Christchurch

TORRES STRAIT
Cowal Creek
Jardine R.
Pandora Reef
Lizard Is.
Cairns
Moa
Darwin
Kakadu
Drysdale R.
Christmas Creek
Riversleigh

NORTHERN TERRITORY

QUEENSLAND

Sydney

VICTORIA
Werribee

AUSTRALIA

Perth
Fremantle

TASMANIA
Lake St. Clair

ANDREW WRIGHT '88

CONTENTS

ILLUSTRATIONS

Key to photographers: JBS = John Blashford-Snell; CS = Chris Sainsbury

ACKNOWLEDGEMENTS

We must record special indebtedness to various members of Operation Raleigh's team of organizers for their continuing work on our behalf.

Dr Robert Muir-Wood, a leading scientist who had been with us in Chile, kindly agreed to head the scientific research programme. Lectures and talks arranged by Dabber and Paddy Davies of Associated Speakers, and by Barbara Snell, were extremely helpful. Michael and Phyllis Angliss continue to liaise with Rotary on our behalf.

John Rayman and Ron Murrell have looked after our legal matters whilst the support of Ernst and Whinney, our honorary accountants, has been of immense value. Nor must we forget the hard work of Peat Marwick McLintock, our honorary auditors. There were literally hundreds of others who helped, many of whom joined our permanent team. The cry was always money, money, money and we were most fortunate to have the backing of a number of government ministers and the Manpower Services Commission. The Foreign and Commonwealth Office could not have been more helpful. We are especially grateful for the support of the Pentagon.

In writing this book, we have relied considerably on the work of Central Headquarters and the expeditions. We are especially grateful to Major Greg Melick, WO I Neil Hampson, Mary Corbett, Peta Lock, Chris Sainsbury and Laurie Karnath and to the dozens of Operation Raleigh organizers and Venturers who sent in contributions, some of which have been used; we hope to use others in follow-up books. Jennifer Watts, our skilful procurement lady, is another whose contribution to Operation Raleigh has been enormous. But the work in CHQ seemed to go on non-stop.

The photographs have been taken by many who risked themselves and their equipment on the expeditions, none more so than Chris Sainsbury. The selection of the photos has been made much easier thanks to the efforts of Operation Raleigh Promotions. Andrew Wright, the talented young artist who accompanied us for the first six months, has drawn the map. Without the help of Sally McGowan-Scanlon, Nadia Brydon, Claudia Lake and Sue Holmes in London, it would have been extremely difficult to amass all the material. In New York, Kathy Williamson transcribed tapes sent by Ann Tweedy from all parts of the world and we are also indebted to June Hall, Operation Raleigh's agent, and her staff for all their sound advice and encouragement. Our thanks also go to John Wall for his kind help in so many ways, from the beginning.

This book is not just the story of the Venturers who came with us on Operation Raleigh, it is a tribute to all those who applied, many tens of thousands, who found the selection process itself challenging. It can only tell part of the tale, but it may encourage many more to follow those who have already sailed on the ships, and gone into the deserts, jungles, mountains and swamps, as Sir Walter Raleigh's colonists did when they went to the New World four hundred years ago.

JOHN BLASHFORD-SNELL
ANN TWEEDY

Harthill Castle, Scotland
January 1988

INTRODUCTION

Blood poured from the deep cut beneath Andy's eye. Fixing a rope to a tree, his axe had rebounded off the log and struck his cheek. 'Get me the medical kit,' Jim ordered. 'Andy, hold this on your eye. I'll stitch it when we get out.'

Peering through the dark forest, twenty-three-year-old British Venturer Sally Armitage wondered once again if they ever *would* get out. Sally was part of the Operation Raleigh expedition in Chilean Patagonia at the end of 1987. For two weeks the eleven young people had sought the rare Huemule deer in southern Chile. The weather had been appalling, with drenching rain and bitter cold.

Eventually they reached an almost impenetrable bamboo forest. The rhythmic sound of their machetes against the curtain of green surrounding them drowned the forest noises. As they battled on, the awful but unspoken thought that they might not get out alive was shared by all. The rations were nearly finished and they were too weak to retrace their steps. Finally, the exhausted Venturers decided that their only recourse was to call for rescue and they radioed an SOS to expedition leader, Major Tony Walton.

Sally's diary records their dramatic escape by helicopter.

> Unless we could cut a landing zone in the thick growth, we were trapped. But hearing the chopper overhead, we knew help was at hand. Terry Egan, the tall American Air Force colonel, and Jim Goodwill, our USAF medic, made a daring jump from the helicopter as it hovered 7 metres above the bamboo. They were our last hope, our link with the outside.

On the fifteenth day of their nightmare, the Chilean Carabineros helicopter pulled the Venturers to safety as Sally recalls:

> I am kneeling on the chopper floor, holding on for dear life to a hand

strap; the side door is wide open. The pilot signals that I should grasp the back of his seat. At last we are getting out. My soul lifts as I look down to the land we had tried to cross on foot. Thick, dense bamboo, dark Tolkien-like forest, and the eerie mist. We are escaping nature's grip in a man-made machine. Her force was too strong, her grip too tight, our attempts to fight her futile. This place was the edge of hell, the forces were evil, the scenery hostile; we would never have got out on foot.

It had all started with the founding of The Scientific Exploration Society (SES) in 1969 when I was an Adventure Training Officer at the Royal Military Academy, Sandhurst. The British Army is fortunate in having a unique Adventure Training Scheme which allows soldiers to take part in challenging, worthwhile expeditions while on duty, and it was my job to encourage officer cadets to do this for the betterment of their characters and, it was hoped, to the least possible detriment of Britain's international relations.

As the expeditions became more complex and far-reaching, the administrative headaches increased. So we set up The Scientific Exploration Society, a permanent organization, outside the Army and with charitable status, through which expeditions could be planned, equipped and financed.

The SES became an international body of servicemen, scientists and explorers, with members all over the world. We have always laid special emphasis on including young people in our projects, and, in 1978, with the considerable backing of His Royal Highness, The Prince of Wales, and the generous support of Mr Walter Annenberg, former US Ambassador to Britain, we launched Operation Drake.

The venture was the most ambitious and imaginative expedition for young people ever mounted. Its launch also marked the 400th anniversary of Sir Francis Drake's circumnavigation of the globe. Its aims were to combine the thrill of adventure with serious scientific research and community-aided projects. Almost 60,000 young people applied to be part of this unique challange, but only 414 could be chosen.

In November 1979 Tactical Headquarters (Tac HQ), which controlled the expedition, was based in Papua New Guinea. The rain had stopped but the heavy night air was no cooler. As I walked up the steps of our wooden office, the radio operator was scribbling messages as they crackled through from England. He looked up as I entered: 'George Thurston's on; says he'd like to speak to you.'

George was our Director of Administration. Slipping on the earphones, I heard his distant voice. Never a man to waste words, he came straight to the point.

'I had breakfast with our Patron this morning.'

'Good Lord,' I said, 'Have we done something terrible?'

'Far from it. The Prince is rather pleased with progress and thinks we should do it all again – on a bigger scale.'

I took a deep breath and sat down. Later that night, sitting on the verandah with my old schoolfriend, Nigel Porteous, I told him of the message. Pouring me a scotch, he said: 'Well, you'll need a bigger, faster ship.' I listened intently while Nigel, a master mariner, put forward his ideas for a larger scale operation with a motor vessel as its flagship.

Drake, Sir Walter Raleigh's cousin, had been a fiercely nationalistic privateeer. Raleigh was more of an internationalist, trying to settle a society in a New World and build something lasting. It was felt that the new expedition should be named after him and that it should set out in 1984 on the 400th anniversary of the founding of English-speaking America in what is now North Carolina. Prince Charles liked the name, so Operation Raleigh it was, and with the Prince as Patron, the new and greater machine ground into action.

Our aim was, quite simply, to develop leadership potential in young people through the medium of expeditions in the hope that they would return home to give service to others. Having witnessed the inner city riots in Britain in 1982, it was clear that young leaders had a far better chance of communicating with the underprivileged than older counsellors – or police.

Each Venturer, as the youngsters came to be called, would spend approximately three months in the field. Weather charts dictated that we should 'go west' and an invitation from Jack Hayward (now Sir Jack Hayward) to visit the Bahamas for our first expedition proved irresistible. To begin with we would go to America, to the site where Raleigh's colonists had landed, then south to the Caribbean, Central and South America and across the Pacific to Australasia.

The scientists were fascinated by what Indonesia had to offer and we also wanted to break new ground in Japan and Tibet. There were interesting possibilities in Pakistan and, from my own experiences in Oman, I knew there would be worthwhile tasks in its challenging desert. Africa, of course, could not be missed from the route of any worldwide expedition, and after that we planned to spend time in South America before returning to Britain in 1988 via the wastes of Arctic Canada.

Before we could do anything we needed some hefty finance. Once again our good friend Walter Annenberg stepped into the breach and provided the necessary seed money. The generous help of the Sasakawa (Great Britain) Foundation was also enormously appreciated, as was the personal help of Captain Robert Maxwell. It did much to enhance Anglo-Japanese relations and goodwill. The next essentials were a dedicated, hard-working staff, who would not expect much remuneration, and a team of experts to advise us on the setting-up of the international venture. Thanks to the generosity of IBM, a giant computer was installed in London to programme finance, logistics and Venturer selection.

Our greatest task was to set up recruiting systems to select the Venturers. Throughout the world the same criteria applied: we wanted young people who were fit, compatible, spoke English and could swim 450 metres. They also needed to have a spark of leadership and a willingness to place service before self.

We planned to select 4000 Venturers worldwide. There was always the danger that Raleigh might become an expedition for the elite, an inevitable criticism. Our selection procedure in Britain, however, was designed to help the underprivileged who had had no previous opportunities to reach their potential. The selection process included an interview and, for the finalists, a weekend in a wilderness area when they were put through their paces under adverse conditions. The young people had to raise at least some of the funds themselves and a large number of companies, as varied as British Rail and Nabisco, sent employees.

Getting the word across in Britain began with a special television programme made by TV South, in which Prince Charles interviewed three ex-Young Explorers from Operation Drake. His Royal Highness called for other young people to apply to Raleigh. Candidates were advised to apply to any branch of the Trustee Savings Bank, the only bank with branches in every part of the United Kingdom. TSB's enthusiastic support and help has been a major factor in the success of the operation.

Applications poured in and the selection process went into full swing. Eager youngsters faced giant pythons in darkened rooms, handled hairy tarantulas and were made wet, cold, hungry, frightened and furious in quick succession so that we could discover just how compatible they were.

Two vessels were acquired to support the enterprise. Our search for a sailing ship had ended with the discovery of the brigantine *Zebu*. She had begun life in a small, busy Swedish shipyard in 1938 and spent the next thirty-five years carrying cargoes of timber, salt and grain across the Baltic. During the Second World War she smuggled arms for the resistance movement and refugees. In 1980 she competed in the Tall Ships Race, but later that year foundered in a severe storm in the Channel Islands. A young couple, Nick and Jane Broughton, bought her and *Zebu*'s new life began.

We found the second ship, MV *British Viking*, in Hull. A 1900-tonne former factory ship, built in West Germany in 1965, she had been converted into a North Sea oil exploration vessel, equipped with submersibles. She still retained the distinctive features of a stern trawler and the massive A-frame across her after-deck, originally used to haul nets up a sloping stern ramp, could lift mini-subs. She had a cavernous hold that would be well suited for carrying expedition supplies and the former submarine base in the hangar could be converted to house landing craft.

The ship's 3000-B.H.P. diesel engine, driving a single, variable-pitch propeller, would give her the required speed, and she was able to hold fuel for 18,000 nautical miles. Her accommodation could carry up to seventy-three crew, HQ staff, scientists and Venturers, and there would be plenty of space for scientific laboratories, computer rooms and all the complex radio equipment we would need.

British Viking was owned by J. Marr & Sons of Hull and it was Hull City Council and the Department of the Environment who donated her to our expedition. Her new name became *Sir Walter Raleigh*, or *SWR* for short. Many companies offered to help equip the new ship and the refit committee in Hull, under the energetic guidance of its chairman, Councillor Jim Mulgrove, and county co-ordinator David Hopkins, did everything possible to keep up local interest. The people of Hull had taken the ship to their hearts, and Alan Marr, chairman of J. Marr & Sons, did much to help.

Merseyside County Council generously provided two water, jet-propelled landing craft and the Avon Rubber Company gave us the very latest of their Searider inshore rescue craft. Robert Glen of E. P. Barrus, a long-time supporter, persuaded Mariner Outboards to become Operation Raleigh's exclusive suppliers. Rover sent us the latest in their line of Land Rover safari wagons, and Gerald Ronson made us a splendid gift of Suzuki jeeps and motorcycles. Aboard the ship was a large diving centre, but we still needed a recompression chamber and this was generously loaned to us by Ric Farrington Wharton in Aberdeen.

There was more. Our marine biologists needed a wet lab, and since the land expeditions would bring back specimens of fauna and flora, there had to be a dry lab and a microbiological lab as well. There was also a vital need for a darkroom, a workshop and computers. Acorn Computers, British Aerospace, Gallenkamp and Pattersons all helped us to fill these requirements.

While *Sir Walter Raleigh* was being equipped in Britain, our international committees were having difficulties of their own. As the United States committee had been allocated 40 per cent of the Venturers, I paid particular attention to their problems. The determination and persistence of Ann Smith and Mark Bensen in North Carolina managed to hold Operation Raleigh USA together, and around the globe marvellous friends gave up their time to help.

On the operational front we were desperately short of qualified staff. Encouraged by The Prince of Wales, the US Defense Secretary, Caspar Weinberger, agreed to assist by allowing members of the American armed forces to take part. The Australian, New Zealand, Panamanian and Portuguese followed suit. In January 1984 the Prime Minister, The Rt Hon. Margaret Thatcher, was our guest of honour at a luncheon organized by our commercial director, David King. Mrs Thatcher became a keen supporter.

As with any non-profit-making organization, fund-raising was vital to our success. David King and his friends in the City were striving to raise as much sponsorship as possible. The Venturers themselves would fund the expedition. We calculated that if 4000 young people brought in $5000 each, the expedition would have $20 m. to spend over four years. Top of our list of priorities was to cut the cost of running the flagship. Here, we were greatly assisted by Occidental Oil and by Burmah Castrol, who generously donated £110,000-worth of lubricating oil.

By September 1984 we were nearly ready. Our chairman, General Sir John Mogg, decided to hand over to a sailor, Vice-Admiral Sir Gerard Mansfield, formerly Deputy Supreme Allied Commander, Atlantic. The Vice-Admiral took over in time for the flagship's commissioning on 4 September. It was a marvellous day. Her Royal Highness Princess Alexandra won everyone's hearts when she commissioned the ship in bright sunshine. Although we only discovered it at the last minute, our royal guest had a special interest in Raleigh; her daughter, Marina, had applied as a Venturer, passed the selection tests and would join us later in Honduras.

On 11 October 1984 *Zebu* was ready. The lovely ship sailed from Tower Pier, London with arch sea-Goon, Sir Harry Secombe, at the helm for a few minutes. Aboard were sixteen Venturers and nine professional crew under the watchful eye of Captain Peter Masters. 'America next stop,' cried Sir Harry as her square sails filled and she left for the open sea and four years of adventure.

Meanwhile in Hull, field director Charlie Daniel and his assistant, Cathy Davies, were driving their teams to work round the clock to have *Sir Walter Raleigh* ready for the royal departure on 13 November.

By dawn of that great day, miracles had been achieved and the master, Captain Mike Kichenside, who had taken *Eye of the Wind* around the world on Operation Drake, seemed well pleased. The Prince gave us a wonderful send-off and, to the cheers of a large crowd, *Sir Walter Raleigh* sailed for New York by way of the Channel Islands where Adrian Troy and his committee greeted us in my home island of Jersey. Next day Mike Duquemin and his team welcomed us in Guernsey.

The first book of the expedition, *Operation Raleigh: The Start of an Adventure* describes the events of 1984 and 1985. Supported by our ships, we carried out twenty-four exciting expeditions in the Bahamas, the

Turks and Caicos Islands, Costa Rica, Belize, Honduras, Panama, Bolivia, Peru, Chile and Hawaii. Some 940 Venturers from many lands and 390 staff, took part. On New Year's Day 1986, *Zebu* was in Australian waters and a new expedition was forming in southern Chile, where *Sir Walter Raleigh*, having served us so well for fourteen months, was refitting.

While we were winning the battle at the front, we urgently needed support at home if we were to remain solvent. I decided to return to London with Charlie Daniel to join the overstretched CHQ staff. Roger Chapman, our hard-working director of plans in Britain, deserved a change of air and with his considerable expedition experience, would run TAC HQ aboard the flagship in Chile during my absence. I hated leaving the field and little did I realize the battles, both political and financial, that I would have to fight to keep the show on the road.

This book is the story of Raleigh from January 1986 to October 1987. Two major expeditions in the field at that time, the second of the projects in the Torres Strait and the Indonesia expedition, will be included in the next volume. Meanwhile, many thousands of hopeful young people were undergoing the arduous selection tests to fit them for the steaming jungle or the freezing fiords of southern Chile.

CHAPTER ONE

Patagonian Pathways

(*Chile Leader:* Major Mike Reynolds, RE)

The Cave of Hands, Southern Chile, 22 March 1986

The laser-like rays of the early sun struck the peak of El Colmillo, turning its serrated edges blood red; then the beam of light penetrated the mouth of the cave, searching out its deepest recesses. On the walls of the cave the paintings of Puma, Guanaco and Nandu seemed to dance in the sunlight and the hundreds of human hands, which give the cave its name, looked as fresh as when they were painted thousands of years ago.

The paintings are the work of the early hunters who migrated across the featureless plains of southern Chile 8000 years ago. The people called themselves the Aonikenk; it was Ferdinand Magellan, the sixteenth-century Portuguese explorer, who named the tall people the Patagones, or 'Big Feet'. For them, the cave was sacred, made more so by the strange phenomenon during the spring and autumn equinox, on 22 March and September, when the sun pierces the cave entrance like a beacon.

Today, at the dawn of the spring equinox, the Venturers waited for the miracle to happen. As the first rays of sun made the paintings live again, the young people shared the timeless mystery with the spirits of the Patagones.

For several weeks, the Raleigh team from Malaysia, Hong Kong, Singapore, Canada, the USA, New Zealand, Australia and Britain had lived in the cave and their camp nearby. Theirs was a daunting task; to build a full-scale fibreglass replica of the prehistoric art gallery, under the guidance of Patagonian-born Harold Krusell, a museologist from the Santiago Natural History Museum. Although few people, other than the shepherds seeking shelter, knew of the cave's location deep in the Andes, the wonderful paintings were gradually being destroyed by sheep rubbing their greasy wool against the lower figures and by present-day graffiti. Once complete, the replica would be carried down the mountain, again by Raleigh Venturers, and exhibited at the museum.

First, however, the materials had to be carried up to the cave. A steep track led up from the base camp on the banks of the Rio Pedregoso. Covered with thorn bushes lying in ambush for the unwary climber, the path zig-zagged up dangerous scree slopes and along volcanic cliffs. Most of the chemicals, fibreglass matting, plaster, sand and cement were carried up by the Venturers on their backs. The heavier loads were brought up by packhorse.

The youngsters shared the cave with more than the ghosts of the Patagonians; as night fell it came alive with rats. With every passing day the sharp-toothed rodents became bolder. They gnawed their way through socks and sleeping bags, scrambling fearlessly over sleeping Venturers. Journals that had been painstakingly kept up to date and protected from rain and turbulent river crossings became their favourite midnight snack.

Although the days were hot, the nights grew increasingly chilly as winter descended on the southern hemisphere. A native of this corner of Chile so near the Argentinian border, Harold Krusell knew that once the spring snows arrived, it would be far more difficult to transport the cave replica down the steep mountain. The weather window could not last. Working against time, the Venturers at the Cave of Hands were spurred on by a new sense of urgency.

Large supplies of expensive silicone rubber had been donated by the West German company, Wacker Chemie GmbH. The cave designs were traced onto the rubber by Ivan Munoz, Harold's assistant, and by Intan Jailani, a Malaysian Venturer and graphic designer. Spattered from head to foot with dust and resin, the Venturers applied the silicone to the cave surface and then covered it with fibreglass matting soaked in plaster. Ice-white, the plaster turned the cave into a fairytale setting.

As the temperature dropped, the ice became real. The butts of water used to mix the plaster froze during the night and had to be melted over a fire. One day the team woke to a blizzard that turned the countryside into a lunar landscape.

They finished just in time. A second group of Venturers arrived to carry down the painted moulds. Racing along the mountain path with the curved fibreglass shells on their backs, the wind lifted the young porters off the ground. They made a stange sight – two-legged tortoises that had taken up hang-gliding. Harold Krusell watched the timeless treasures flying past. The Venturers made three round trips a day, and Tim Murray, one of the fittest, whittled down the usual hour-and-a-half run to the cave to a record thirty-eight minutes. 'Please don't drop the moulds!' the museum deputy director begged. 'They're so valuable.'

Indeed they are, and the replica of the Cave of Hands can be seen today in the museum in Santiago. Although electric light and not the morning sun illuminates the figures, the hands of the early artists and the bounding animals they drew have been preserved for another 8000 years.

Directly west of Argentina to the south of Peru – and south of just about everything else as well – Chile hosted four Raleigh expeditions in 1985 and 1986. Her jungles and snowcapped volcanoes, glaciers, deserts and vast Patagonian plains yielded a wealth of challenges. In 1986 the different phases of the expeditions in Chile were ably led first by Major Mark Bentinck, a former Royal Marine, and later by Major Mike Reynolds, a fellow Royal Engineer.

Their efforts were backed up by Pablo Calderon, the popular Chilean liaison officer, with Roger Chapman as field executive director. An old friend and superb organizer, Roger's home for the last few months had been on *Sir Walter Raleigh* as she refitted for the Pacific crossing. Nearly ready, and eager to be off, she strained against her anchors in the blue waters of Puerto Montt.

Roger and ship's captain, Mike Kichenside, had the massive job of readying our flagship for the crossing. They were lucky in their crew: Second Officer John Pearn, Quartermaster Cathy Davies, Purser Adrian Turner, radio wizard Nick Perrott, Chief Engineer John Manley-Tucker and US Navy Lieutenant Ceil Mckinney among many others. As Chilean customs held up essential engine parts and the barnacle colony on the ship's hull seemed to multiply despite daily scraping by diver Eric Primeau, flagging morale was lifted by the exceptional dinners provided by the Chilean chef Luigi Toro and pint-sized but big-hearted 'Cokie'.

Among the new members of the crew gathering in Puerto Montt to take part in the Pacific crossing were a great bunch of lads from the Shell oil company fleet. They included twenty-three-year-old Neil Carmichael from the Isle of Lewis in Scotland. Six months later, off Australia's Great Barrier Reef, it was with a heavy heart that I read his memorial service; on night watch aboard ship, Neil had fallen overboard. His body was never recovered.

But now, as they worked in the sunshine of southern Chile, the crew had no premonition of the tragedy to come. *Sir Walter Raleigh* supplied the expeditions with their tools, tents and rations, and welcomed the Venturers on their return from the field. No matter how well stocked she kept the hold, however, even Cathy Davies couldn't rustle up saddles and packhorses on demand. And that was just what New Zealand Venturer Julie Hale wanted.

When Julie and three companions decided to end their expedition with a 70-kilometre horseback ride, they found more adventure than they had bargained for. The mini-expedition had made a rendezvous with the rest of their group for two days' time, but Julie soon began to wonder if they would ever leave the mountains alive. The horses bolted, dumping ration packs in the mud, and within hours the little band was lost in the Andes. As Julie recounted in her diary:

> The first night, we found reasonable shelter from the rain. Although there was no grazing for the horses, it was the last possible spot before the mountain pass. Dehydrated macaroni was on the menu that night; little did we know it would be our last meal for two days.

The next day dawned cold and wet.

> Countless times we lost our way. When we finally found a track, we doubted it was the right one. The rain fell all day and into the night – we had little sleep in our 'waterproof' sleeping bags. We still couldn't make radio contact and we were now completely lost. My thoughts frequently wandered to another expedition rowing to the glacier of San Rafael. We couldn't be much worse off than they, I reckoned. It had rained for most of the three weeks they had spent in the open sea, and I knew they must be constantly wet, cold and hungry.

26

Suddenly, whoever was directing Julie's Chilean Western, brought in the hero. A horse and rider appeared through the mist. Dressed in a long woollen cape, he could have stepped straight out of a movie script. Without a word, the handsome gaucho wheeled his horse and led the sodden group to the mountain track they had despaired of ever finding.

It was not the first time that Raleigh's plans had gone awry when four-footed transport was required. Nor was it the last. In April another expedition had spent a month on horseback in Coihaique, a region in Chile's far south.

'We were asked to discover whether a road could be built through the mountains to the isolated village of Villa Castillo,' explains Brette Jones, a New Yorker. 'There was no track through the mountains and the route was slick with mud and snow: the horses had to lock their front legs together and slide down on their haunches. We woke one morning to 15 centimetres of snow. The thermometer was 4°C. The snow wasn't easy to ride through, but it made a nice change from the freezing rain.'

Headed by Sergeant Len Whitten, US Air Force, the Castillo group was an international mix of Malaysian, Chilean, British and American youngsters. 'Most of us took several tumbles,' said Venturer Gonzalo Vallouta, ruefully rubbing his backside as he recalled the trip. 'Only a few of us had ever ridden before, but in a week's time we were jumping 1–2-metre logs. We had to; there was no way around.'

San Rafael glacier, 9 January 1986

The group of Venturers that had kept Julie going in spirit had survived their rainy ordeal, but the 300-nautical-mile voyage had tested them to their limits. Twenty-nine Venturers and six staff had set sail in open boats from the tiny fishing village of Melinka. Their guides were local fishermen; their destination, the frozen lake of San Rafael.

It was to be a month of incessant rain and bad weather, high seas and freezing winds. As they edged into the mouth of the Fiordo Elefantes they encountered drifting ice. At first the floes were small, merely the tips of the icebergs to come. Finally the five small boats emerged from the narrow channel into a wide expanse of sea. For a moment, everyone stopped rowing. Ahead lay massive islands of floating ice, each lit by a soft blue light.

'It was as if some ageless light had long ago been imprisoned there,' wrote archaeologist Rowland Reeve. Later that day, the Venturers caught their first glimpse of the San Rafael glacier; they were nearly at the end of their voyage. Suddenly a sharp 'Crack!' like artillery fire rent the stillness. A slab of ice the size of a building dropped from the face of the glacier and disappeared beneath the sea. Seconds later it burst through the waters like a breaching whale, lifting the small boats high into the air and pushing them away from the shore.

The exhausted voyagers needed their last ounce of energy to reach their destination; now they could see the beach and the jetty, built by other Venturers. The shore teemed with tiny figures, their shouts of welcome transformed into the merest whisper as they drifted across the water.

The boating skills the Venturers had learned *en route* proved useful later during the science programme conceived by Dr John Pethick. The project set out to investigate the environmental change that had taken place in the area over the last 10,000 years. Under the stewardship of Eibleis Fanning, Raleigh's Scientific Coordinator, scientists and Venturers explored the remote waterways of this desolate region, logging tidal cycles, glacial discharge and currents. Another of the science projects, under Dr Robert Muir-Wood, was to study the history of earthquakes in the area. Its findings have important implications for a heavily populated part of North America which has tectonic similarities.

At nineteen, Joe Lane was an accomplished thief. He was also tired of living. When the police caught him breaking into a store in Alberta, Canada, he didn't run away. Instead he ran towards them, swinging a machete.

'I just didn't care. I was ready to die,' recalls Joe.

The emergency task force was called in. Overwhelmed by tear gas, Joe collapsed and woke up to find himself in jail.

'Joe,' said the guard at the jail, 'there is a God. If you had died, you'd have found that out.'

That was four years ago. 'I did find that out,' says Joe. He also read an article in the *Toronto Sun* and walked brazenly into the publisher's office. 'Hi. I'm Joe Lane, I'm from Toronto, I'm an ex-con and I want you to sponsor me to join Operation Raleigh in Chile.'

Only Joe was not surprised when the newspaper did just that.

On 3 March, Joe boarded a plane for Santiago. He was a strong, good-looking young man, with a bit of a chip on his shoulder. It wouldn't stay there long. Working as a labourer had built up his muscles and toughened him physically, but it was Joe's eyes one noticed first. Beneath thick lashes, his right eye was deep brown and his left eye the colour of slate.

From Santiago, Joe and the other Venturers travelled twenty-four hours south to Coihaique. There, Joe became part of a gang unlike any he had come across before: 'Babyface Mitchell's Gang'. Under the leadership of bearded Steve Mitchell, the expedition became known as the 'Manihuales Patrol'. The plan they hatched was to traverse the extensive river system from Lago Roosevelt to Puerto Cisnes, fishing for dinner in crystal-clear waters and swimming in meltwater streams. Next, they would attempt the 2225-metre mountain, Volcan Cay, and spend a week at the massive Quelat glacier with its subterranean hot springs.

Like most plans, it worked in part. Before they set off, survival expert Jim Bozeman gave the 'gang' a lecture on cold-weather hazards and hypothermia, and Pablo Calderon helped bridge the culture gap with a briefing on the customs of Chile. Four packhorses and two cart-pulling bullocks transported most of the rations and heavy gear to where the river deepened enough to launch the three inflatables. They were off.

Leeches, rapids and swimming the horses across the river – Joe Lane's speciality – became familiar, but hardly routine. Chilean guides Jorge and Lulo were some of the best rivermen in the country. Good enough to show off a bit sometimes – and get away with it – as the Venturers soon learned.

'The first stretch of white water was over very quickly,' remembers Adrian Mumby, a UK Venturer. 'The rapids were easier than I had anticipated. Now comes a U-turn to the portage site for another load, I thought. The engine revved and Jorge's hand twisted further and further to the right. The boat was heading back up the rapids! We hit the rapids at what seemed like full speed and took off like the Varig 747 that had brought us to Chile. I shut my eyes and waited to start swimming, but amazingly enough that cold feeling never came. We were back up the river for a second load, and that next trip felt like a Sunday afternoon stroll.'

Maillen Island, southern Chile, 22 April 1986

Lumbering oxen dragged the beams along the beach to the blue-and-yellow church. The pace was slow enough for the Venturers guiding the oxen to pocket handfuls of shellfish for supper. From the small boat anchored off the island, building tools and bags of cement were lowered to others standing waist deep in water. All the materials needed to build the bridge for Maillen Island, together with food and equipment for three weeks, had to be offloaded before the ebbing tide stranded the supply boat.

Crossing and recrossing the beach of shell and seaweed with their loads, the workers sized up the job ahead: clearing a wide stretch of bamboo, gorse and mud, and building an 18-metre bridge over the tidal marsh to the gaily coloured church. The bridge was one of several that Raleigh had been asked to construct. We seem to be spanning most of Chile, thought Mike Reynolds, who, as a Royal Engineer, was the perfect choice for expedition leader.

Indeed, Raleigh did seem to be leaving a legacy of bridges and buildings in southern Chile. As the group on Maillen Island lugged their materials up the beach, bridges were going up on two other sites, Chinquihue Alto and Posta Panitao, while piles for a jetty were being driven into a lake deep in the Alerce jungle. At the village of Puelo, accessible only by boat, Venturers were moving an entire school from its frequently flooded site, while another school was extended at the fishing village of La Arena.

At Maillen Island curious children came down to the shore to watch the international team at work. Seeing them gave expedition doctor, Tan Chi Chiu from Singapore, an idea. There was no doctor on the island and visits from anyone with medical knowledge were rare. Why not start a free clinic while we're here? he thought.

30

A few days after the new clinic opened its doors, twenty-six-year-old Chi recorded his first patients.

1. Village chief
2. Seventy-eight-year-old lady who sells cheese
3. Fifty-seven-year-old lady living near the football field
4. Various cases of migraine, tonsillitis and angina

News of Dr Chi and his clinic spread rapidly through the small island community. Soon the expanded practice requisitioned an old bamboo desk for a medical cabinet while the shed holding the hand tools and chainsaws for the bridge construction became a waiting room for the steady stream of patients.

On board *Sir Walter Raleigh* Roger Chapman and Mike Kichenside held daily meetings, Morning Prayers we called them, to keep the crew informed of current projects and the plans for the Pacific crossing. The cast of characters for the crossing was nearly complete. Scientists, radio operators and crew from all over the world had assembled at Puerto Montt. David King and Tony Walton, who, with Captain Mike Kichenside, would head the long expedition, gradually scored lines through the long list of jobs that had to be done.

In the field work was also drawing to a close. The construction projects completed, the Venturers returned to Puerto Montt with many a blackened thumbnail. Soon the ship echoed with the exuberant shouts of a new group of young men and women who would cross 7500 nautical miles of often stormy seas and visit a dozen islands. Together they would explore the mysteries of Easter Island and study the rare nautilus in the deep waters of Polynesia.

CHAPTER TWO

Pacific Overtures

(*Pacific Crossing Leader:* P. David King)

Robinson Crusoe Island, 25 May 1986

The Life and Strange and Surprising Adventures of Robinson Crusoe, the famous eighteenth-century novel by Daniel Defoe, was inspired by the true adventures of Alexander Selkirk of Lower Largo, Scotland. As they sailed through the Juan Fernandez group of islands, a quarrel arose between Selkirk and his captain and the strong-minded Scot was promptly put ashore on the nearest island. There he lived for four years and four months, aided by Friday, whom he had saved from the island cannibals. His story has since captured the imagination of millions.

The story was of special interest to *Sir Walter Raleigh*'s ship's officer, David Taylor, one of the members of the Shell tanker crew on the expedition. Having lived near Selkirk's birthplace and heard his story so often, David was keen to see the famous island. In fact, the Scottish sailing master has two Pacific islands to his credit, one named after him and one after his fictional double. Raleigh would visit both, but our first port of call after Chile was Robinson Crusoe.

The Raleigh group chose to set up their base camp on the very spot where Selkirk had kept his four-year vigil: a narrow ledge on a ridge rising 600 metres behind today's settlement of Cumberland Bay. Commanding views on both sides of the volcanic island, the ledge, only 4.5 metres wide, provided an ideal lookout point both for Selkirk and, almost 300 years later, the young Raleigh seafarers.

The task throughout the long nights on Robinson Crusoe was to capture as many different moths as possible. The tools the scientists provided seemed a real Heath Robinson collection: a large white sheet, a tilly lamp, two Nescafé tins and a length of hose. 'The idea was to

32

attract the night-flying moths onto the illuminated sheet and then pick them off the material by sucking them up the hose – without swallowing them,' wrote journalist Mary Corbett. 'The next step was to blow the moths out of the hose into a tin. Howling gales and driving rain, rats and spiders were all pretty distracting and made it an extremely unproductive effort. We left the site with only fifteen moths to our credit.'

Alexander Selkirk Island, 27 May 1986

From a distance Selkirk Island looked as though a giant had taken a carving knife and slashed deep wounds in the land. The image proved horribly apt. As *Sir Walter Raleigh* drew nearer, the crew could see the small slipway surrounded by corrugated iron shacks and the island's fourteen inhabitants frantically rushing about. 'It was only when we landed that we realized why,' wrote Mary Corbett. 'The island is inhabited for only ten months a year and we just happened to arrive on the day of the annual evacuation to Robinson Crusoe Island. Landing was precarious. The small boat had to wait for just the right roller to sweep it to shore. Passengers clung to a thick yellow rope to guide the boat in, and only perfect timing ensured that we would avoid the sharp rocks that meant certain disaster.'

Once ashore, a new shock awaited the group. The people of Selkirk were slaughtering their animals '. . . left, right and centre. Cows, goats and dogs had their throats slit and were left to die, while two bulls had their horns knocked off with a sledgehammer so that they could be crammed into the bottom of a small boat,' wrote Mary. Oil drums, crates and carcasses were stowed one on top of the other; a macabre cargo and a grisly sight.

Easter Island, 4 June 1986

Bad-tempered but sure-footed horses carried scientists and Venturers around the island in search of insects. They didn't have to look far, for hundreds of miniature snails fell from the branches and the riders' faces

33

and bodies were soon covered by ants which they had to scrape off their skin. The mysterious, frowning countenances of the giant Easter Island statues seemed to delight in the visitors' discomfort, with a glimmer of a smile on their stone lips.

Heading for the inland lake of Ramo Kao crater, the going became even more difficult. Bamboo barred their path around the edge of the lake and they had to scramble up steep mudbanks through thick, prickly undergrowth. Once at the water's edge, the horses had an equally hard time, for reeds that had looked like a grassy verge from far away towered 3 metres high.

The combination of mud and marsh made the group's other objective – to capture and identify the crater fish – almost futile. It was well worth the trek, however. Emerging from the dark bamboo jungle, the party was greeted by a huge double rainbow which arched across the entire width of the crater, splashing its colour against the sky.

Trials of a different nature loomed ahead. As the ship continued across the ocean for Pitcairn – one of the world's most inaccessible islands, and chosen for that very reason as a refuge by the mutineers of HMS *Bounty* – Tony Walton radioed some bad news to HQ in London. The second mate, John Pearn, had come down with hepatitis. No great catastrophe under normal circumstances, it was akin to the Black Death should the infection break out in a remote island community. Pitcairn's entire population had nearly been wiped out by relatively mild flu some years previously. It looked as though we would never meet the descendants of the *Bounty* crew.

As discussions continued with the New Zealand Government, which administers Pitcairn Island, Captain Mike Kichenside changed course for uninhabited Henderson Island, 118 nautical miles to the north-east. So inaccessible is Henderson, protected from intruders by lethal reefs and strong currents, that few boats ever land there. The hazards ashore are equally daunting, and no previous expedition had succeeded in traversing the island from one end to the other. It was Operation Raleigh's aim to do just that, and they nearly made it. A scientific survey of Henderson provided some new information on the island: a Pacific paradise untouched by man, whose wildlife, like the flightless Henderson rail and the multicoloured fruit dove, are not found on other islands.

The savage coastal currents that had saved the pristine island and its wildlife, however, proved nearly fatal for David Taylor and others. David's job was to ferry the landing parties from *Sir Walter Raleigh* to Henderson and to run resupply trips. He remembers the boat runs as a real test of seamanship. 'The swells on the reef were enormous and the troughs literally laid the coral bare. You had to time the passage through the reef to the last second. If you missed the channel, you were doomed.'

At one stage the skiff, laden with supplies, was swamped by the high swells. Two of its crew were hurled into the reef and dragged 100 metres out to sea by the undertow before they could fight their way back. For David, however, the most terrifying time was when he took the skiff out to rescue Venturers trapped on a reef. Walking round a headland, they had become stranded by the fast-rising tide. David had only one choice and he took it without hesitation. Plunging into the sea, he dragged the youngsters through the current to safety. 'It was one of the most frightening moments in my entire life,' he recalls.

Henderson Island was also a particularly memorable stop for the radio experts aboard the flagship. John Layton, Nick Perrott and Alastair Turner were determined to be the first to cross the airwaves from the remoter parts of the Pacific. The contribution of amateur radio enthusiasts to Raleigh has been enormous, and with the backing of the Japanese company, Yaesu, they have kept us in touch with the world from many an unknown spot.

This is John's story of the adventures of the radio hams, or Gannets as they are known in Raleigh code. (Those readers who find radio jargon difficult to understand, may need a translator!)

> We set up base camp on the only suitable spot – the seashore. We had to bring everything ashore, including fuel and water for a week. A trickier bit of equipment to transport was the 12-metre mast which carried the marine band whip and wire aerial as well as providing support for the VHF and UHF Yagis. Since lugging the heavy radio equipment up the steep cliffs was impossible, at least we were on the north side of the island and had a reasonably tall mast for our inverted V aerial.

We planned to use the two Yagi aerials for our first satellite operation through Oscar 10. The beacon was heard on our Mutek transverter at good strength, but we couldn't hear any other signs of activity. Our reluctant conclusion was that the transponder must be out of action. As a normal VR6 licence only permits operation on the HF bands, we had been lucky to get special permission from the New Zealand administration to operate on 435 MHz from the Pitcairn Island group. The failure of the satellite to respond was, therefore, an enormous disappointment.

News of our radio activities spread quickly through the world and pile-ups occurred both on SSB and Morse. All our equipment worked perfectly – with the exception of the generator – and that proved a frustrating exception indeed.

Nick had waited for hours for 40 metres to open into Europe. Finally the channel cleared, but, as the second contact was completed, the generator stalled. Working with lightning speed, Nick stripped down the faulty generator and repaired it – just as 40 metres closed again.

Our time on Henderson, however, had been well spent. Over 1500 QSO's (amateur radio conversations) had been completed, and a CW expedition frequency established on 14.023 MHz. We would use this for the rest of the Pacific voyage.

Pitcairn Island, 23 June 1986

As the airwaves resounded with the Gannets' gossip, the question of whether or not we would be allowed to land on Pitcairn was resolved. The answer was a cautious yes. Richard Parkin, the ship's doctor, laid down stringent rules for the visit: personal hygiene was more important than ever, and everyone going ashore must take their own eating utensils with them to avoid any chance of infecting the islanders with the hepatitis virus.

Once again, reaching shore proved to be a test of courage.

Venturers and scientists lined up on the ship's deck and one by one climbed down the port side. It was quite a drop to the islanders' longboat and the 4.5-metre swells made climbing down the rope ladder even more hazardous. The boat below rose and fell on the rough sea, crashing against the ship; to descend one rung too many would lead to a smashed leg.

Venturers on the San Raphael glacier in southern Chile.

Above: When the *Sir Walter Raleigh* visited Mitiaro Island in the Cook group the peace of the Pacific was broken by local engineers blasting to create a safer landing place.

Below: Byron White from USA and Phil Moran from Surrey in the laboratory on board the *Sir Walter Raleigh* studying Cook Island eels.

Above left: Ham radio operator Nick Perrott from Orpington adjusting an antenna on Henderson Island during the Pacific crossing. *Above right:* Third officer Steve Mackin from Bury, Lancashire, one of the *Sir Walter Raleigh* crew sponsored by Shell, driving an Avon Searider off Robinson Crusoe Island in the Pacific Ocean. *Below:* American Venturer Jane Ayers measuring the nose of a *moai* on Easter Island.

Above: *Moai* heads in Anakena Bay, Easter Island.

Below: A demonstration of fishing methods on a Western Samoan reef.

Above: Villagers welcoming Operation Raleigh at Mauke Island in the Cook group.

Below: An inquisitive child in the Solomon Islands stares up at *Zebu*.

Above: Venturers and locals worked side by side on the Mount Mase flora and fauna survey in the Solomon Islands.

Left: Nigel Daly hacking his way through the dense jungle in the Mase region of New Georgia, Solomon Islands.

Below: The Red Cross Centre built by Operation Raleigh on Giso Island.

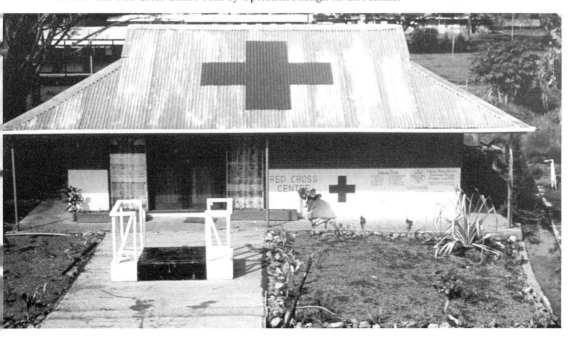

Above: Staff and venturers looking out of their temporary home during an orchid project in the Solomon Islands. *Below:* Farewell feast at Paradise Village, Solomon Islands.

The Pitcairners shouted a stream of instructions, terse in the extreme. 'Come!' 'Jump!' 'Stop!' To 'Jump!' was to hurl yourself backwards through space into their arms far below. It was like leaping blindfolded into the unknown.

At first the people of Pitcairn were reserved. They had waited all year for Raleigh to arrive and their fear of the virus was evident. Tension soon evaporated, however, and the hospitality of the isolated Pitcairn community was unsurpassed.

Tales from Andrew Young, the island's oldest inhabitant, and from Tom and Betty Christian, Len Brown and Brian Young kept everyone spellbound, and the last evening with them was perhaps the most moving of the entire voyage. The islanders' song of farewell, 'We will miss you as you journey on your way, We do wish that you were evermore to stay', left not a dry eye on the island.

Later that night, Raleigh's small boat bucked through the ocean swells for the last time to unload seventy-five barrels of oil provided by Shell which we had brought from Chile. Supplies on the little island were critically low and the oil would see the islanders through for another few months.

Pago Pago, American Samoa, 20 July 1986

Rarotonga, Atiu, Mitiaro and Mauke were the exotic-sounding islands the expedition charted on its way to the next stop, American Samoa, the only US territory south of the Equator. Pago Pago Harbour is reputed to be the best in the Pacific. Its straight, narrow entrance bends at a dog's leg and a cordon of steep mountains protects it from rough weather. It was the first time that the ship was able to 'go alongside' since leaving Chile two months previously. For the Raleigh crew, the arrival was perfectly timed. We had only two days' drinking water and fuel was running low.

We stayed for eight days, climbing volcanic peaks into the steamy jungle and gathering samples to complete the science projects. In Western Samoa, the Venturers and islanders found each other's customs equally strange. For the young sailors of both sexes, however, one part of the culture took some getting used to: transvestism.

It is all perfectly natural in Western Samoa. 'If a family has three sons and no daughters,' reported Mary Corbett, 'the youngest son becomes a "daughter", taking a female name – Rose is popular – dressing in women's clothing and doing the domestic chores.' Venturer Phil Moran learned about the practice the hard way. Sound asleep under his mosquito net, he shifted, and was awake in a flash. He was not the only one under the net. A young transvestite had taken 'her' role to extremes and crawled in beside him. As the heavily made-up young 'lady' snuggled closer, Phil's loud shriek could be heard clear across the island.

Before leaving Western Samoa, the Venturers underwent a tough survival exercise organized by Cathy Davies. To their surprise, and possibly hers, they lived to see another day. This one dawned on the Kingdom of Tonga.

Nuku 'alofa, Tonga, 11 August 1986

Just west of the International Dateline, Tonga is the first nation to usher in each new day. It is said that here, 'the roosters are so confused they crow all day to be safe.' The ancient island kingdom is unique in many other ways: it is the only remaining monarchy in Polynesia; it is the smallest kingdom on earth; and it is the only Pacific nation never to fall under foreign rule.

Sir Walter Raleigh docked at Tongatapu and the Venturers and scientists were ferried to another island, Eua, to complete the extensive scientific projects and to take part in a festival organized by HRH King Taufa'ahau Tupou IV, King of Tonga.

Then the ship sailed on. Missing his girlfriend after so many months at sea finally became too much for Shell crewmember Steve Mackin. Once in Rarotonga, Steve dashed to a telephone box and proposed. Half a world away, at some ungodly hour in the morning, the bemused young lady could only accept.

Quick to spot a good idea, Venturer Joe Duffy from Glasgow tried it out on his girlfriend, popping the question from Western Samoa. She accepted too. With wedding bells echoing in the salty air, ship's engineer, Geoff Lee, completed the hat trick on board *Sir Walter Raleigh* by proposing to our exhibition manager, Karen Smith. Yet again the champagne corks popped. In November 1986 they were married and *en route* to Geoff's homeland, New Zealand.

Suva, Fiji, 21 August 1986

And finally, Fiji. Here most of the Venturers and staff departed for home, leaving only a skeleton crew to bring *Sir Walter Raleigh* on to Australia on 6 September. Docking at HMAS *Cairns*, the elegant white flagship received immense hospitality from the Royal Australian Navy. It was a time for refitting and review. At Tac HQ the scientists briefed us on the excellent results of the crossing.

In his report author and conservationist Andrew Mitchell noted that the Pacific voyage had netted (literally) a unique collection of night-flying moths, as well as spiders and shrimps, both freshwater and marine. Never before had these been systematically collected across the Pacific; the material would be of vital importance for biogeographers.

For the first time, too, a living fossil, the nautilus, had been found in the Samoan Islands, extending the range of this rare and lovely mollusc further across the Pacific than had previously been recorded. The medical team had come up with good information as well, and their study of the incidence of beta Thallasaemia, a genetically inherited disease, would help to indicate the relationship of one island group to another. The geologists too were pleased with their findings. The rock samples hewn from island cliffs and valleys will help to determine the origins of the islands themselves, and the fibreglass copies of Easter Island petroglyphs will be displayed at the Santiago Natural History Museum, along with the Cave of Hands replica made by the Venturers in Chile.

'The coming of man to the Pacific Islands meant extinction for many species, but he brought new animals along: pigs, chickens and rats are now common on most Pacific archipelagos,' Andrew Mitchell wrote.

Like the rats, fruit bats were uninvited travelling companions – or perhaps the Polynesian seafarers brought the flying foxes along as lunch, for they are highly prized as food. The Tongan variety, *Pteropus tonganus*, is found as far east as the Cook Islands; such bats do not make a habit of flying thousands of miles across open ocean.

Particularly tasty evidently, are the wide-winged Samoan bats, *Pteropus samoensis*; those in the nearby Mariana and Caroline Islands have already been put on the endangered species' list. Only in the Kingdom of Tonga are bats relatively safe. Here, on the islands of first-edition dawns, they are protected by Royal decree – exclusively for the King's table. No doubt a few find their way into his subjects' stews.

There were no bats in our Australian stew that evening, but I wouldn't have been surprised if I had found an eye of newt or toe of frog, or any of the Macbeth witches' other ingredients which flourish in northern Queensland. Certainly the Venturers, now in the Solomon Islands and Papua New Guinea, would encounter many an 'adder's fork and blind worm's sting' if herpetologist Mark O'Shea had anything to say about it.

Reviewing the Pacific crossing and finalizing plans for future expeditions, Nick Horne and I talked late into the night. As I picked up Defoe's book to read in my tent, it seemed to me that the young voyagers had encountered many a real-life adventure of a modern-day Crusoe. Theirs was, as Andrew Mitchell had said, perhaps a last glimpse of a rapidly vanishing Eden.

CHAPTER THREE

Adventures in Paradise

(*Solomon Islands Leader*: David Parker)

Ferguson Passage, 10 June 1986

'The sea is getting rougher,' shouted David Parker to me as our small boat bucked against the swell.

'Do you think the dugout will make it?' I shouted back to the tall, sandy-haired expedition leader.

David nodded with a confidence that his eyes betrayed. Our flotilla of small craft heading for Paradise – the name of the village on New Georgia – included two motor boats, two canoes and a long wooden dugout. It was the latter which was in imminent danger of overturning and providing the white-tipped hammerheads with a late breakfast. I remembered the grisly tales of their feeding frenzies here during the Second World War when ships broke up, spilling their crews into the sea.

I peered into the rain. Visibility was now less than 6 metres. Waves crashed over the sides of the boats and the torrential rain washed the salt from our bodies. Rivulets of water ran into our eyes and made it even harder to see the hazards ahead: floating logs and the innumerable sprouting coconuts, a sea of trees seeking dry land.

Conditions deteriorated when we reached the break in the sheltering lagoons. Now we were in the open sea; in places the water plunges to a depth of 6100 metres. Between us and Australia to the south was nothing but hundreds of kilometres of whitecaps.

We manoeuvred the boat as close to the dugout as we could with safety. Thigh deep in water, the eight Venturers in the canoe looked remarkably cheerful. Lisa Peach, a zookeeper from California, passed the bailer to Jane Nicholls, just as a tiny flying fish landed in Jane's lap.

41

You picked the right boat, thought Jane as she slipped the fingerling back into the sea. There's enough water in here for a whole family of fish.

It wasn't far to Paradise. In good weather the motor-powered craft could make the trip from the Raleigh base camp at Gizo in under three hours. We had left Gizo at nine that morning and planned to join the rest of the Venturers and staff for a farewell feast with our friends at Paradise. Together, the islanders and Venturers had hunted wild pig, trekked through the thickly forested mountains, unearthed the remains of an abandoned village deep in a mountain crater, searched for orchids, and gathered information on local medicines. Now the Kusage people had bidden us to their feast and we were determined to be their guests.

As quickly as it began, the storm stopped. The sky cleared and the sun's strong rays glanced off the sea, turning the clouds to silver. Our feast-bound flotilla breathed a collective sigh of relief and regrouped for the final run into Paradise.

Later in the day Claire Tregaskis put on a red sarong, here called a 'lap lap', and tucked a red hibiscus behind her ear. The other Venturers and the ebony-skinned islanders were similarly dressed in brightly coloured cotton. Some of the men had painted streaks in yellow clay under their eyes. There was a feeling of growing excitement as final preparations were made and people scrambled down the ladders of the houses built on stilts. Claire eased herself over to the door, 3 metres above the ground, and slowly began her descent. She had cerebral palsy. The young UK Venturer knew that it would take her longer to climb the hill and had decided to start early.

'Claire!' called Rowland Reeve, the handsome archaeologist from Hawaii. Completely at home in whichever jungle he happened to find himself, Rowland had headed Operation Raleigh archaeological teams in Costa Rica, Honduras and Chile, discovering many unique archaeological sites. I was delighted to be with him again. We would need all of his experience.

Claire turned with a smile as the lithe figure ran easily up the hill. A strong bond had grown between the two. Rowland spoke with admiration of how Claire had set out to climb from Paradise to the Mase River, and made it. Claire wrote later:

42

I can never describe the euphoria and the determination to succeed for each other which carried us along during the seven hours it took me to reach the river. We crossed streams, clambered under, over or along fallen trees and slithered up and down treacherously muddy slopes.

I must have spent as much time skidding along on my backside as I spent on my feet, but it was such great fun that it didn't matter. For me it was probably the single most gratifying thing I have ever done – and the whole team had made it possible. I've proved to myself that I can do anything if I want it badly enough.

Now, as she waited on the hillside for Rowland, Claire knew she would take home with her all of these memories and more. Like helping to build a centre for the Red Cross in Gizo. Or working at the home for disabled children in Honiara when the deadly Cyclone Namu struck, and then helping to evacuate the hospital's leprosy and polio patients to safety.

Below Claire lay the scattering of leaf-thatched houses and the reef beyond. Sinuous palms stretched over the water, reaching out to sea. The children of Paradise ran up and down these natural ladders, gathering coconuts. Claire watched as they jumped down to join the throng, heading for the feast. One of the smallest slipped his hand in hers: Paradise is well named, thought Claire.

The table – huge leaves placed on the ground – had been set under the hot Solomon sun. A table big enough to seat the entire village and their Raleigh guests, and laden with mouthwatering dishes: roast wild pig, chicken, several kinds of fish and an extravagant speciality: turtle, chopped into heads, tails and flippers. There were also sweet potatoes, squares of grated and fried coconut and fresh coconut milk to drink straight from the shells. All had been provided by these handsome and generous people as a thank you to Operation Raleigh.

There was another thank you, a telegram from Prince Charles. He had learned of the help the Venturers provided when Cyclone Namu raged across the islands, leaving over 100 dead. Addressed to David Parker, 'The Leader, Operation Raleigh, Gizo Red Cross, SI', the message read in part: 'Please convey my best wishes to the local community and my congratulations to all members of the team on their good work.' The telegram was signed simply, 'Charles, Patron'.

Once we had tucked in to the feast, Ian Willing, the tall, handsome headman of the village, started the proceedings. In a Solomon Islands version of after-dinner speeches, Venturers, staff and islanders alike stood and said a few words, sometimes in the local language, sometimes in English and sometimes in the universally understood Pidgin. Chief Billy Kikobule from the neighbouring village of Tamurai, had the last word. 'We have lived together and worked together and eaten together,' said the old chief. 'We are friends. Although our skins are of a different colour, we have the same face.'

As the evening sun dropped behind the jungle canopy, Ian Willing stood again. A frown creased his brow. Beside him his little daughter wrapped her slim arms around his knee. Motioning the villagers to make way, the headman cleared a path.

'An ancient one wants to join our feast. It would not do to refuse him.'

A hush fell on the chattering crowd. Children edged closer to their mothers, and their mothers didn't look much braver. Suddenly the crowd shrank back. Walking towards us was a terrifying sight: a tall figure in grass, rags and feathers, with a huge wooden mask on his shoulders.

Not too long ago, the people of this island were noted for their head-hunting skills. Even as late as the Second World War Japanese soldiers hiding in the jungle had died in this macabre way. I couldn't help wondering if this creature was a relic of the old days. Beside me, Roy, a hunter who had put many a pig in our pots, chuckled softly. David Knowles, the competent quartermaster from the Bahamas, glanced at Roy and relaxed his massive frame. Then others laughed as they heard the creature's voice.

'I am the spirit of the bush. I have come to join your feast.' The loud thrum of the cicadas underlined his words. 'I have seen many young people come to my ancient land. I have followed them as they hunted the wild pigs and gathered the white orchids. I have lifted them when they fell, fed them when they were hungry and cared for them when they were ill. But I am a spirit and they could not see me.'

As the 'spirit' warmed to his theme, Roy rocked with laughter. Beside him, David Parker joined in. The 'spirit' was Hapi, the oldest of our Kusage guides and as cheerful as his name. A wonderful flash of island humour which had us all worried for a while.

44

Mase Crater, 4 May 1986

For over 1000 years the Kusage, our generous hosts at Paradise, had lived high in a mountain crater. Cannibals themselves, they had a healthy respect for the opposition and their remote eyrie provided some protection.

Then, one day in 1905, Methodist missionaries arrived on New Georgia and built schools and churches. The Kusage chief sent an envoy to the shore. Would the strangers climb up to the crater and teach the Kusage too?

The missionaries, brave folk all, considered the suggestion. Head-hunting had been outlawed only a few years before, but the Methodists knew that the practice was still very much in vogue.

'We will teach the Kusage if they come down to the shore,' they replied prudently. 'But we will not come up.'

Twelve years later the Kusage came down, leaving the crater to be reclaimed by the jungle. Shell money, sacred sites and everyday tools remained just as they had left them but only the ghosts of the ancient chiefs walked the abandoned settlements. For almost seventy years, time stood still in the Mase Crater.

The crater was an archaeologist's dream. 'Even now there are a few Kusage who remember living here,' said Rowland. 'Their memories keep the past alive.'

Sweating heavily in the 32°C humidity, the Raleigh group, which had climbed to the top of the volcano, uncovered massive stone terraces, ancient settlements, shrines of worship and of war. They found tools, ovens and shell money. In the old days five of the discs made from giant clam shells and whales' teeth would have bought a bride for Indiana Jones.

'We drew maps and pictures of everything we found,' explains Rowland, 'and, when we returned to Paradise, we could actually ask the old people how they were used.' The archaeology project provided a rare opportunity – the chance to recapture a history that would otherwise die.

Among the tools and terraces, the Venturers found other relics that made them shiver in the tropical heat: human skulls. Rowland had

45

warned them never to touch any bones or burial sites they might discover. The spirits of the past are powerful in the Solomon Islands. On
nearby Rendova Island another expedition was learning just how strong.

Rendova Island, Solomon Islands, 28 May 1986

The sea was our highway between expedition sites. The Solomons are a
scattered archipelago of mountainous islands and coral atolls. Happily,
our boatman, James Longden, a yacht master and, at twenty-two, a veteran of three Fastnet races, managed to manoeuvre our Mariner-engined
craft without mishap. He had been recruited by Anthony Agar, one of
the hardworking team at CHQ in London, himself a valuable member of
any expedition.

James could read the water like a book, a colouring book. A light turquoise colour speckled with brown meant reefs ahead; a dark blue
stretch meant safety. Throughout these lovely waters were the remains
of many ships, some the tragic reminders of the Second World War,
others ripped apart by unseen rocks.

One Monday towards the end of May, James had ferried a small
group of Venturers from Gizo to New Georgia. With conservationist
Margaret Dickson, whose gentleness of manner concealed a will of iron,
the group would go deep into the rainforest, collecting orchids for London's Kew Gardens. The orchids came in a rainbow of colours: varia-
tions of white, pink, green, orange and, Margaret's favourite, the blue
invorara.

Some blossoms are no bigger than a diamond, while others are larger
than a man's hand. The trailing orchids used at island weddings form a
gorgeous garland over 30 metres long.

Margaret was sure that the moss forest on top of Rendova volcano
would yield a wealth of new orchids. What she couldn't know was that
the route to the summit would take them through sacred Tambu sites,
the secret burial places of ancient chiefs. According to local folklore,
people who disturbed the sites sometimes lost their memories and, unable to find their way home, died in the jungle.

There are other stories. Several years ago a man who had violated a
site went mad. The villagers believe he still wanders the jungle, preying

on travellers. More recently a child searching for honey stumbled upon a Tambu site. He returned home with gobbets of honey running down his arms, completely insane.

Each time the rain had followed. Torrential rain that fell for days, flooding the land and destroying crops. Unaware of the stories, the group that reached Rendova Island that sunny May morning put on their packs and began the steep trek to the mountain peak. They would never reach it.

Among the Venturers heading up Rendova were two British science students, Richard Watson and Louisa-Jane ('Lou') Pritchard, and an American, Ed Ritchie, a builder from Kansas. Fit though they were, it wasn't easy to keep up with the fast pace of the guides and hunters: Alfred, André and Kennedy.

'Aren't those burial mounds?' asked eighteen-year-old Lou as she came back to camp, dragging jungle firewood behind her. She pointed a green stick at a pile of stones just visible in the jungle. Busy building the shelter and preparing supper, no one paid her much attention.

Lou shrugged and went back for more wood. The evening light filtering through the thick canopy was so dim that at first she doubted what she saw. Slowly, she turned full circle, then quickly walked back to camp, the firewood forgotten.

They were camping in the middle of a Tambu site. The guides found a large stone cairn nearby. Inside were the seven skulls of seven generations of chiefs – one of the most sacred places. There were stone pots filled with shell money and shark's teeth. Rifles, more recent symbols of power, lay rusting on the jungle floor.

In the bright, hot morning sun all thoughts of the supernatural seemed unfounded. That day the group found orchids they had never seen before. So dense was the canopy and so intense her concentration on the plant in front of her, that at first Lou didn't feel the rain.

Then it became a deluge, battering through the jungle with extraordinary force and drenching the orchid hunters in minutes. The Venturers returned to their base where they spent a very wet night. All thoughts turned to the Tambu sites. The guides were sure the rains were the result of disturbing the spirits, but finally the rains stopped and nothing more was said. Tomorrow they would climb to the top, they decided.

They reached the rainforest late in the morning, and, as if on cue, the rain began again. Undaunted, Margaret and the others were happy with the results of their day's hunt: six new species. Marcus Pugh got a round of applause when he discovered he was sitting on two of them.

The rain fell in rods. Still the group continued up the steep mountain, reaching cloud level wet and cold. Once there, the floodgates opened and practically swept them off their feet. Although they were only 100 metres or so from the top, it was impossible to go on. They turned and went back to camp.

Now everyone began to feel uneasy. The spirits gave us two more hints of their displeasure – but pretty strong hints.

First, Roy, an experienced hunter who was familiar with the jungle, became inexplicably lost. Following a ridge that he knew was a two-lane highway for potential pork chops, Roy looked up, confused.

This is impossible, he thought. I don't recognize this place. It took all of his experience and skill to find his way back to camp. He arrived late at night, exhausted and more concerned than ever.

The final warning came as the Venturers attempted to climb Rendova for the third time. The sky was blue and the jungle hummed with humid contentment. The storm came out of nowhere, this time complete with thunder and lightning. Rain fell with such force that the drops bounced like spearheads hurled on hard ground.

'The message was very clear,' Margaret told me later. 'As soon as we decided that the storm was too wild to risk climbing the peak, the skies miraculously cleared to a beautiful, sunny, hot day.'

It was strange too, that when the photographs taken by Margaret and the others were developed, they were, without exception, blank. There are indeed a great many more things in heaven and earth than we have ever dreamed of. Thankfully, we managed to avoid most of them.

Gizo, Western Province, 9 June 1987

If there was one word which crossed the Venturers' lips more often than 'food', it was 'custom'. In the Solomon Islands anything described as 'custom' can be loosely translated as 'traditional'. The feast at Paradise was a custom feast. Families that kept to the old ways were custom families and the traditional remedies were known as custom medicines. There were custom medicines for everything from VD to earache. With the introduction of Western medicine, however, some of the old cures had already been forgotten. Just as Rowland sought to record the history of the Kusage, Hugh Bramwells, who led the Bioresources project, hoped to document custom medicine, a resource which, once lost, is lost for ever. Experts believe that a quarter of the earth's plants will be wiped out by the year 2050.

Conrad Gorinsky, the director of Bioresources, London, is a realist as well as a scientist. The world's wild places, he believes – its jungles, plains and forests – will survive only if governments become convinced that the wilderness areas are of economic value. If the cure for Aids, for example, could be distilled from a jungle shrub, retaining the jungle might raise the country's GNP more than a luxury hotel on the same spot.

One day, some of the custom medicines recorded by Bioresources might well be used in the Red Cross centre which the Venturers were building in Gizo. The building was a massive undertaking but I was impressed to find it almost complete when I arrived. London builder Trevor Newland, a wiry, red-haired project leader, was sharpening the scissors for the Governor-General's ribbon-cutting ceremony in twelve days' time.

To reach Gizo I had flown from Tac HQ in Cairns and stopped for the night in Brisbane with my good friends Nigel and Jenny Porteous who ran the Queensland Operation Raleigh committee. The newspapers in Australia had headlined birthday greetings to the Queen – 'G'Day Your Majesty!' – as well as Bob Geldof's famine relief in Africa and the recent Chernobyl nuclear disaster. But what concerned me most that morning were the accounts of Cyclone Namu in the Solomon Islands.

The news was grim. Over 100 people had died in the savage cyclone and more than 100,000 were homeless. In three days of wanton destruction, Namu's winds had reached 208 k.p.h.; 100 knots. The jungle had been ripped from the hills and entire villages torn apart.

International response was immediate. Operation Raleigh Venturers on Guadacanal, one of the hardest-hit islands, had immediately joined the relief effort. It was the tireless work of Claire Tregaskis, Lisa Peach and the others which had elicited the telegram of congratulations from the Prince of Wales.

David Parker and Charley Kelly, Secretary-General of the Solomon Islands' Red Cross, met me at the airport. Waiting on the hot tarmac was a four-seater Aztec Piper to fly us on to Gizo. Once airborne, I could see for myself the havoc Namu had wrought. The wind had uprooted hundreds of trees and swept them up the rivers and far out to sea. Bridges and dams had been severed, leaving huge pools of stagnant water which could easily bring on a malaria epidemic.

As the little Piper climbed to over 1800 metres, we flew over the outer islands which had escaped the worst of the cyclone. Ahead were the Russell Islands, dark shards of green glass in the ocean with carefully tended plantations of coconut palms. We passed Kennedy Island and countless lagoons, Second World War airstrips and submarine volcanoes. Finally, we spotted the tiny airstrip of Nusatupe, about the size of a pocket handkerchief. We would land there and continue by canoe to Gizo.

Ailerons down, the Piper began its descent. 'Look!' exclaimed David, pointing out of his window. A tiny boat was racing out to meet us with the flags of Operation Raleigh and the Red Cross streaming in the wind. Brian Smith, our pilot, buzzed the craft and the miniature figures waved energetically. Boatman James Longden set the magistrate's 'canoe' into perfect circles, slicing through her silver wake in a dozen places.

We landed on the coral runway and Brian braked hard. Gaping holes in the bush ahead showed where other pilots had not judged the extreme shortness of the runway so accurately and had shot into the sea.

The Red Cross centre built by the Raleigh team is the first thing one sees from the wharf at Gizo, cheek by jowl with the church run by a wonderfully tough Australian nun who wears a baseball cap and careens about the island in a Toyota pick-up. Sister Christopher had been a great help to David Parker and the entire expedition. In return they had repaired the church tower.

As the crowds of laughing black children parted to let us up the wharf, I saw the final touch being put onto the new medical centre: a bright red cross on the roof. As the Venturers came up to say hello, my delight at seeing them turned to dismay. The whites of their eyes were as scarlet as the cross they were painting. Lit with supernatural brightness, the eyes of the Venturers would have been coveted by the director of a horror film. Before the expedition was over, just about everyone had contracted the tropical 'red-eye'. Although the painful infection sealed its victims' eyes for a few days, most people recovered, thankfully, in about a week.

The conjunctivitis spread through the village, striking islanders and Venturers alike. Nigel Curtis, the expedition doctor, soon ran out of his store of antibiotics. Perhaps Conrad Gorinsky knew of a local cure, but he was in Papua New Guinea with another Raleigh expedition and I was heading off to join them. The red-eye epidemic brought home the importance of the Bioresources project. Most villagers had forgotten the ancient cure for the infection. Some Venturers were offered fresh milk from the breast to ease the pain! A little custom medicine would have gone a very long way.

Well before dawn James Longden piloted me through the black lagoons to the tiny airstrip. I was sad to leave the beautiful island country but eager to reach the expedition in Papua New Guinea. Reports had reached me of recent sightings of an elusive monster which had long captured my imagination. We were on the trail of the giant Artrellia.

CHAPTER FOUR

The Dragon's Tail and
Points West

(*Papua New Guinea Leader*: Lieutenant-Colonel John Swanston, RAMC)
(*Malaysia Leader*: Lieutenant-Colonel Sulaiman bin Yosof)

Kunini Village, Papua New Guinea, 30 May 1986

New Guinea, the world's second largest island, is shaped like a huge sea dragon. The western half, the creature's head and shoulders, is the Indonesian province of Irian Jaya; Papua New Guinea is the dragon's tail. Only the Torres Strait saves the rugged island from being impaled on the sharp spear of Australia's Cape York Peninsula.

The geographical setting of PNG mirrors part of the country's diverse culture; here in the Western Province, spear-hunting is still the quickest way to put something in the pot, and the country is thick with reptiles: blind snakes and blue-tongued skinks, death adders and dragon lizards. In a region of superlatives – towering mountains, raging rivers and vast jungles – I was familiar with the rumours of witch doctors' curses, cannibalism and mountains of copper capped with gold. This time, however, something else held my interest. Mark O'Shea, the red-headed herpetologist who had been on expeditions with Operation Raleigh in Honduras and Borneo, had relayed fresh accounts of an old story: a dragon, 7 metres long.

'It's probably our friend the Salvadori dragon, the giant Artrellia,' Mark told me when I arrived in Kunini village. 'A local hunter, Dawo, told me he had seen the lizard just north of his village, Giringarade, in the upper reaches of the Bini Turi River.'

Dawo's account was substantiated by Essex Venturer Mark Swift on a herpetology patrol on 21 June, near the same spot. Walking through the savannah on the edge of the bush, he froze. 'The creature saw me first and ran out of the tall grass 100 metres to my right, running faster than you could sprint. Its heavy body smashed the grass out of the way and it disappeared into the bush. If it had decided to charge me, it would have caused a bit of damage – we've been told that the Komodo dragons in Timor have recently killed and eaten two Japanese tourists!'

As I listened to the accounts, I sketched a drawing in my notebook and showed it to Mark. It was a prototype of a cage. Baited with carrion, it worked on the principle of the African game traps which capture but do no harm to wildlife. We sat around the fire discussing the Artrellia and the many mysteries that remained in this beautiful and strange country which had shot out of the Stone Age only decades ago. In the morning we would go back to the village of Giringarade. I wanted to meet the monster again.

The Artrellia was no stranger to either Mark or myself. During Operation Drake, I had investigated a story about a mysterious 'dragon' in south-west PNG which was said to climb trees, walk upright, kill men and even breathe fire. With the help of the people of Masingara, we had mounted an extensive search and captured a young Salvador's monitor (*Varanus salvadori*) and seen an adult. Records of 3-metre monitors have been substantiated, but there are reported sightings of Artrellia 7 metres long.

Unlike mythological dragons, the Artrellia is not poisonous. The only lizards with that distinction alive today are the gila monster (*Heloderma suspectum*) and the Mexican bearded lizard (*Heloderma horidum*). It does, however, have other anti-social habits. Sometimes confused with a tree-climbing crocodile, the Artrellia will wait on a branch and drop onto its prey or pursue wallabies and bandicoots with the incredible speed that had surprised Mark Swift. Its sharp, pointed teeth, claw-tipped legs and powerful tail, which it uses as a whip to keep attackers at bay, also command a healthy respect.

By now snakes and insects dropping down on the Venturers in PNG had become an everyday occurrence; a particularly nasty leech had fastened itself to the eye of Australian Venturer Kathy Kelly. Used to the

53

jungle though they were, I noticed the Venturers carefully scanning overhanging branches as we trekked through the bush in search of the monster. I did too.

This time luck was not with us as far as the 'dragon' was concerned, but Mark O'Shea and his team were more than happy with their herpetological haul. They had collected, identified and recorded eighty species of reptiles and amphibians during the expedition, including 116 snakes of twenty-six species.

There were two snakes which Mark and the PNG Venturers sought with special enthusiasm. One they did not find, the very rare Boelen's python: the other, the deadly 'Papuan black', found them. 'The Papuan blacksnake (*Pseudechis papuanus*), known locally as the "Pap blak", is without doubt the most feared snake in southern Papua New Guinea, and most fatal snake bites are blamed on the species,' wrote Mark in his report. Although its bite is usually fatal, the 'Pap blak' comes second to the coffin-headed taipan (*Oxyuranus scutellatus canni*) in the *Who's Who* of poisonous snakes. During the expedition, three taipans were captured, each with enough venom to kill 100 men.

'Nurse Saves Snake Victim in Jungle Drama!' ran the headline. But for the quick reaction of Gillian Kaye, a British nurse and Venturer from Bournemouth, the villager would have died of the poison or of the local cure, slashing his leg to bleed out the venom. Either way, the result was usually fatal.

'We met someone in the jungle with a machete. He was going to bleed a hunter who had stepped barefoot on a Pap black,' remembers American Venturer Michael Sparks. The Venturers raced ahead of the machete-carrying messenger. Gillian immobilized the victim's leg, applied a pressure bandage, and, with the village chairman, embarked on a hazardous, four-hour boat journey across rough seas to Daru hospital. Luckily, the man survived both the bite and the boat ride; expedition leader Lieutenant-Colonel Swanston, of the Royal Army Medical Corps, reckoned that the poison would have killed him in another hour.

Traditional antidotes for snake bite have always been one of Conrad

Gorinsky's special interests. The director of Bioresources had just left our expedition in Paradise, and, with the Venturers and assistant Rebecca Hughes, had been gathering information on the living pharmacy of Papua New Guinea.

In India Conrad had recorded a cure for snake bite and he was intrigued to learn of a similar remedy in PNG. The bark of a mango tree, taken internally and applied directly to the bite, appears to stabilize body tissue against the haemolytic poison. Certainly a vast improvement on the kill-or-cure machete method currently in vogue amongst the villagers.

American biology students Serena Wilson and Jenny Bond – a marathon runner – together with Canadians Krista Hanni and Alon Gelcer, were among those who spent many days in the remote river villages learning the traditional ways. They hunted cassowary, wild pig and wallaby with bows and arrows and learned the easy way to catch a fish supper; some sap from the sadi bush stunned the fish and floated them to the surface. They learned, too, how to navigate the crocodile rivers in outrigger canoes and to spear fat prawns. At night they helped the women cook sago and cassava and joined in the rhythmic dances that recounted the stories of the past.

Most important for the Bioresources project, the Venturers recorded over 500 remedies used in Papua New Guinea. Undoubtedly some would save lives in the future, but the ingredients were enough to make a high street chemist nervous: ants, bark, soil and fungus were all part of the bottomless reserve of biological treasure.

'Red and black ants crushed together release something like formaldehyde to relieve fevers,' explained dark-haired Serena. 'Then there's a riverside plant, a relative of the iris, whose root helps to cure diarrhoea and stomach problems, and a tree bark which makes an excellent anaesthetic, good for everything from toothache to a good night's sleep.'

There were other diseases which modern medicine had already managed to control: tuberculosis, polio, measles and tetanus, for example. Venturers like Jean Smith, twenty-two years old and from Edinburgh's Royal Infirmary, and Alison Farmer, a nurse from Southampton, took part in government-supported medical patrols to inoculate villagers along the Fly River. PNG Venturers Chris Togui and Thomas Kuluwebano found the adventure down the twisting Fly River as challenging as did their foreign friends.

Fifty kilometres wide at the mouth, the river soon narrows to a ribbon of water that winds through the jungle. Anthony Agar reduced the speed of the Mariner engine and steered his small outboard around a tangle of vines and bamboo. The jungle scent enveloped them in a thick, rich soup. Overhead, fruit bats hung like dark plums, and pink and grey corellas screamed as they sought refuge for the night. As the shadows deepened, only the slim outline of a dugout canoe nestling among the sago fronds indicated a nearby village.

Picking up information for Bioresources as they journeyed upriver, the young people had yet another mission; to win the trust of the many people blinded by cataracts and convince them, and the members of their families, to come to Daru hospital. Venturers Jean Smith, Sue Jamieson, Donna Croft and others would be waiting to give them eye tests. Some would merely need glasses; others would be given a sight-saving operation by the medical team known as SEE International.

Daru Hospital, PNG, 2 June 1986

SEE is shorthand for Surgical Eye Expeditions, the name of the US-based group of ophthalmic surgeons which works with local doctors to perform free operations in remote areas of the world. Two-thirds of all blindness is surgically correctable and cataracts, one of the most common causes of blindness, can be removed by a simple operation that takes thirty minutes.

On 2 June at 8 a.m. the international team of four surgeons, an optician and a nurse arrived at Daru airport, led by Dr Harry S. Brown. One hour later, working with hospital surgeon Dr McKup, matron Kathy Attu and PNG ophthalmologist Dr Bage Yomanoa, they began examining patients. By 1 p.m. fifty-two pairs of spectacles had been issued and the first patient was in surgery.

Eighteen-year-old Ibia Mada had been totally blind since the age of two. It had taken Ibia and his brother three days to travel to Daru by dugout canoe and, when his bandages were removed the following morning, the tension in the air was palpable. There was total silence. 'Ask him if he can see you,' said Dr Brown to Ibia's brother.

'It was only when his brother spoke that Ibia's bewildered look slowly turned into a smile,' said American nurse Paula Urschel. Paula, a petite but tough lady who had accompanied me on many expeditions, had previously supervised clinics in Panama and Chile when SEE International and Raleigh joined forces in 1986. 'We realized that until he heard the familiar voice, Ibia did not know who his brother was. How do you recognize a brother you have never seen?'

The hard work of the medical patrols had paid off. The young people had visited over fifty villages in the Western Province and given eye tests to over 150 people. Most importantly, they had managed to win the trust of the Papuans and convince them to make the difficult river journey to a place they had never seen for an operation of which they had never heard.

By 2 June, the morning that the doctors arrived, long queues of patients had formed at the hospital doors. Two days later, when the SEE International team set off for another village hospital, it left behind a gift more precious than all the gold in New Guinea. In only a few hours those who had lived for years in the shadowy world of the blind could see.

Kunini Village, 28 June 1986

As he did every evening, Mareame Isase Dagi, the village councillor and head man of Kunini, circled the grassy patch that formed the centre of the village. His strong voice rose and fell as he related the day's news to the people of the village. Often it was about the snakes found by the Venturers living with them, or about a wild pig the hunters had killed for the communal pot. This evening, however, the message was exciting enough to make the women weaving armbands and pounding sago put down their work.

'There will be a wedding in the new church we have built with Operation Raleigh,' chanted Mareame. 'All the villages will come: Garingarade, Boze, Ture Ture and Irupi. People will travel down the river in their canoes to Kunini to join our feasts. There will be bow dancing and sing-sing and we will give prizes to the best. We must send out

57

the hunters for wallaby, pig and cassowary, and catch many sea turtles, dugongs and prawns. Every night we will practise our dances so that Kunini village can be proud.'

Not even Emily Post's *Book of Etiquette* could have sorted out the social niceties of the wedding Mareame announced to his people. The bride wore a pale grey lap lap and carried a bouquet of purple bougainvillea. Drums announced the arrival of the groom, who was carried from the riverbank to the church in a cane chair, and the guests wore grass skirts and face paint. Pastor Moresby Waia presided, wearing a shirt and tie and trousers covered by a white lap lap. The mounds of gifts for the happy couple included drums and bamboo spears, beautiful carvings and woven feathered fans.

It was all Babette's idea. Our young Anglo-French photojournalist had been part of the group that had built the new church the Kunini villagers wanted so badly. What better way to end the expedition and inaugurate the new church than with a traditional Papuan wedding? Babette wrote to her fiancé, Ray Gallard, proposing the idea. His enthusiastic reply had brought him halfway round the world and was the cause of his now being carried shoulder high under the hot sun of Kunini.

The wedding was the social event of the year. In Pidgin English, or 'Tok Pisin' so widely spoken in this country which boasts over 700 languages, Ray and Babette were about to 'kissim ring' or get married, and live happily ever after, which was 'bel i-gut' or very good indeed in any language.

The preparations had taken weeks. The stilt houses of Kunini were festooned with flowers, new mats and armbands had been woven, and there were enough plantains, sago and yams to feed the hundreds of guests whose canoes jostled for space on the mudbanks. Mareame had thought of everything and his nightly chants and exhortations had become more and more detailed as the wedding date drew nearer. On the day, Stephen Eagle, a forestry student at Aberdeen University, had been detailed to catch turtles in the morning and cut down coconuts in the afternoon. Well suited to the job, Stephen scrambled up the tall, straight palm trees with ease. He had raised his sponsorship money from Salvesen Drilling, James Scott and Son and other companies by spending a week living in the highest branches of a Scottish sycamore tree.

Geoff Ford, a police sergeant in the Leicestershire constabulary and the popular deputy leader of the expedition, had purchased a lap lap in Daru; it would serve as the symbolic dowry which every bride must have. Brenda and Philip Willmott-Sharp, members of the local Operation Raleigh Committee, who had provided such generous hospitality for so many Raleigh participants, had picked up Ray at the airport and sent him safely on his way to Kunini.

The service in the little white church went without a hitch. John Swanston didn't lose the ring and the vows were made in strong, clear voices that were easily heard over the noise of the cicadas and correlas. That night, after the wedding feast, as the huge tropical stars began to appear in the black sky, the dancing began. Dancing that the small village common had never seen before: traditional Japanese dancing by Hozy Yamada and Shuji Hasegawa, Morris dancing by Sara Blizzard, sword dances over razor-sharp machetes by the New Zealanders and reels of Strip the Willow, The Dashing White Sergeant and the Gay Gordons all performed to the unfamiliar beat of the native kundu drums.

Then the villagers took over and the rhythmic beat of bare feet on the hard-packed earth lured the Venturers to join in the steps they had practised so long. Cassowary feathers at the ankles and wrists of the dancers caught the flickering firelight; people of all skin colours and nationalities wove circles within circles as they danced in the jungle clearing of Kunini.

The sun is up at 6 a.m. in PNG, and the Venturers were up with it on the day they were to leave. A breakfast of rice, fruit pudding from the ration packs and tea was hastily consumed, but no one felt much like eating. In half an hour the white river boat that was the spitting image of the *African Queen* was anchored off the mudbank to take the Venturers to Daru, and finally home.

There were tears on Mareame's cheeks as he helped the Venturers across the log gangway onto the boat, and they shared his sorrow. All the villagers lined up to say goodbye, and, watching them, John Swanston remembered the words Serena Wilson had said at the first service in the new church.

'We came without much understanding, but we have been given so much by the people of Papua New Guinea. It is said that so many things pass, but these things remain; faith, hope, and charity. These are the foundations of this community, and you have taught us that the greatest of these is indeed charity.'

Sadly, the harmony of the remote villages of Papua New Guinea could not be found in all countries, and, as war raged in the Persian Gulf and chaos reigned in Sri Lanka, we were forced to relocate three major expeditions. About a year after Babette's wedding in Kunini, Operation Raleigh was back in the equatorial Far East – this time in Malaysia.

Singapore, 6 August 1987

Fortunately, it all fell into place. The Malaysian committee, driven on with almost fanatical enthusiasm by Miss Chiang Siew Lee, who had already visited us in Chile to see her young people in action, were able to help. Siew Lee wrote for the *New Straits Times* and attained considerable coverage for the operation. Malcolm Hyatt and various members of CHQ flew to Kuala Lumpur (KL) and in a remarkably short time some excellent projects were arranged for 132 Venturers from Australia, Britain, Canada, West Germany, Italy, Japan, Kenya, Malaysia and the USA.

The expedition leader, a resourceful and charming Malaysian Army officer, Lieutenant-Colonel Sulaiman bin Yosof, was assisted by Major Nick Thompson, Royal Signals and Anthony Agar from CHQ. Sadly for me, my PA, Peta Lock, had fallen in love with the dashing Marcus Wilkenson, former ship's exhibition manager and they were to be married. So my wife Judith persuaded our old friend Nadia Brydon, who had herself endured the jungles of South America, to take over. Nadia's cheery attitude was a breath of fresh air and together we flew to Singapore to see the committee and Venturers before going on to Malaysia.

Bob Powell, a veteran of the Zaire River expedition, and Anthony Cheong, the highly efficient secretary of the Raleigh committee, met us. Anthony, of accountants Ernst and Whinney who have done so much to support Raleigh all over the world, briefed us on the way to Chairman Gordon Benson's house for dinner. The Singapore team had done extremely well in providing both Venturers and staff. Much of their success was due to some first-class local publicity created by Ilsa Sharp, a freelance journalist whom I had first met in the jungles of southern Nepal.

Next day Anthony Agar whisked us across the causeway connecting Singapore Island to the Malay peninsula and, as night fell, we drove into the coastal town of Mersing. Sitting at a plastic-topped table in an open-fronted bar, we listened to Colonel Sulaiman's description of the expedition activities.

Malaysia comprises the peninsula and, to the east, on the great island of Borneo the States of Sarawak and Sabah. The tropical climate gives rise to dense jungle, but along the south-east coast there are lovely beaches and the island of Pulau Tinggi has a beauty of its own. It was there that we sailed that night to visit the groups doing marine and biological surveys.

The next evening we drove to KL, arriving after midnight at Sulaiman's HQ. As usual on Raleigh expeditions, a small band of administrators was working desperately hard, their job made especially difficult by the huge distances between projects. Fortunately Malaysian Air Services (MAS) were a generous sponsor and helped us enormously. To add to their worries Ley Kenyon, our chief artist, was seriously ill in one hospital with typhus, while a Venturer with appendicitis was in another. The previous month Christian de Souza, a popular British Territorial Army officer, had died in a road accident. Chris was the deputy leader of the Sabah project and his sad death had been a real blow to everyone in the expedition.

Flying in to Kota Kinabalu, capital of Sabah, a few days later with MAS, we were greeted by David Hammond, an Army Catering Corps officer with a zest for adventure training. His teams were involved in searching for the Sumatran rhinoceros, diving, building an observation tower in the rainforest canopy and a host of community projects. In addition they were constructing trails on Malaysia's highest peak, Mount Kinabalu, which rises almost 4100 metres above the sea.

*

Tambunan, Sabah, 11 August 1987

As our landcruiser reached Kampong Makatip, lightning flashed momentarily, illuminating the black afternoon sky and surrounding landscape. Rain fell in sheets, pelting the rich, fertile earth. Braced against the rocks, the Venturers fought the river's swift current to remove the last of the bamboo they had earlier floated down to the building site of the village hall.

Even in fine weather the bamboo's 0.8-kilometre voyage proved a difficult task. It was chopped down with local help and the Venturers then rode the logs, keeping them free from boulders and other obstacles. Clinging on for dear life, the team soon found themselves entangled among the bamboo lengths and battered against the rocks. At the construction site they fished out the poles and also any stragglers. Meanwhile village children glided expertly by, three astride one thin bamboo pole. As we arrived the Venturers were, amazingly, smiling. Then, clothes plastered to their skin, the group laboriously made their way back to the relative dryness of the base-camp hut. Their leader, Dina Wheatcroft of London, was firmly in control, rapidly organizing hot coffee and dry towels.

The hut was already overcrowded when two latecomers arrived. Space was cleared for the drenched pair who gratefully slumped down. Closer inspection of the bedraggled travellers revealed camp medic Maureen Bird, accompanied by a local girl draped in a colourful sarong through which peered the bright eyes of a newborn baby. It had taken Maureen and Jasmine Binda three hours to reach camp. Persistent rains, driven by gale-force winds, blew incessantly, blinding them as they struggled over rocky ledges and through marshy rice fields. As much of the terrain proved too perilous to traverse, they were frequently forced to cross the river. The torrent raged past, gripping their legs and making their balance precarious on the slippery rock. On several occasions Maureen feared they would drown. The baby was twenty-seven-year-old Jasmine's seventh child, five weeks old. The infant had been stricken with fever and diarrhoea since birth. The young mother had given birth on her own and was now suffering from a severe breast abscess. Maureen had decided that immediate medical attention was necessary and set out to lead them through the storm to hospital.

Once at the camp, she was delighted to find David Hammond's truck. The remaining 12.8 kilometres were quite a journey too. Wheels spun and the vehicle listed dangerously as it sought to gain traction. At several points the track had been completely washed away but miraculously the rugged four-wheeler managed to get through. Elsewhere water buffalo blocked the way, requiring coaxing to the roadside. Throughout, Jasmine sat stoically erect, masking her pain and clutching the child to her.

Finally David pulled up at the neat row of recently painted brick buildings which formed the hospital. Flocks of geese, immune to the weather, waddled happily in the flooded driveway. Jasmine and her baby were immediately ushered into a room. A sign with the admonishment 'Jagan Berludah – Do Not Spit' hung behind the examination table. As the doctor proceeded with his examination the other patients quietly crept in to gaze in astonishment at the fair-skinned, light-eyed 'foreigners'. The infant, who had never received any immunization, was given standard shots for diphtheria, whooping cough and tetanus. Both mother and child were then admitted to the hospital.

Tears welling in her eyes, the frightened girl turned to Maureen who promised to let her husband know that she would not be returning to the kampong that evening. The nurse knew that the native people associate hospital with death and dying and rarely travel the distance to it until their condition is beyond treatment. Understanding her fears, it was with great reluctance that she left the terrified Jasmine.

Heading back to camp they were once again confronted by the storm. Suddenly only metres ahead, the steep embankment began crumbling. As if in slow motion, an enormous slab of rich red earth hit the roadway, narrowly missing the vehicle. With trepidation they continued, negotiating several more landslides. Maureen realized that if David's truck had not been available, this was the route they would have travelled on foot.

Although there was a local midwife, Maureen found that there was more than enough work to keep her busy. One night, returning late from her rounds, she met Michael, a head man, who requested that she see his wife, Roming. Maureen quickly identified the problem as premature labour. The couple were extremely nervous, since only a year before Roming had given birth to a stillborn child. Assisted by the husband and

Dina Wheatcroft, Maureen safely delivered the 2-kilogram baby boy, whom the couple named Walter Raleigh Michael!

This community project was arranged by the Sabah Foundation with the aim of improving the quality of day-to-day life in Sabah. It was hoped that it would serve as a model for other villages and, following the departure of Operation Raleigh, the programme is scheduled to be continued through the foundation.

Later I visited the beautiful thirty-storey aluminium and glass foundation headquarters, overlooking the waters of Likas Bay. The director, Dr Jeffrey Kitingan, discussed the tasks and praised our efforts. He made it all seem so worth while.

A week later Maureen returned to check on the expedition namesake. Stooping to enter the small, two-room bamboo hut where Roming had given birth only a few days before, she found shafts of light passing through the small window, illuminating the face and hair of the petite mother as she sat demurely next to the batik sarong which hung from the ceiling, serving as a cradle for her child. Despite a temperature well in excess of 32°C, Walter Raleigh Michael slept peacefully, swaddled in blue woollen mittens and a pink ski hat. Maureen emptied her medical bag, assembling the necessary components to form the baby scale and measuring device. The baby's healthy 2-kilogram birth weight had increased to a full 2.2-kilograms, pleasing everyone.

Stepping out of the hut into the bright glare of daylight, Maureen saw several hundred metres away a woman carrying a child. Turning, the woman looked back towards the village. Before beginning her ascent up the mountain, she raised her arm in triumph. Jasmine was going home.

Meanwhile, high on Mount Kinabalu, blonde Anja Ball from Britain was leading a trail-building team. Having just taken part in Operation Raleigh as a Venturer she had been lucky to get a staff post so quickly, but she was a talented climber. The mountain, although radiant by sunlight, is swiftly transformed to a place of darkness and danger at the onset of the sudden, violent storm. The unpredictable weather tested all her skills, especially as several of her team were novices. Nevertheless, assisted by experienced climber Guido Bonvicini of Italy, Anja got everyone to the summit and safely down again.

Mark Bowsfield of Australia later described the rope descent: 'Terrifying . . . we were beginning to suffer from hypothermia, little gullies became crashing, churning torrents, making it impossible to gain any footing on the sheer granite. We were so wet and cold, we hardly noticed.' After more dramatic river crossings and traversing steep waterfalls, they reached camp. Thawing out, they realized that there was a great deal of work to be done if they were to make the route 'safe for tourists' as they had been instructed.

SEE International also joined us in Malaysia and CHQ staff Simon Headington and Penny Knocker flew out to help with the administration of the group. Working in Sabah and Sarawak, Dr Harry Brown's team of Malaysian and American doctors tackled the job with their usual enthusiasm and energy.

Posters describing the programme had been printed in four of the region's languages and to make maximum use of SEE's operating time, the Venturers travelled to the remote longhouses and screened prospective patients for bilateral cataracts and squints. Once this was done, they tramped back along the treacherous paths to base, leading the blind candidates for surgery. This required courage from both parties and the blind Malaysians had to trust foreigners who did not speak their language.

Over a period of three days 900 patients were screened and 143 operated on. This was the largest number of operations SEE had performed in one expedition and certainly the greatest number of patients they had screened. In addition they arranged for an optician to supply 300 pairs of glasses.

Despite the difficulties encountered and the dedication required for the SEE project, 70 per cent of the Venturers asked to take part. Sara Oxley from Britain described their attitude:

Our sole concern was for the people we had brought down and we would move heaven and earth for them! This was a project where we were able to give Malaysia something in return for the experiences on other projects. We all felt honoured to be part of it as what we gained is something that we will never be able to repeat.

65

Off the coast of Malaysia there were brushes with real danger. Becky Lewis of Henley-on-Thames remembers her first night dive when carrying out a survey of the Fishing Department: 'My torch had gone out and I was holding on to my partner. Suddenly two eyes appeared out of the darkness and I saw my first shark only a few metres away.'

It was fortunate for Becky and her diving companions that the streamlined machine built for killing had other things on its mind. Ignoring the terrified girl, the shark swam on, and, long after the danger was over, Becky would remember the creature's cold stare.

As the Venturers in Australia during the summers of 1986 and 1987 were to find, one cannot reason with a shark. So pleased was nature with her first model, created some 300 thousand years ago, that she hardly bothered to alter the shark's morphology except to improve its feeding and swimming abilities. In Australia, the Great Barrier Reef and the waters off every coast were patrolled by large numbers of sharks – as well as by crocodiles and a host of other hazards that members of the expeditions would have to literally learn to live with.

CHAPTER FIVE

Of Billabongs and
Bush Camps

(*Northern Territory Leader*: Captain Peter Herden, RA INF)
(*Cape York Leader*: Major David H. Hudson, RA INF)

Peter Herden's Flying Circus, 15–19 June 1986

David Bennett tucked his crutches securely under his seat and settled back against the side of the olive-green De Havilland, the military tactical aircraft called a Caribou. The noise of the engines made earplugs essential and the small group ranged along the side benches of the aircraft could only communicate in sign language. In any case, the breathtaking sight below robbed David of speech.

The Caribou tailgate yawned open. Below ran a ribbon of acid green. It was the Drysdale River which snakes its way some 400 kilometres through the rust-coloured wilderness of Australia. The Venturers waving from the boulders lining the river had just completed the first-ever descent by canoe of the river.

Flying Officer John Turton brought the Caribou low over the river, buzzing the group below. For the next few days John, along with Flight Lieutenant Tony Bennett and Flight Sergeant George Owens, would fly our small group and an ABC Television film crew to expedition sites in the wilds of Australia's Northern Territory.

Thanks to the enormous effort of our Australian Director of Operations, Lieutenant-Colonel Robin Letts, a challenging series of expeditions had been planned for Raleigh down under. We were fortunate indeed to have the backing of Australia's Defence Department at Darwin and I was grateful to the Royal Australian Airforce base and to

67

Lieutenant-Colonel Neil Weeks, commander of NORFORCE, for their unstinting support. Over the next four days the motley group, which came to be known as 'Peter Herden's Flying Circus', would span several hours' time difference as we visited the various expedition sites.

The rock-strewn Drysdale did not permit a landing. Nevertheless, a small orange windsock flew hopefully below. The plane dipped its wings in greeting and banked again, steep and low. The slipstream wrenched the message of congratulations from my hand and sent it spiralling down to the young people from Singapore, Hong Kong, the US and Britain.

The river descent had taken fifteen months of planning. Urged on by the banter of leader Clive Richardson, the hardy international band had paddled over 320 kilometres in five weeks, desperately chasing the water which decreased each day. 'Our lives acquired feral dimensions,' wrote one Venturer in his log. He continued:

> Evening Prayers [briefings] were held around a campfire festooned with strips of grilling donkey or fresh fish staked on sticks. Even tortoise soup was downed with relish by most of our merry band. Only when it was dehydrated Chinese rations did some choose to 'eat out'.
>
> As the veneer of consumer society peeled away, we became fully absorbed in the moods of the river landscape. A land of contrasts: harsh yet soft; beautiful yet dangerous; full of ancient wonders. Never to be taken lightly, but for all of us, home.

The Caribou made a final pass over the Drysdale. Ahead loomed the white curtain of Jim Jim Falls. David Bennett grinned at the memory of a freezing swim a few weeks earlier. David has had cerebral palsy from birth. Without the use of his legs, even his powerful arms and skill with crutches could not get him over the boulders that blocked his path to the falls.

'When the trail ran out, project leader Barry Taylor carried me on his back. We found a carrying position less painful than the others, but the going was too treacherous. There was a better solution. Barry threw me clear of the rocks into the deep river pool. I swam towards the falls in the cold, brackish water beneath the gum trees.'

Above left: American Venturer Serena Wilson with one of the local children from Kunini, Papua New Guinea. *Above right:* Lance Corporal Raju Gurung of the Queen's Ghurkha Engineers, on the tower during the Lambir project of the Malaysian expedition. The tower enabled scientists to study the rainforest canopy. *Below:* Nurse Alison Farmer of Hampshire visiting her patients in Papua New Guinea.

Above: Venturers building a new church at Kunini in Papua New Guinea.

Below: Photographer Babette Seymour-Cooper and Ray Gallard, both from Bristol, being showered with rice after their traditional wedding in the church at Kunini, Papua New Guinea.

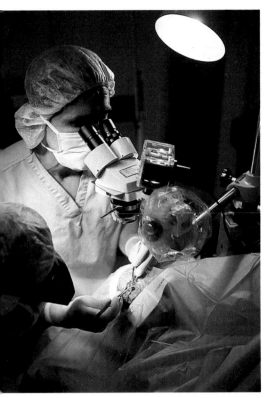

Above left: An American SEE International surgeon performing a cataract operation in Marudi, Malaysia. *Above right:* Nurse Sara Oxley from Sussex cooling off in the Andaman Sea after the SEE International project. *Below:* Venturers portaging an inflatable canoe along a shallow stretch of the Drysdale River in Northern Territory, Australia.

Above: The Operation Raleigh landing craft *Prince Harry* and *Prince William* in rough seas at Pandora Cay. These excellent boats were donated by the Merseyside County Council.

Below: The 20-foot whale shark 'Nellie' which frequently visited the wreck site and nudged the giant Avon inflatable diving tender *David Gestetner*. Perhaps she considered it a likely mate!

Above: View of the HMS *Pandora* wreck site. The anchor is thought to have been from HMS *Bounty* and was being carried back on *Pandora* as evidence. *Below left:* Ron Coleman, Curator of Marine Archaeology at the Queensland Museum, with a bronze wheel from *Pandora*. *Below right:* Alastair Brown of the Western Australian Museum with what may be an ink bottle. Copper cooking pot in foreground.

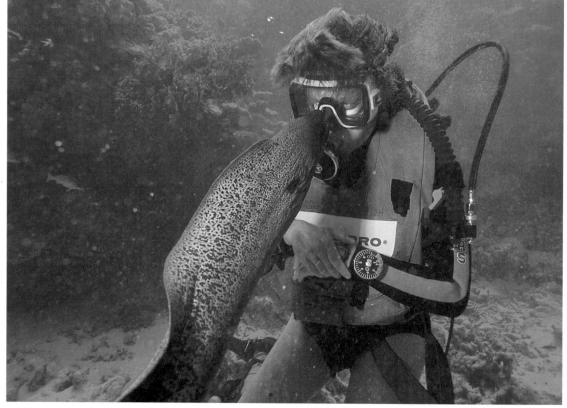

Opposite above: Robert Taylor from Cornwall watching the sunset from the top of Obiri Rock in the Kakudu National Park, Northern Territory, Australia.

Opposite below: Marine biologist Elizabeth Gimmler from Hampshire encounters a friendly Moray eel near Lizard Island on the Great Barrier Reef, Australia.

This page: Aboard *Zebu* off Mayotte Island in the French Comoros *(above)* James Usher, a Nabisco-sponsored Venturer from Liverpool, working aloft and *(below)* Canadian Venturer Stephanie Hughes sorting rations.

Above: Australian archaeologist Dr Peter Bindon and his assistant Bob Scott during a search for Dingo remains at Christmas Creek, Western Australia.

Below: American Venturer Burt Warren with Australian rock art expert Percy Trezise in the Cave of the White Lady, Quinkan, Queensland, Australia.

As the plane soared on, David watched the terrain turn snowy white. These were the salt flats where nothing grows but crystals: salt, quartz and diamonds. Two hours later, after refuelling, we arrived at our next destination, the 404,700-hectare cattle station called Christmas Creek.

With a loud hum, the ramps at the rear of the Caribou opened again. Shorthorn cattle and sleek horses raced our shadow as we came in for a landing. It was mustering time in the Poole Hills and the noise of our engines sent the animals into wild confusion.

In the days of the lighthorse campaigns in the Middle East, the Australian stock horse, called the Whaler, was the most famous war horse in the world. Today the breed excels at other jobs; Prince Charles praised its speed on the polo field, and here the ringers value the horse for its skill at working cattle.

The Caribou landed roughly in the Great Sandy Desert, 1280 kilometres south-west of Darwin, and a few metres away from a dead kangaroo. Through the dust David could just make out the sandstone hills that marked the horizon. Walking towards the plane was a willowy figure surrounded by tiny black children. He recognized Julie Monroe, an unemployed twenty-two-year-old from Liverpool. Like many others, including Jane Pares from Glasgow, who would later join our London HQ, and Brooklyn-born Mark Sardy, Julie had developed close ties with the community at Christmas Creek.

The Aborigines at this station only came out of the desert in 1968 and their way of life is much the same as it has been for centuries. Several of the luckiest young people had been invited on hunts, taught to carve boomerangs and told part of the knowledge of the past – the 'Dream Time' of the Aborigines.

If the Venturers at Christmas Creek were able to win the trust and friendship of the Aboriginal community faster than they had dared hope, it was largely due to Peter Bindon, a huge, bearded man, in the spirit of the legendary American lumberjack Paul Bunyan. Peter had worked with the community for years and had built up a strong rapport with the elders and families of the cattle station.

'This is an Australia the Australians don't see, the best side of Aboriginal life,' said Peter. The scientist was dressed in a lumberjacket and thong sandles. He sported a watch on one wrist and a compass on the other. 'There are plenty of reports about the worst side, the drunkenness and the unemployment and the illness. While they are here, these young people can make their own judgements.'

Listening to the Australian scientist, Californian nurse Paula Urschel felt the stirrings of a new idea. It was an idea which would soon bring her back at the head of an unusual team concerned with the problems of Australia's first people.

Peter Bindon can look at the charcoal of an ancient fire and tell you what was for dinner. Ethno-archaeology, the study of present-day activities which help to interpret the past, was an important part of the work of this desert expedition. Another project attempted to bracket the age of a unique fossil find, the calcified bones of a dingo, to within 150 years. Ultimately, the study of man's earliest 'best friend' may yield new information on the first migrations to Australia.

That night, under the low-slung stars, we swapped stories and sang until we exhausted our repertoire. Peter Bindon strummed his guitar and belted out songs from the Beatles to the classic Australian poet, Andrew Barton 'Banjo' Paterson. As the last strains of 'Tie Me Kangaroo Down, Boys' and 'The Pub with no Beer' drifted through the air, all but the hardiest made for their sleeping bags.

Away from the fire, the desert temperature plummeted. Pulling a heavy jersey over her clothes, Troni Merrylees wondered how she would manage to wake by five the next morning. The station stockmen, Aborigines and Europeans, had asked Mark, Jane and Troni to ride with them for the morning muster. The girl who had earned her spurs riding unbroken ponies in Nepal and Cyprus, knew the invitation was a great compliment; they couldn't be late.

Never had David Bennett spent a colder night in Australia, but he woke to the most glorious sunrise he had ever seen. Not content with a hasty dash of pink across the horizon, the dawn had filled the overturned bowl above with peach-coloured clouds. Once airborne, the Caribou's ramp opened again, and, ramp-riding with Nick Horne, David was the first to catch sight of the 10,500-square-kilometre Gregory National Park.

Together with the Conservation Commission, Operation Raleigh was conducting flora and fauna surveys within this virgin land. We watched as Venturers ringed rare crimson finches, jabirus and the beautiful dancing brolgas. I particularly admired the huge python which herpetologist Paul Edgar and North Carolinian Venturer Steve Vaughn brought into camp. This one was 1.8 metres long and as thick as my arm.

The flies covered us like blankets. The buzzing, black insects crawled around our lips and eyes and into every uncovered crevice. Only evening brought respite. The jungle clock seemed set for 7 p.m. As the sun went down, bats filled the skies, the beautiful white corellas came home to roost and the torture of the flies came to an end. It was the hour to slip down the river with Ford Cristo and Joe 'Crocodile' Macdonald to watch the jungle curtain rise.

Crocodiles have a crystal-clear third eyelid like a scuba mask. With it they can see through surface glare, spotting bullocks drinking at the water's edge or a careless swimmer. Freshwater crocodiles are relatively harmless and many a Venturer shared their river pools. It is the broad-snouted salties, or estuarine crocodiles that are the killers. No one swam in the rivers of Gregory.

'Have another grub,' urged Singaporean Venturer Frances Chee Chu, popping the segmented, deep-fried delicacy into my mouth. 'It's 16 per cent protein.' She passed round a tin plate of the deceased's nearest neighbours. In pride of place was the chartreuse eucalyptus grub that takes on the piney flavour of the tree it feeds on.

David Bennett sucked a green grub from its nut. 'It's fine,' he said, chewing slowly, 'but not as nice as the witchity.'

Deep in the lost spaces of Arnhem Land, the Bullman camp was made up of only eight Venturers and a handful of staff: Major Chris Burgin, whom I had last met in PNG in 1980, helped by District Veterinary Officer Dennis Thomson, and Henry and Tex the Aborigine guides. By a stroke of fortune, the day the flying circus came to Bullman, a special guest walked into camp: Captain Les Hiddins, a bush survival expert.

Buffalo steaks rounded off our lunch of grubs, green ants and river prawns. Had the famous mid-1800s expedition of Burke and Wills learned from the Aborigines, I reflected, they certainly would not have starved. But the buffaloes, imported 150 years ago from Timor, came later than these explorers. Grazing the black spear grass and just about everything else, the feral creatures destroy the land they live on. One of the projects of this isolated Raleigh oupost was to count the feral beasts and estimate the damage they cause.

At Kakadu ten years previously, the buffalo had left the land a dusty range devoid of vegetation. Now, according to Dennis, the buffalo in the arid land of Kakadu have been controlled: lilies and lotus blossoms were among the first flowers to return to the top end of the Northern Territory.

Counting swamp buffalo is a hazardous affair. Dennis, who 'can pick a bluebottle off a bull on a dark night', packs a .357 as insurance against a charging bull. As he says: 'A tonne of beef that decides it doesn't like you is extremely dangerous.'

Speaking from experience, I would rather face an enraged buffalo at Bullman than a hungry mosquito. The most savage 'animal' of any jungle or forest, the mosquito comes without warning and kills with a stealth Jack the Ripper would have relished.

At Kakadu Nasser al-Suleimany from the Sultanate of Oman, came face to face with a different dilemma, a dilemma with a long tail, a broad snout and rows of jagged teeth. After weeks of swimming in the Kakadu river pool Nasser saw a long floating log where no log had floated before. Shooting up through the water like a rocket, Nasser, closely followed by Sean McCormack and Joe Dellert, heaved himself onto the rough river boulders. The Omani and the Americans had just shared a bath with a saltie.

Kakadu is famous for its beauty and its wildlife. One of its mountains, Ubiri Rock, harbours the sacred Aborigine site known as 'Jabiru Dreaming'. It was also the site of one of the happiest and most extraordinary events of the expedition.

One of our expedition staff members, Robert Taylor of Taunton, Somerset, has been paralysed from the neck down since the age of seventeen following a motorcycle accident. Handsome, moustached, and with a twinkle in his eye, Robert came to Australia with his lovely friend and nurse, Alison Saltrese, to help with communications and to do access

surveys in the national parks and in Darwin for the handicapped.
Together they had covered a number of the expedition sites, but
although Alison had climbed the rock-clad mountain of Jabiru, Robert
thought it was impossible for him to reach the sacred summit in his
wheelchair. He was wrong.

With his arms around the massive shoulders of fellow staff member,
1.9-metre-tall American Craig Bush, Robert reached the top tied to
Craig's back. The American's long stride got them over the gaps between
the rocks, while two other friends carried the wheelchair up the steep,
barren hill. It was exhausting but they arrived as the sun set over the
flood plains below.

'The sunset lit the sky with a warm, burning orange,' recalls Robert.
'Far below, I could see the silver streak of the receding waters and the
bright green stripe of forest. All was quiet. I understood now why Jabiru
Dreaming was such a sacred place; I knew it would forever be part of me.'

Only two more stops remained for the Flying Circus: the islands of Melville and Bathurst, home of the Tiwi tribe. As the passengers jumped
from the Caribou they were met by Melville Council President
Pularunpi Ciril Rioli not far from the ruins of Fort Dundas. Here, 150
years ago, the British had tried to build a second Singapore. It was a
brave idea but a tactical diasaster: starvation, illness and well-aimed
Tiwi spears won the day. The competing colonial powers of France,
Germany, Holland and Portugal soon lost their appetite for northern
Australia.

The Northern Territory Museum of Darwin and the Western
Australian Museum in Perth had asked Raleigh's help to clear and map
the historic fort. The job was hard, hot and tedious. In spite of the heat,
flies and dust that were an everyday part of the job, Bahamian Sophia
Pintard looked immaculate. As always, expeditions are about people, not
places. For Sophia and the other island Venturers, learning the ways of
the Tiwis was the highlight of their stay. Painted by the Tiwis, Sophia
and British Venturer Ralph Pannell had danced at a funeral corroboree
and the girl from Freeport had hunted with the islanders for crab-
flavoured mangrove snakes and tree-climbing possums. 'Chewy,' was
Sophia's verdict on possum. 'Like steak.'

On 4 July the American Venturers on Melville and their international mates celebrated Independence Day by rowing to Bathurst in boats laden with tucker. America had already commemorated its bicentennial; on 26 January 1988 Australia would celebrate the 200th anniversary of the arrival of the First Fleet at Sydney's Farm Cove. The commodore of the fleet of eleven square-rigged ships retracing the voyage would be Captain Mike Kichenside of *Sir Walter Raleigh*. As the bicentennial approached, everyone in Australia hoped they had a first-footer – convict or not – somewhere in the branches of the family tree.

The arrival of that fleet was low on the list of happy historical moments for the Tiwis of Bathurst. Here the people 'go bush' for several months every year. Each year too, they are plagued by drought. Under Lieutenant Chris Reynolds of the 14th/20th King's Hussars, the Venturers were building a concrete dam and laying nearly 4.8 kilometres of pipeline to bring water to the bush site.

Sweat dripping from their lean, brown bodies, and dressed in little more than bathing suits and water bottles, the Venturers on Bathurst broke from their labour only for lunch or when they heard the shout of self-appointed snake watchers Phil Grice and Jim James: 'King brown coming down the track!' The call would have sent shivers of delight down the spine of herpetologist Paul Edgar.

For David Bennett Peter Herden's Flying Circus had been far more than just a way of seeing all of the far-flung expeditions. As the Caribou came in for landing after bumpy landing, David, like Paula and the others, had occasionally left his lunch behind. His earth-bound friends were thrilled that he had cadged a ride no other Venturer had managed – and had actually flown the plane.

'Excellent to hear David's cheerful voice and to see his green but smiling face,' wrote one unsympathetic expedition member. For the young man whose father was in the Airforce and who loved to fly, ramp-riding the DAC-4A and taking over its controls had been a particular achievement. It was David who had flown the Caribou into Melville as herds of buffalo scattered at the plane's approach.

'The big aircraft felt steady in my hands and I was soon able to stay level and keep to a given height and compass bearing. John, beside me, seemed completely relaxed (he must have nerves of steel) with his feet clear of the rudder pedals and his hands in his lap. I was really beginning to enjoy myself . . . It was good to get into the clouds and free of the earth.' Amen to that.

Quinkin Country, Cape York, August 1986

'I plan to live till I'm ninety-five, then get shot by a jealous husband,' said Percy Trezise, author, painter, pilot and one of the greatest authorities on the art of Australia's first people. Tough as a dingo and burned the colour of old mahogany, Percy was one of the project leaders of a remarkable series of expeditions which took place thousands of kilometres east of David's flight path: the Cape York wilderness.

On the north-eastern edge of Australia, youngsters from twelve countries were deployed over vast distances and diverse terrain. David Hudson and his skilled project leaders mounted expeditions in the rainforests of Bellenden Kerr, the river systems of the Mulgrave and Johnstone, and the arid bush of Rokeby which bristled with crocodiles and feral bulls.

At Lizard Island, named by Captain Cook after the monitors that guard its sandy beaches, Venturers dived on the Great Barrier Reef. On the dusty ranges of Old Laura, a once proud cattle station boasting 800 head, they restored the historic homestead built by a pioneer family. At Chillagoe and Lakefield they explored the famous labyrinthine caves and trudged through swamps and billabongs, and, as they climbed the mountains of McIllwraith, some turned their hand to panning for gold.

The gold of Quinkin country was of another sort: paintings of crocodiles, kangaroos, serpents, people, emus and echidnas on the walls of hidden caves. Black silhouettes of hands, and figures of men and women painted in blues, ochres and white are frozen in time. The paintings are the stories and culture of a people. Frequently they are powerful symbols of love and hunting magic as well as sorcery.

When Japanese Venturer Kazu Kayada from Fukushima City and Juliet Needell, a British girl born in Hong Kong, stumbled upon a gallery of bright blue figures, they felt a mixture of elation and fear. The cave was overgrown with shrubs and if a flash of blue had not caught Julie's

75

eye, it might still be unknown. Inside was a painted tangle of people who had never seen the sun.

The Venturers had woken that Sunday to a different world. The dawn chorus – some would say shriek – of rainbow lorikeets on the scrubby quinine trees was louder than any church bell. Someone had fetched water from the river and the billy was on the fire. As the smell of frying sausages and eggs rose in the morning air, Kazu, Juliet and the others swung out of their hammocks with an acquired grace and landed, fully dressed – for they had not undressed – and ready to go.

Some would climb high in the hills with Percy to his 'White Lady', a Cézanne-like outline painted with a sure hand in a fluid, continuous line. Percy had discovered her in 1969 with Dick Roughsey, now deceased, an Aborigine who was Percy's long-time colleague, friend and co-author, and who received an OBE for his services to Aboriginal arts. Others, like Kazu and Juliet, would head off in search of new discoveries.

When the last Quinkin Venturer piled into Percy's dilapidated Land Rover and headed out of the bush to Old Laura, the young people had found over forty new galleries and built a 32-kilometre track through the tortuous dry riverbeds. Their tools, in Percy's words, were 'chainsaws, axes and bloody backbone'. The track would enable the rugged Australian to bring in a series of 'Earthwatch' teams the following year for longer periods of study.

Lizard Island, August 1986

Nearly all the 192 Venturers on the Cape York expedition wanted to go to Lizard Island, a rocky outcrop of granite and coral about 4 kilometres long and 3.2 kilometres wide, but there was room for only 89. Among those who did go were Italian Paolo Scalvi, a future vet who had learned to scuba dive as soon as he heard he was on the expedition, and Edinburgh-based Dougie Potter who had accepted a job as navigator with the RAF to start after the expedition.

From the Laura Homestead project, came lovely Takako Takano, a graduate student of political science who played a mean electric guitar, ski'd like a demon and had agreed to be Tony Walton's right hand during the Japan phase in a few months' time. Like all Japanese Venturers, Tak had been sponsored by Nippon Denso Ltd. The support of the manufacturing giant would enable ninety Venturers from Japan to participate in Raleigh. At a Tokyo reception at the Akasaka Palace for Raleigh members, Tak had met Prince Charles.

'Use your natural ability to the fullest – Raleigh will provide the experience,' our Patron had advised. 'Japan will need your leadership in the years ahead.'

'Before he said that, I hadn't taken Raleigh very seriously,' said Tak. 'I resolved to do my best.'

Jasmina Hilton, who had joined as camp administrator and diving supervisor, was part of the team assembled by Major Peter Ormerod. Peter is adept at wearing a variety of hats: leader of the Lizard Island expedition, he is also Raleigh's chief diving officer.

A good 12 metres below the sea near Lizard Island is the home of the famous potato cod; huge, thick-lipped groupers which grow to almost 2.1 metres. Circling the divers expectantly, the potato cods would nudge and bump the Venturers, waiting to be fed. 'Overhead hovered shy Maori wrasse. The Moray eels were braver,' recalled Jasmina.

'On one dive,' she continued, 'I was kneeling in the sand feeding the cod when, unnoticed, an eel slid round the air cylinder, curled under my arm and pushed his nose into my lifejacket pocket.' Within seconds the long, thin thief had devoured the sausages the diver had kept safe for future fish picnics.

Under the water marine biology projects were led by Dr Charles Anderson of the Maldives as well as reef and seabed surveys. Under the sun the Venturers had built walkways and a bridge over a mangrove swamp. They had christened their efforts 'Mickey's Footbridge', after Michele Brew's big toe was broken when the bridge was accidentally lowered onto it.

The one great sadness for all on this island paradise was caused by something no one could control. When Venturer Ronnie Guy complained of a constant headache, he was flown from Lizard Island to hospital. A brain tumour was diagnosed: his aunt from Scotland was with him when he died weeks later.

All of us echoed Jasmina's thoughts: 'It was a terrible waste of a fine young man who could have made a good life for himself and those who shared it.'

*

Once in the azure waters of the Coral Sea, it was hard to prise the scientists and divers from its fascinations. As Peter Ormerod and his team on Lizard Island hosed down their diving gear in fresh water for the last time, a new international team of divers and archaeologists was assembling in Cairns. HMS *Pandora*, the oldest-known wreck in Queensland waters, had cast a potent spell.

CHAPTER SIX

In Australian Waters

HMS *Bounty*, August 1791

'Never fear, my boys, we'll all go to hell together.'

These words of encouragement, growled by HMS *Pandora*'s master at arms early one August morning in 1791, were almost the last that the imprisoned mutineers from the *Bounty* ever heard. But as the ship which held the captives began to sink to her grave on the Great Barrier Reef, the boatswain's mate opened the wooden cell and most of the men scrambled into the sea if not to safety.

This great saga of the sea had begun in 1787 when HMS *Bounty* was sent to Tahiti to collect breadfruit plants for the growing slave population in the Caribbean. Finding the attractions of the Tahitian ladies greater than service under the infamous Captain William Bligh, the British sailors seized the ship and started the most notorious mutiny in naval history.

Led by Fletcher Christian, the mutineers put Bligh and eighteen loyal crew into an open boat off the island of Tonga. Then they sailed back to Tahiti where the 'pirates' rejoined their ladies, many of whom were pregnant. Christian, however, with eight shipmates and a number of local men and women, sailed to Pitcairn, an uninhabited island, which, he knew, was wrongly marked on the charts. Their chances of ever being found were slight but they set fire to the ship as a precaution. As far as the world knew, it had simply disappeared.

Perhaps maligned as a leader of men, Captain Bligh was, however, an acknowledged master of the sea. Set adrift in an open boat, Bligh and his crew reached Timor in forty-one days, having navigated *Bounty*'s tiny launch 3618 nautical miles through terrible seas and the Great Barrier Reef. Their bold sea run is still a record. On return to England, Bligh acquainted their Lordships of the Admiralty with the news of his ship's fate. They were not amused.

Meanwhile, Fletcher Christian's paradise had soured. Quarrels with the Polynesians led to blows and all save two sailors were killed. By 1808, when the first ship called at Pitcairn, only one Englishman was alive to tell the tale, kept company by a large 'family' of women and the descendants of shipmates. These were the founders of the colony that exists to this day, and to whom Operation Raleigh's flagship, *Sir Walter Raleigh*, brought much-needed supplies and fuel in August 1986.

It was a strange fact that as our gleaming, 2000-tonne exploration vessel rode at anchor in the turquoise seas off the tropical isle, she was linked through history to the wreck of the *Bounty* 15 metres below, since the home port of both ships was the city of Hull.

Back in 1790 the Royal Navy had come to investigate the disappearance of their ship. HMS *Pandora*, a twenty-four-gun frigate captained by Edward Edwards, arrived at Tahiti in November and found the fourteen mutineers foolish enough to have remained on the island. They were dragged aboard *Pandora*, clapped in irons and incarcerated in a small cell. 'The heat was so intense that the sweat ran in streams to the scuppers and soon produced maggots . . .' ran the account of one unfortunate. The prison was called Pandora's Box.

The prisoners had no chance to bid farewell. Overcome with grief, their women stood in canoes holding their babies aloft as the man o'war sailed for England and the inevitable courts martial. The only sign of *Bounty* that remained was an anchor that Edwards had hauled aboard as evidence.

It was late in the day. Sailing for home on a westerly course, *Pandora* sought a passage through the Great Barrier Reef near what is today Cape York. She struck the knife-edged coral wall hard, hurling crew and captives alike on to the deck. During the frantic effort to save her, two of the ship's pumps broke: she sank at sunrise at a spot now known as Pandora's Entrance.

Thirty-one sailors and four of the mutineers drowned in the Coral Sea. The ninety-nine survivors, including ten mutineers, swam to a nearby cay where they erected sailcloth tents against the relentless sun. The mutineers had no such luxury. Their skins were lily white from five months of confinement in Pandora's Box: without protection they would die agonizing deaths. Midshipman Peter Heywood, one of the prisoners later to be pardoned, recorded, 'We had to bury ourselves up to the neck in the burning sand which scorched the skin entirely off our bodies . . .'

The hapless band that had survived the relentless forces of the sea and sun, had yet another test ahead. Like Bligh, the sailors managed to row to Timor and eventually reached England. Some of them need not have bothered. Six mutineers were condemned; three were hanged at the yardarm.

Pandora rested under the waves until 1977 when Australians Ben Cropp and Steve Comm, aided by RAAF anti-submarine aircraft using an aerial magnetometer, located the wreck in only 30 metres of water. The local museum's Curator of Marine Archaeology, Ron Coleman, followed up the discovery and soon well-preserved artefacts were brought to the surface, including the surgeon's watch. One of the earliest timepieces to have a second hand and a stop-watch control, it has now been restored to near working order.

In 1986 a larger expedition was planned to the historic wreck. A large support vessel with a recompression chamber was needed for the forty divers who would take part, and our Queensland Chairman, Nigel Porteous, suggested that we cooperate with the museum in this exciting venture.

Sir Walter Raleigh was the perfect ship for the job, he argued, and the project would be ably assisted by Tommy Smith of Brisbane as captain and by New Zealander John Parsloe as mate. I liked the idea. The six-week expedition would provide information of great value for our hospitable Australian friends, and at the same time offer some really advanced diving for ex-Venturers.

The crew, which included young men and women from Operation Raleigh and some superb US and Royal Australian Navy personnel, needed all their skills for the challenging project. Our square-rigged, 21.9-metre brigantine, *Zebu*, also supported the expedition with sixteen Venturers and nine crew, while back in Cairns, energetic operations officer Nick Horne and Adjutant Major Hawk Freeman organized sea planes to resupply the expedition. Again we experienced the unstinting generosity and enthusiasm of Cairns as a great many companies and individuals donated supplies.

One tragedy marred the great success of the expedition, however.

Pandora claimed yet another life, that of *Sir Walter Raleigh*'s popular able seaman, Neil Carmichael, who had sailed with *Raleigh* across the Pacific. On a calm, warm night, whilst on anchor watch, Neil disappeared without trace, despite an intensive search. It can only be assumed that he fell overboard attempting to adjust a mooring line on a boat secured astern.

Pandora is 'the most significant wreck in the southern hemisphere', according to archaeologist Dr Margaret Rule, Research Director of the Mary Rose Trust. Agreed a museum officer, 'We are only scratching the surface of this remarkable wreck which will give us an unrivalled collection of late eighteenth-century naval artefacts and much more information about shipboard life of the period.'

Certainly it was clear that *Pandora*'s officers were enthusiastic collectors, for stone implements, wooden clubs, cowrie shells and carved fishing lures were found in abundance, one of the finest collections of datable ethnographic material in the world.

Captain Edwards' underwater cabin also yielded historical treasure. Parts of sextants, hour glasses and what appeared to be a complete flintlock pistol, were brought to the surface. Soon *Sir Walter Raleigh*'s deck was covered with bottles, plates, wine glasses and even a stone water purifier. Human bones were also found – the sad remains of the thirty-five men who met their graves when *Pandora* sank in the Coral Sea.

The Coral Sea, 22 July 1987

The stars hung like chandeliers over the dark Australian waters. Separated by the boom, two young sailors sat on the aft deck of *Zebu*, gazing at the sky.

'How many stars on your side, Shirley?' asked Asoka Markandu from Singapore. There was a long pause.

'Five hundred and thirty-four billion,' Shirley King replied.

'Aha! I have one more than you,' retorted Asoka.

Suddenly a star streaked across the sky and disappeared.

'Not any more,' said Shirley. 'Now we're even.'

By the time *Zebu* arrived in Cairns for a 'shave and haircut', as Captain Peter Masters called *Zebu*'s refit before she joined the *Pandora* project, she had covered 28,000 nautical miles and visited seventeen countries, among them Portugal, the Bahamas, the Canary Islands, Panama, the Galapagos Islands, Hawaii, Fiji and New Zealand. Almost more impressive, 4000 loaves of ship's bread had been baked in the galley. I wondered which hungry accountant had made that calculation, but I supposed it was an indication of how important food became to these young sailors. Prince Charles would have chuckled to see his portrait in the galley – draped with parsley.

By now she knew the Australian waters well. The last expedition had used *Zebu* as a diving platform prior to their 3520-kilometre run from Adelaide via Tasmania to Sydney. Anchored over the nineteenth-century wreck of the *Zanoni*, the Baltic trader became a treasure chest of solid silver cutlery and ironstone plates which had last seen the light of day 120 years ago.

When Asoka and Shirley joined *Zebu* in May 1986, they knew little about sailing and less about square-riggers. Neither did Martin Webb, a twenty-one-year-old technician with British Telecom, or Tim Stevens, a sandy-haired graduate from Allentown, Pennsylvania. They soon learned the ropes – literally. *Zebu* has about 100, each with a different name. There are halyards and sheets, clews and brails, but within a week the new crew had mastered the language of the sea as well as the words to Nick's sea shanties, like 'The Son of the Son of a Sailor' which turned the air such a vivid shade of blue. They also became adept at serving up supper from the narrow galley, keeping the route to the deck clear for seasick customers. 'The only way to cure seasickness is to sit under an oak tree,' said Peter Masters ruefully.

On board *Zebu* the old sailing skills were kept alive; the ropes were made of natural fibre, so the miles of rigging required continuous maintenance. So too did the woodwork and brass. Watches were split into four hours on and eight hours off, but no matter how deep asleep, the shouted 'All hands on deck!' galvanized the Venturers into action.

The call rang out in the middle of the night as *Zebu* began her run from New Zealand to Cairns. The crew had unfurled the topsails for a run down Queen Charlotte Sound and tacked southwards towards Auckland. At dinner that night the watch on deck spotted whales to starboard, gliding through the gentle swells. Tim Stevens curled his long body onto the driest part of the mattress and fell sound asleep. The shout of 'All hands!' knocked him from his bunk and he scrambled into any clothing he could find. On deck the coarse sheet flapped freely, making a thundering din. The high winds had torn it loose and the whiplash of the sail could have easily knocked a sailor off the yards.

'It took twenty minutes to gain control of the sail, and another hour to stow it properly,' remembers Tim. The winds rose higher as *Zebu* continued along the eastern coast of North Island. The huge swells made Tim feel queasy down below, so again he climbed on deck for fresh air.

Some premonition made him look up. Just in time he saw the metal shrouds crashing down. There was the deafening sound of a breaking sheet as the vang lines, which support the gaff, broke. The gaff snapped in two and the huge beam swung madly back and forth. A metre from where Tim stood, heavy blocks smashed into the aft cabin and one fell into the sea.

Rob Bradley's bosun's knife flashed as he swiftly cut the sheet to the knock staysail. You don't cut a sheet unless the situation is drastic; here, the sheet had become entangled with one of the other ropes and the untamed sail was deadly. Finally the bulky beam was lowered down the mainmast and lashed to the boom. The danger fled into the darkness as quickly as it had come.

During the late night watch, a school of dolphins chased the bow of the tall ship, splashing and playing in the silver waves of phosphorus. 'It seemed as if Walt Disney had animated the *Fantasia*-like spectacle,' wrote Tim that night in his log. 'The dolphins continued to romp in the frigid waters they call home as I retired to my warm sleeping bag below.'

'Set the squares!' boomed the skipper. It was the moment everyone had been waiting for. Asoka, Tim, Lana Wedmore and the others sprang into action, climbing swiftly up the rope ladders and along the yardarms that bucked and swayed high above deck. The sails billowed out, catching the south-westerly wind, and *Zebu* surged ahead, rejoicing in her speed.

In calmer waters, the brigantine sailed down moonlit paths to fantasy islands: Tanna, with its sacred volcano glowing orange in the night; Malekula, home of the Big Namba tribe, who knock out their women's front teeth as a sign of affection; and Martyr Island, where scores of early missionaries were massacred. Anchoring off wide bays fringed with palm and papaya, the Venturers had their pick of coral atolls for snorkling and scuba diving. At night their barbecues were shared with locals who filled the night with the rhythm of their drums.

Tom Thumb, Cairns, 28 July 1986

As *Zebu* unfurled her thirteen sails for the run into Cairns, two people waiting on shore watched with special interest. Only a few days earlier, Mark Darby, a 2-metre-tall Australian from New South Wales, and Michelle Theis, a naturalist from California, had navigated the harbour buoys in a craft which could not have been more different to *Zebu*. The *Tom Thumb* was a 4.8-metre catamaran; two bright yellow sea canoes strapped together, carrying a mainsail and a jib which would take them round the huge continent of Australia.

Both Mark and Michelle knew Operation Raleigh well. Mark, an outward-bound instructor with a degree in parks and recreation administration, was a popular member of the Raleigh team in North Carolina, working with my tireless friends, Ann Smith and Mark Bensen. Michelle held a degree in the same subject and had helped out on many selection weekends in California.

Together the two had planned the thirteen-month trip. Leaving Sydney Heads on 3 May 1986, and covering some of the same waters as *Zebu*, Mark and Michelle had sailed 1500 nautical miles in the fibreglass catamaran by the time they reached Cairns. Although backed up by a Yamaha engine, the little craft had other, less regular equipment like the silver aluminium bladders from wine casks which they ran up the mast as radar reflectors so that other boats could spot them.

The trip from Cairns around Cape York and into the Gulf of Carpentaria would, the young couple knew, bring hazards of a different nature. Drinking water would be in short supply, inhabited areas few, and there would be tidal currents of up to 5 knots. As the Raleigh expeditions on the isolated cape would also learn, the tropical temperatures and intense humidity would take their toll. With the heat would come the 'Wet': the season of torrential rains.

There would be other, uniquely Australian hazards ahead too. 'The crocodile mating season starts in October and makes them very aggressive,' explained Mark. 'It's also the season of the box jellyfish. A sting from one of its transparent tentacles, which reach 9 metres, can kill you in minutes. Then there are the sharks, so we will have to be very careful where we throw food scraps, where to go to the toilet, things like that.'

'Our policy will be not to go near the water,' laughed Michelle.

Mark and Michelle had called their catamaran after the boat of the early British sea explorer, Matthew Flinders, who named Australia and was the first man to circumnavigate Terra Australus. Later in the 1850s he set off with George Bass, a ship's surgeon, in a 2.4-metre whaler, the *Tom Thumb*, to explore the southern coast.

I congratulated Mark and Michelle on their research and their spirit; Raleigh expeditions in the wilderness of Cape York would be keeping one eye out for crocodiles and the other for a small yellow catamaran.

CHAPTER SEVEN

It's Tough at The Top

(*Torres Straits Leader*: Major Charles Daniel)

Northern Territories, Australia, July 1987

It isn't heroin, coke or pot that Aborigine parents worry about. It's petrol sniffing. Cheap and readily available, petrol can be sucked from the tank of a car, motorbike, outboard or even a lawn mower. The short-term effects are dizziness, violence and addiction. The long-term effects are brain damage and death. The children have cause to worry too. Their parents can usually find the money for alcohol, and eventually the entire family suffers from the disease which often leads to more violence, homelessness and early death.

Paula Urschel's idea, conceived while she and I talked to Peter Bindon and to the Aborigines living at Christmas Creek, did not take long to become a reality. In a few months' time, the Santa Barbara nurse had made a proposal and received the blessing of the Australian Government, and in July 1987 she came back to the Northern Territories under the auspices of Raleigh with her team of paramedics.

One volunteer was an old friend of mine, Eric Niemi, a biology teacher with long years of experience in counselling young people, who had also been with Raleigh in Panama and Costa Rica. The other two, Tony Barlow and Juanita Dixon, were outstanding counsellors for young people and families suffering from addiction. Both American Indians, they had seen their own tribes suffer many of the same problems the Aborigines now face.

The situation is fraught with political and emotional issues. Too often, for example, the addictions of any people in the world are regarded as a feature of their personalities. Raleigh's special project in the Northern Territories could not become involved in these complex matters, however. Our aim was to work with the Council for Alcohol Programme Services and the skilled team at the Gordon Symons Centre: near Darwin, where we hoped to take an active counselling role and to exchange ideas.

During the summer months Paula, Juanita, Tony and Eric lived in villages and towns and 'went bush' for weeks on end in the remote areas of the Daly River, Bathurst Island, Jabiru, Galiwin'ku and Maning Grida. They would be the first to recognize how limited their help could be, given the enormity of the problem. But help they did, and their contribution could stem the growth of the addiction in a few cases. Without such assistance there is a real fear amongst all the people of Australia that the twin addictions of petrol and alcohol will not be defeated, and that 30,000 years of 'the dreaming' could evaporate with this generation.

Jardine River, Cape York, 30 July 1987

As Paula Urschel and her team worked with the Aborigines in the western part of Australia, my friend Charlie Daniel, a brave soldier and dedicated bachelor, was mounting a far-flung expedition on both the Cape and the Torres Strait islands. At the close of the expedition, he had, with equal grace, won the battle of logistics, but lost his bachelorhood.

Cape York is the northernmost point of the world's smallest continent, or largest island, depending on one's view of Australia. North of the Cape itself lie the island jewels of Naghir, Moa and Thursday Island, made famous by the stories of Somerset Maugham.

Conventional seasons don't exist at the top end of Australia. While the southern states were blanketed in the largest snowfall in thirty years, the north, which, with simple mathematics, divides the year into 'the Wet' and 'the Dry', was enjoying bright warm days, clear skies and moonlit tropical nights. It was tough at the top.

In fact the Venturers exploring the unknown reaches of the Cape's Jardine River were really finding it tough. The aim of the expedition was to navigate and explore the west-flowing river to its source, making biological surveys *en route*. At the end of one long, steamy trek through the jungle, Brian Seymour noticed that Andrea Jackson had a pronounced limp. There was blood on her socks when she put new plaster on her feet.

88

To keep her blisters dry, the gallant lad offered Andrea a piggy-back across the river.

The idea was to go two by two across the Jardine, home of huge crocodiles. As Brian and Andrea set off, everyone else scanned the river for salties, which can bite a boat in two. That was why they didn't see the snake. No sooner had the pair gained the far shore, than something hit Andrea's ankle hard, plunged into the Jardine and headed upstream at speed.

'Snake!' called the tousle-haired Scot somewhat weakly.

'What snake?' replied the next pair in midstream, looking about the swirling waters. Suddenly the streak of silver made an about-turn and came straight for Leicestershire Venturer Yvonne Cook, up to her waist in water.

'Oh, that snake!'

'I'd step out if I were you,' said Australian leader Martyn Swain in his cool, 'no worries, mate' style. 'It's a king brown.'

They flew up the bank with the viper right behind.

Having chased the intruders from his watery kingdom, the king brown plunged back into the river. It took a bit of courage for the rest to make the crossing.

The three bushmen leading the Jardine River expedition certainly looked the part: handsome, rugged and at home in a slouch hat. Martyn Swain, Mark Geyle and Dave Fell had been with Raleigh on earlier Australian expeditions to the Johnstone River and the McIllwraith Range. The trio had an easy style of leadership and the happy combination of long experience in the bush and scientific backgrounds. The former enabled the Venturers to go with confidence where few had gone before; the latter provided answers to the myriad questions posed by the jungle plants and animals.

In addition to the snakes and crocodiles, bats, birds and botanical wonders, there were wild boars, a legacy from Captain Cook, which provided many a supper for the Venturers. The four-year-old brindled pig now cooking on the fire weighed about 87 kilos; it would supplement the dried rations for several days to come.

Around the evening campfire, set at a respectful distance from the crocodile slides, the three Australians told tales of the explorers who had gone before. Indeed, the Venturers walking through the vine-tangled trees sometimes came across an ancient axe blaze; the cut probably marked the passage of the Jardine brothers 100 years ago. Since then only a handful of people had travelled the upper reaches of the river. A continent of 7,700,000 square kilometres, much of it desert, jungle, rainforest and dense scrub, is not easily explored.

While the names of the great Australian explorers are known, their stories often remain mysteries. There were Bass and Flinders, in whose wake Michelle Theis and Mark Darby now sailed their little yellow catamaran. There were Burke and Wills, who crossed the continent from south to north in 1860 only to die in the desert when their companion left seven hours before they reached the rendezvous.

Then there was Ludwig Leichhardt, the Prussian draft dodger with a bad sense of direction whose disappearance – and that of his seven men and seventy-seven beasts – remains an untold tale, and Harry Lasseter, who died in the 1930s after finding a reef of gold a metre deep and 16 kilometres long. Or so he claimed in his sand-encrusted diary.

But one tale around the campfire was as familiar to the Venturers as their own, for the story of Edmund Kennedy and his Aborigine guide, Jacky Jacky, had unfolded here on the Jardine. This was the land called the 'Wet Desert' by the explorers since it had plenty of water but no feed for the horses. In 1848 spear-carrying natives, lack of supplies and hostile terrain forced Kennedy to send his companions to the east coast, while he and his guide pushed on. It was a courageous decision, but not one to grow old on. The natives came in for the kill and Kennedy died in Jacky Jacky's arms. Speared himself, Jacky Jacky nevertheless made it through the jungle, found the schooner that was to take them off the peninsula, and rescued the others stranded on the coast.

The young Venturers, whose footsteps must have literally crossed those of the Kennedy expedition, were a diverse bunch. Mushtaq ('Mushie') Kazi, Paramjit ('Pram') Bhogal and Primalyn ('Prim') McLean were part of the terrific group of Birmingham inner city Venturers. Others were Jimmy Kaighin from the Isle of Man, Charles Smith from Yorkshire, and popular Lim Chin Hwee from Singapore, a triathlete and a student at Ngee Ann Polytechnic. Chin is quick to tell a funny story, especially against himself.

Under a canopy of acacias, Liverstonia palms and flowering paperbarks smelling of cinnamon and honey, Chin demonstrated the technique of simultaneously slapping stinging ants off his arms and stir-frying the butchered boar. The others, having tried to roast and stew the tough meat, waited patiently for the only palatable solution. 'I had no idea Raleigh meant this when they said we were going to the jungles of Australia,' says Chin. 'I read the kit list, but dismissed it; instead of jungle boots, mosquito nets and thick trousers I brought bathing trunks, shorts and sunglasses. Oh, and a cap for the river. I looked more like I was going to the pub than to the jungle.'

Chin's only complaint was the food, which was why he took over so often as cook and even carved chopsticks for those who had lost their Western utensils. 'Even the fish tastes different here,' said the young athlete. 'Beef and bread are totally alien to me. Noodles and chicken are mainstays in Singapore, but when you're hungry, everything tastes good.'

Food was not one of the three real concerns of the expedition, for the jungle and river could always produce emergency rations. Crucial to survival were communications, safety, and fresh water, especially once the expedition moved inland. Along the way the young people would learn the skills of map-and compass-reading, navigation and boat handling and how to survive in some of the world's most hostile terrain.

The group's radio was being repaired and the lack of access to airwaves made boatman Bill Arnold's resupply runs between Bamega and the expedition even more vital. A Raleigh veteran – he had been on the Black River expedition in Honduras – Bill had an uncanny knack of finding a way through water, no matter what the river conditions. The Mariner engines that Raleigh has used from the start, can cope with as little as 45 centimetres of water – which helped.

Once they left the river to head for the coast, twenty-year-old Venturer Chris Maund from Shrewsbury, Shropshire, would lead one of the small teams. I know he has the survival skills, thought expedition leader Charlie Daniel, but if Chris is at all weak on leadership, taking his group through the rainforest, tropical jungle, swamps and woodlands will do the trick. It was a 'no worries, mate' situation. Chris and the rest of the Jardine expedition came through with flying colours.

Riversleigh and the Gulf of Carpentaria, 20 July 1987

It was Bruce Leach who introduced me to marsupials. When Tac HQ first came to Cairns, the caretaker of our borrowed Australian headquarters had been told that a 'Pommy colonel' was on the way. The tough-talking Australian, who could drink anyone under the table, tell the bluest of blue stories and quote pages of 'Banjo' Paterson's poems, was expecting a real stuffed shirt.

I decided to rumble that expectation as soon as we met.

'Where's your bloody kangaroo, then!' I bellowed, stretching out my hand.

Without batting an eyelid, he produced one – a tiny, chocolate-coloured joey, or baby kangaroo, which hopped about at his heels, feasting on coconut biscuits.

But even Bruce would have been startled by the Joey's prehistoric relatives that Raleigh sought at Riversleigh. If you could slide down the west side of Cape York Peninsula, you would land not far from one of the world's greatest fossil deposits. Riversleigh, just south of the Gulf of Carpentaria, is a private cattle station and a treasure trove of creatures that writers of fiction could not invent: marsupials the size of Toyotas preyed upon by tree-climbing marsupial lions. Ten years ago the only treasure to come out of this land was copper, silver, lead and zinc.

Today Australia has the world's prize collection of marsupials; mammals born prematurely that develop in their mother's pouch. The best-known are kangaroos, wombats, koalas and bandicoots, but they range from the recently extinct Tasmanian wolf to tiny moles and mice. Australia's share of Noah's Ark was discovered only a few years ago by Dr Michael Archer, and the fossil deposits at Riversleigh will do much to change our conception of the early world. Giant kangaroos, diprotodonts (gigantic beasts sporting huge tusks), and 7-metre pythons roamed this land, which was once part of Gondwana, a huge continent which also included what is now Africa, South America, India and Antarctica. There dolphins played, in areas which are desert today.

Riversleigh was the habitat of creatures so odd that serious scientists have given them light-hearted names like 'Bizarrodontia' and 'Thingodontia'. Asked how 'Thingodontia' got its name Henk Godthelp of the University of New South Wales, who was working with the

Venturers, grinned. 'It was a very strange thing, and it don'ta resemble anything else.'

With such a rich motherlode at Riversleigh, palaeontologists are hopeful that the surrounding country will yield more discoveries. Project leader John Courtenay had organized a second scientific project in the gulf savannah country along Colless Creek, Lawn Hill Gorge and Musselbrook Creek. In the dry wilderness of spinifix plains and open grasslands, often the only way the Venturers could get to the different sites was by canoe.

Twenty-two-year-old Beatrice Retchford knew the country like the back of her hand. The pretty, straight-talking Aboriginal ranger, a member of the Lardil tribe, is at home in the bush, and knows its secrets: where to find the wild passion fruit and berries, the red pig weed, wallabies that taste like chicken, and, of course, the witchity grubs that, by now, most Venturers had come to enjoy.

Beattie, as she is known, maintains a healthy respect for the sacred places of the bush: some are so sacred that to enter them would be breaking tribal law. And that is very dangerous. 'I've seen far too much to underestimate the power of the spirits and what they can do,' she says. One power in particular, called 'boning', is a tribal way of killing those that break the law. A group from the tribe wear feathers on their feet and track the outlaw. When they find him – and they always do – they point a special bone at him and sing; within days the person dies.

She and Jock Pedro, a tribal elder living with the Venturers at Riversleigh, often accompany them in the bush. Jock knows all the sacred places. 'If he doesn't want them to go into a place,' said Beattie, 'I'll do anything in my power to keep them from going.'

As she spoke, the young ranger bent down and casually picked up a spear head from the ground. 'This was used for wallabies,' she said, almost absent-mindedly, holding the 8-centimetre serrated flint. She put it back exactly where she found it. It will stay there because things are only of importance if they are viewed within their context. The small spear head was part of the larger story of Riversleigh.

*

Moa and Naghir Islands, August 1987

Many kilometres away, but still on the mainland, there were other expeditions near Charlie Daniel's headquarters at Bamega, and at Eliot and Fruit Bat Falls. Here the primary projects involved construction, although plant and animal surveys, bioresources projects and crocodile counts were all part of a week's work.

The Venturers were building a community centre for the Aboriginal village of Cowal Creek and, with the National Parks and Wildlife Service, making barriers to keep cars from delicate conservation areas and constructing tourist facilities. The morale and energy levels of the young builders were high; it was the supply of tools and materials that was often low, held up by government red tape and the long distances it had to travel.

There were no such supply problems at the building sites on Moa Island. And for a very good reason. Here, the Venturers were building two substantial houses for the islanders, using only materials available on the island: trees, stones and mortar made from termite mounds.

Moa Island is a round, hilly punctuation mark in the island-studded sea between Papua New Guinea and the tip of Cape York. Washed by the Arafura Sea to the west and the Coral Sea to the east, the island is whipped by typhoons and high winds, and the corrugated-iron structures, which house up to fourteen people, are expensive to build and do not last well.

Working with the islanders and a gentle, sunburned bush architect, Paul Haar, the Venturers were building more substantial houses which would also serve as examples for others who wanted do-it-yourself shelter. The stone, mostly white quartz, comes from the hills and beaches. The timber is found in the bush: bloodwood, hard and durable; mangrove, tough and stright; and brown pine, also called mast wood, which is used for window and door frames.

The mortar holding the structures together was an interesting mixture of fifteen parts ant hill and clay, and one part cement, which the Venturers mixed with river water by tramping on the sticky stuff barefoot. If it wasn't for a few extras like palm trees and coral reefs, it could have been a scene from an old French village during the *vendange*.

On neighbouring Naghir, an uninhabited island owned by Martin Nakata and his family, the Raleigh youngsters had practically gone feral.

They and project leader Glen Wyatt, a survival expert and deep-sea diver, had been put ashore, Robinson Crusoe-like, with only enough water for fifteen days. The sea was a well-stocked larder: the top priority was to find the wells that Martin said were there, now overgrown by vines and shrubs.

Their first view of their island home was of palm trees, white beaches, rocky outcrops and lagoons. Along the sand grew blue-flowering vines, and huge green turtles slithered into the water at their arrival. They could see immediately that the coconuts, gourds and bamboo would serve as useful receptacles, as would the giant clams and bailer shells washed up on the shore.

Pulling the boats onto the beach, the Venturers kept a wary look out for crocodiles. Although none were seen that afternoon, they did make a more startling discovery. A human shinbone lay under a magnolia tree. Bleached by the sun, its stark whiteness contrasted with the wild poinsettias, the colour of blood, which grew beside it.

It took the Venturers only two days to find the water that would determine the success or failure of the island expedition. Search parties had been out all day, clearing the thick undergrowth with machetes in an attempt to spot a tell-tale depression that would indicate an ancient well. Stewart Shirley was the first to find one. It was curious to see palm trees growing out of scrubland, thought the eighteen-year-old student from North Carolina, and deduced that it must be getting more water from somewhere. He was right. In the next few days the Venturers found a second well and knew the expedition would be successful.

Rebuilding the old school, clearing and restoring the island cemetery and building a track to the top of Mount Ernest were some of the Naghir projects, but even these paled in comparison with one that had not been scheduled: the wedding of Jasmina Hilton and Charlie Daniel. All the Venturers were invited.

Tropical fruit and island food was spread out in a long buffet, and Jasmina, bedecked with flowers, had never looked lovelier. It had taken some Venturers five hours to get to Naghir by boat, and the huge waves at the end of the day made the return journey seven hours long. But clearly this was a social event not to be missed. From far away I toasted my friends and wished them the happiness of a lifetime.

95

CHAPTER EIGHT

From Cradle Mountain
to Great Kosciusko

(*Tasmania Leader*: Lieutenant-Colonel Greg Melick, RA INF)
(*Victoria Leader*: Warrant Officer Neil Hampson, RAEME)

Cradle Mountain, Tasmania, 23 December 1986

'Snake bit her on the bum; died before she got down,' drawled the ranger, stirring his coffee as he recounted the tragic tale of the death of a young walker in the National Park some years ago. Tramping ankle deep in pre-Christmas snow, we found it hard to imagine this a land of snakes, but much about Tasmania is a contradiction.

Falling like a teardrop from the south-east edge of Australia, the island state of Tasmania is, in reality, fiercely proud of its geographical independence from the continent. Its isolation and what a newscaster might call 'variable' weather, a euphemism for the stormiest climate anywhere in the world, were a double disincentive to early explorers.

Like New Zealand's South Island and Chile's Patagonia, Tasmania is below the 40th parallel and the playground of furious winds – the Roaring Forties – that our flagship would later encounter as she made her way home from Australia to Hull. Eventually, of course, some explorers did stumble upon Tasmania, and local names like Flinders Island and the Banks Strait give tribute to the most famous of them: Tasmania itself was named after the great Dutch navigator, Abel Tasman.

Once they'd found the island, no one quite knew what to do with it. The aggressively hostile terrain, a backcloth of black mountains, steep ravines and rivers liable to sudden flooding, do not, at first sight, seem an inviting proposition. These, however, were the very characteristics that made Tasmania a perfect choice for an expedition. The geography is as

96

diverse as the rest of the country's, ranging from humid rainforests to near arctic tundra. Without doubt, it is some of the toughest country I've ever known.

We had arrived at the height of summer down under to find ourselves struggling up the 1816-metre-high slopes of Cradle Mountain. As night-fall approached, I realized we were not going to reach the Venturers' camp that day, and I was thankful to see an emergency hut ahead, a welcome shelter from the storm.

As we entered it, Joel Schmiedeke, my cheerful USAF adjutant, did a classic house search worthy of any private eye. He didn't have far to look. Inside was a large but moving sleeping bag. Joel poked it cautiously and the heads of a honeymoon couple emerged.

'G'day,' said the man. Joel asked if he'd mind sharing the nuptial bedroom with four weary travellers.

'Make yourselves at home, mate,' grunted the Aussie, disappearing back into the bag.

Twelve hours later the pair were still inside and had not once left their cocoon.

'What stamina these Australians have,' remarked Rodrigo Noreiga, our Chilean mountaineer, admiringly.

We awoke to a blanket of new snow that would have made even the most sentimental dreamer of a white Christmas reconsider. It was Christmas Eve and we trudged on to find the Venturers. Two large wallabies hopped across our path, clearly unhindered by the snow.

Eventually we reached the tented camp where Randy Galloway, a USAF para-rescue specialist, and nine Venturers were constructing a track on ground above the route that the thousands of hill walkers had churned to mud. Shivering in the biting wind, Abdul Qadir, a twenty-two-year-old clerk from Oman, assured me of a warmer reception in his country. But Abdul and everyone else was cheerful enough and glad to have the mail and Christmas wine that Rod had lugged up in his pack.

*

Lake St Clair, 26 December 1986

Not far away more Raleigh builders were constructing an impressive suspension bridge over the Narcissus River. In the distance, a movement caught my eye and we turned to see the huge black figure of a man approaching through the pines. Curtis Lonie, twenty-one years old, was from Chicago and an inner city member of the expedition. Over 1.9 metres tall, Curtis was massively built and weighed in like a Sumo wrestler. Happily his great size was matched by his gentleness and good humour. By the time he went home, he had shed 38 kilos. Raleigh has that effect on people.

The expedition leader, Major (later Lieutenant-Colonel) Greg Melick, an officer of the Australian Army Reserve, had been plucked from the Tasmanian Court, where he is a crown counsel. Greg had been thrust into the position of expedition leader because someone discovered that he had once spent time in a commando unit. With much help from local organizations, he had put together a programme of community work, scientific exploration and adventure which would take the Venturers into some of the most demanding environments in Australia.

There was understandable concern about sending young people with limited survival skills into this potentially dangerous wilderness area, especially given the vagaries of the Tasmanian weather. Assurances of the selection procedures that winnowed the fittest for the project relieved some of the worries but, with Murphy's Law hovering in the air, the organizers were on edge for much of the expedition. As insurance they had an excellent group of servicemen from Australia and the United States to assist.

The north-western part of the island was one of the most testing areas of any in Tasmania: its tip is tellingly named Cape Grim. Staff Sergeant Gary Byington, US Marine Corps, fought to keep his team resupplied despite the lack of roads and the abundance of foul weather, bad enough even to rule out air support. Gary's first-aid training came in handy treating hypothermia cases and burns, but his calmness in a crisis really showed when he surprised a gang of bandits looting the base camp. Held at gunpoint, he reasoned with his captors whilst making mental sketches of their appearance and memorizing their vehicle registration number. Thanks to his quick-wittedness the gang was quickly caught.

Meanwhile an archaeology team was working at an old convict settlement site on Sarah Island. During Raleigh's stay, Venturer Patricia Ortenzi, a nineteen-year-old civil servant from Harrow, was often seen greeting the tourists and directing them to the Raleigh camp. There the welcome would be taken over by Jim Redgate of Nottingham, fetchingly attired in turn-of-the-century prison clothes. To my chagrin the youngsters had quite an enterprise going, selling 'Genuine Convicts' Rations for just $3'. The 'historic artefacts' bore a distinct resemblance to the tins of beef curry and beans from our Australian Army ration packs.

Early in the New Year the continuing severe weather conditions brought us more than our fair share of snow and floods. Even when the floods abated and the camps settled back into some kind of normality, the insects and leeches remained.

Pulling on her socks, Jackie Irvin of Humberside felt something warm and sticky on her leg. Leeches don't hurt as they suck one's blood and it is often hard to tell that they are attached. Judging by the engorged body of this particular one, it had been enjoying its dinner for quite some time. Jackie's involuntary scream got everyone's attention. The Venturers watched with amazement as Rodrigo Noreiga nonchalantly flicked the leech off with his razor-sharp machete. That was nothing; the Chilean variety, he explained, sometimes required some real convincing.

Franklin River, 6 January 1987

The worst spell of rain in seventy years hit our exploration team on the Franklin River. Twisting through deep gorges, the river rapids challenge even the most expert rafters. Australians Alan Shaw and Clive Richardson, who had led the Drysdale River run at the northern tip of the continent, were white-water professionals.

Looking for a way through the torrent, Jim Brotherton of Hull found himself dumped unceremoniously in the middle of the river while his inflatable raft suffered a nasty rip on the sharp rocks. As the rain continued into the third day, Venturers woke a little wetter than usual to find their camp awash and their kit disappearing downriver. Overnight the water level had risen by a staggering 4.8 metres.

Nevertheless, projects continued apace. Bridges were built and tracks laid, crustaceans collected for Hobart University and tasks completed for the National Parks and Wildlife Service. There had been reported sightings of the Tasmanian tiger, a marsupial generally believed to be extinct for about fifty years. Although unidentified yelps were sometimes heard at night when the young people camped in the dense bush and wild mountain ranges, no evidence of the stripe-backed creature was found.

Due to a mix-up in the Raleigh joining instructions, some Venturers turned up with kit for the desert, while the Omanis arrived equipped to undertake a trans-Polar expedition; they only needed a couple of huskies to complete their arrangements. In the end, however, all of the equipment came in handy since Tasmania offered the expedition ample extremes of cold and hot weather in the island's worst summer for many years.

Werribee, Victoria, 21 December 1986

Across the Bass Strait, a waterway hyphen between the Indian Ocean to the west and the Tasman Sea to the east, Nick Horne had moved Tac HQ thousands of kilometres south to give support to the expeditions in Tasmania and Victoria. Aided by Garry Krauss, secretary of the Victoria committee, Nick had re-established the on-site headquarters in Werribee Park Mansion, a partly restored property of impressive size on the outskirts of Melbourne.

The sixty-room Italianate residence had been built in 1874 by Thomas Chivside who arrived in Australia from Scotland in 1839. Now open to the public, it is a remarkable reminder of the splendour of country house life enjoyed by wealthy Victorians in the boom years of the 1800s. Nick, Joel and Cathy Davies filled one wing with an armoury of machines that Thomas Chivside could never have imagined: Acorn computers, fax machines and radios were essential to keep in touch with the expeditions, with the two ships, with CHQ and with me as I travelled from one location to another.

*

100

Above: Major Charlie Daniel from Suffolk and Clive Barrow from Cornwall on the Jardine River, Cape York, in Far Worth, Queensland, Australia.

Below: Venturers climbing the strange volcanic rock formations of the Hazard Mountains, Tasmania.

Above: Craig Darby from London abseiling in the Grampian Mountains, Victoria, Australia.

Below: Disabled Venturer Colin Price of Manchester diving in his wheelchair off Wilson's Promontory, Victoria, Australia, during a marine biology survey.

Above: Alex Rigg from the Orkneys painting a mural depicting the variety of Fiordland wildlife in the Te Anau Children's Nature Programme Education Centre. *Below:* British Rail Venturers John Lucas of Yarmouth and Jim Redgate of Nottingham by a dramatically eroded boulder in the Hazard Mountains, Tasmania.

American Duane Whitcomb and a local Australian Venturer resting during a trek across the Snowy Mountains in Victoria, Australia.

Linda Thompson directing a helicopter at Manapouri base camp in Fiordland, New Zealand.

Opposite: Looking across Lake Wakatipu towards the snow-capped peaks of the Humboldt Mountains in southern New Zealand.

Right: Venturer para-sailing on Lake Te Anau in Fiordland, New Zealand.

Below: Operation Raleigh's flagship SES *Sir Walter Raleigh* in Sydney Harbour.

Above: Landing craft *Prince Harry* being loaded back onto *Sir Walter Raleigh* at the end of the Pandora project on the Great Barrier Reef, Australia.

Below: SES *Sir Walter Raleigh* enters the Albert Dock, Hull, after her successful circumnavigation.

Sir Walter Raleigh had sailed south too, spending the end of 1986 in Melbourne to unload vehicles and stores for the forthcoming expedition in Victoria. Thanks to Garry Krauss and his friends, the ship's crew enjoyed a memorable feast at Christmas. Australian hospitality is hard to beat.

Robin Letts had selected Neil Hampson, an extrovert efficient Australian Army officer, to head this next phase. With the backing of Brigadier Brian Wade, who commanded this military district, preparations were going ahead well. Brian was also Operation Raleigh's Chairman in Australia, and with his feet in both camps we had the best of both worlds.

Although Victoria is Australia's smallest mainland state, it is also the most densely populated. In 1834 land speculator John Betman arrived at Port Phillip Bay, the notch at the base of Australia where Tasmania broke away, and declared it 'the place for the village'. With blankets and apples to barter, he 'purchased' 242,800 hectares from the Wurundjari Aboriginal tribe and named it after the British Prime Minister, Lord Melbourne. The settlement was founded, not as in Sydney, by recalcitrant convicts, but largely by farmers from Tasmania.

Victoria contains some of the most formidable territory in the subcontinent. The bush horses, gorges, and 'beetling cliffs' of Kosciusko celebrated by 'Banjo' Paterson in 'The Man from Snowy River' are still there:

He hails from Snowy River, up by Kosciusko's side,
Where the hills are twice as steep and twice as rough,
Where a horse's hoofs strike firelight from the flint stones at every stride,
The man that holds his own is good enough.

This was the country over which the Venturers in Victoria would raft, scuba dive, climb, build refuge huts and undertake scientific projects ranging from researching the wild brumbies to the tiny, mouse-like marsupial, *Planigale paucident*. The land would test them and tire them; by the end of the expedition they would have reached some of their limits and learned if they were indeed 'good enough'.

*

Puckapunal, Victoria, 4 March 1987

Working with the staff at Wilson's Promontory National Park, which includes important underwater conservation areas, the Venturers lived on 'tins, tins and more tins!' 'We were given a refresher course in diving since we would be collecting statistics on abalones,' says Mary French from Sussex. Abalones are marine snails that the Australians call 'earshells', logically enough since they look like ears. They have a tough, muscular foot which Japan and many other countries consider delicious. Here, abalones are protected but some are still poached. Mary recalls the project:

> Then the expedition in Victoria began in earnest – a six-day walk from our base camp at Morka Gorge to Bogong National Park. We'd heard horrific tales of how difficult it was; I'd never even walked 15 kilometres before! Carrying all our stuff on our backs, we went up mountains and down gorges. We are talking blisters!
>
> Somehow we all managed it. Our group split in two at the end, and mine went to the High Plains to research herds of brumbies. This was my turn to be leader for four days. I was with three guys and we were away from all staff – and all civilization. For four days we didn't see one other person.
>
> I did everything wrong, but I learned from my mistakes and it was exceptional. I saw my first shooting star, and satellites moving across the sky. We climbed to the Plains in a raging blizzard, and, when the sun came out, watched the grass blades sparkle in their coats of ice.

The Snowy River became an important part in the lives of the young Victorians. Some groups studied the ecology of the rock wallaby that lives by its shores, while others, like Sarah Turner and her group, canoed 176 kilometres, mapping the climbing and camping spots for future canoeists and conducting a conservation survey *en route*.

Like the Drysdale River expedition in the north of this great country, the southern challenge forged particularly strong bonds between the Venturers and the waterway. 'We were very sad to leave the river,' wrote Sarah. 'There was a feeling of excitement and anticipation at every turn.' The young people came to know the river well, its moods and its pleasures.

'It was the experience of a lifetime,' Sarah had said. I had heard other Venturers in other countries say the same about other Raleigh expeditions. Not particularly original, perhaps, but the very reason we were here.

Finally, I reached Neil Hampson's group at Lake Tyers' Aboriginal settlement where they were restoring the weatherboard church built in 1880. Black swans paraded on the mirror-like waters as I was introduced to the local community. All of the Venturers had made good friends with the local people but the Aborigines and the black youths had some especially interesting conversations. It was a unique intermingling of cultures.

'Tell me,' said the chief, Murray Bull, 'is there much good grazing land in Manchester?'

After some thought and a sip from his tin of Fosters, the young man replied: 'It's getting in short supply.'

The chief pondered on this, then commented: 'I suppose the white folk took it.'

More deep thought until the Venturer replied, 'Yes, you could say that, but we call them the city council.'

CHAPTER NINE

Kiwis and Kakapos

(*New Zealand Leader (A)*: Charles Burton)
(*New Zealand Leader (B)*: Major Tony Walton, TD RA)

Fiordland, New Zealand, September 1986

The Jet boat nosed its way into the sheltered cove and my nimble friend, Margaret Henderson, leaped ashore. 'Come on,' she said, 'I'll show you where your mother took us girl guides sixty years ago.'

We clambered up the rock and came face to face with the Princess of Lake Hanroko. For some 300 years her upright skeleton, still dressed in funeral finery, had stood sentinel in the cave beneath the old rata tree. My parents had first seen the Princess in the 1920s, when my father was vicar at Otautau on New Zealand's South Island. They had visited her cave with the scouts and guides of the parish for a 'field day'. Indeed, it was my mother and father's enthusiasm for young people and the great outdoors that had started me on my own expeditions, and I hoped they would have approved of our activities. Now, led by one of those former scouts, we revisited this unique Maori site.

Under the energetic leadership of Marshal of the Royal Air Force Lord Elworthy, and of Major-General Rob Williams, formerly Chief of New Zealand's Army, the national committee had done stalwart work in selecting, funding and sending out Kiwi Venturers and staff to our other expeditions. Now they gave handsome support for two Raleigh expeditions in their own country.

Sir Robertson and Lady Stewart of Christchurch provided generous backing and their company, PDL Holdings, became one of our leading sponsors. Considering the economic problems New Zealand faced at the time, the contributions to Raleigh made by this grand nation were even more remarkable. The committee appointed a splendid Mr Fix-It with much experience in the Antarctic, as their executive officer. Major Norm MacPherson was largely responsible for setting up the expedition and liaising with hundreds of different organizations.

Norm, an energetic administrator, organized a base camp near the town of Te Anau on the edge of the Fiordland National Park. This remote region is one of the world's major wilderness areas. Two hundred years after Captain Cook first stepped onto its mountainous shores, some of the interior valleys have still to be explored. I'd asked Charlie Burton, who had taken part in the epic British Transglobe Expedition and is one of only two men ever to have reached both poles over land, to lead the first of two phases.

We always need medical officers and I'm extremely grateful when hardworking doctors offer their services – and pay all their expenses. As a tribute to the Operation Raleigh MOs, I've taken a few excerpts from an account by Dr Rob Stephenson of his experiences in New Zealand.

We were all exhausted by the thirty-six-hour flight to Christchurch and the long coach ride through the mountains to base camp, but the next morning we surfaced to find ourselves in a big army-style camp with 140 Venturers from all parts of the world: Britain, New Zealand, America, Canada, Hong Kong, Singapore and Japan. There was a solitary Australian whom we all adopted.

We spent nights bivouacking in the bush and sampled Fiordland's main delights: rain and the hungry sandfly. The vegetation is dense rainforest and a constant battle. Much of the park is unexplored because of its inaccessibility, and most of the peaks are unnamed.

I made use of the first week to organize my 'surgery' – in reality the kitchen of a prefabricated administration building. I had to compete with the New Zealand radio men who used it for making coffee and washing up.

One project was assisting the National Park Authority to build hiking trails for the public. On our days off we managed to bag several snow-covered 1500-metre peaks. The views of mountains, forest, lakes and fiords were impressive and memorable.

Another exciting project was exploring a group of limestone caves above Te Anau. The formations were very beautiful and some of the passages had undoubtedly never been seen before. There were also bird surveys of yellowheads, blue ducks and kiwis, the last the flightless emblem of New Zealand which sleeps by day and forages at night and uses the sharp claws on its feet as weapons. Transport in and out of the remote areas was by boat, helicopter or light plane.

Many Venturers helped at outdoor pursuit centres and at schools for problem children, teaching skills and talking about their own countries. I think that by the time we left, the whole of South Island had heard and seen Operation Raleigh in action.

As Christmas approached, Venturer Diana Spivey described the glories of freeze-dried Christmas fare:

Rations are dropped by helicopter into the rugged bush and mountain regions where we carry out scientific and community projects. The food may not appear very appetizing, but everything here can be used to create adventurous feasts, different from home cooking, but you just have to accept this on an international expedition. Christmas fare comes in the form of freeze-dried, sweet and sour New Zealand lamb.

As the year ended I flew from Tasmania and its snowcapped mountains to Te Anau. There I joined the new Venturers of Expedition 8B. Tony Walton, formerly my adjutant aboard *Sir Walter Raleigh* in Central America, and lately returned from crossing the Pacific on our flagship, flew in to take over from Charlie Burton.

There was a marvellous party on New Year's Eve. The Japanese team carried a special New Year house shoulder high around the fire and the Venturers dumped poor Charlie Burton in the water tanks to 'wash away the past'.

Two London Venturers on the second New Zealand expedition, Peter Wilson and Dennis Horsely, had been selected as part of the Inner City scheme. We launched the scheme in 1986 to give young leaders from Britain's urban areas an opportunity to take part in Operation Raleigh. Now, with backing from both national and local government, we would

recruit 200 underprivileged youngsters. The setting up of this prog-
ramme owes much to the then Secretary of State for the Environment,
Kenneth Baker, who had been with the Prince of Wales at Hull when *Sir
Walter Raleigh* first sailed in 1984.

Both Peter and Dennis had led lives all too typical of teenagers
brought up in urban areas of high unemployment where crime is often a
career. 'The selection process dragged me off the streets and helped me
put my head together,' said Peter. 'I knew I would be the only black
geezer on the expedition and I thought I would be left out. I talked to as
many of the other Venturers on the flight as possible. We had brought
London with us, but I soon realized that we had left the world of dope
and drink behind.'

When they arrived at Christchurch airport, Peter was disconcerted
to find that being black made him an object of curiosity. 'I looked about
and everyone was just staring me out, man, they kept looking at me as if I
was from another planet.' An overnight bus journey gave him time to get
to know the New Zealanders he would be with for the next three months.
Soon all his initial suspicions about Kiwis faded away.

In the cold light of dawn the youngsters arrived at base camp, bleary-
eyed and weary. Rows of green army tents glistened in the early morning
sun which lit the snowy peaks of the surrounding mountains. It was
Christmas and midsummer all at once; the Kiwi weather was as confused as we were for there had been a fresh fall of snow just before our
heatwave. The 147 Venturers hardly had time to unpack before they
experienced the unique South Island hospitality. Everyone was asked to
join a Kiwi family for Christmas.

Peter, however, was in a very dark mood:

> I was waiting for a totally unknown family to take me away from all my
> new-found friends. As every car drove into camp I looked up and
> thought, I really don't want to go with them. Then I began to believe
> that because I was black, no one would really want me.
>
> Eventually I was called over to an ancient Morris 1100, the likes of
> which would never be seen on the streets of Wandsworth, and to my
> surprise found it was a Mrs Wilson asking for me. At the farm the work
> was hard and unpleasant: this was obviously not going to be a holiday.

107

Both Peter and Dennis were overwhelmed by the way the families made them feel at home. Dennis said: 'They became my family. They adopted me and even took me with them to another family for Christmas lunch.'

Peter surprised even himself when on the second day he started calling Mrs Wilson 'Mum'.

When I get back home to London, Dennis thought, the only thing that will have changed is that most of my friends will probably be in prison. You don't need drugs to get a kick, man, a natural buzz is just as good.

One of Dennis' projects had been working at a camp for children from broken and disturbed homes. 'The kids kept crying all the time, they were constantly seeking attention and it kept me on my toes keeping them occupied. By the time I left, I had become a big brother to them – I wish I had had one when I was a kid.'

While Dennis was working at building paths in the National Park, he surprised everyone by reciting a poem he had made up in his head:

> What does Operation Raleigh mean to me?
> It's a chance to show what I can really be.
> To build a pass or mountain track,
> Or walk for weeks with pack on back,
> To climb a mountain to the peak,
> Or lend support to those who are weak.
> And although we won't be here for long
> We must stick together
> And it won't go wrong.
> Because if we don't, it won't be fair
> On those who try and really care.
> When it's time to head homeward bound
> And leave all the friends I have found,
> And if there's a time when I am sad
> And everything seems blue and bad,
> I'll cast my mind back to here
> And I'm sure it'll fill my heart with cheer.

Peter and Dennis did not have a monopoly on the hard life. Among the Venturers in New Zealand were others who had struggled all their lives with one form of handicap or another.

Two young Kiwis made an incongruous sight as they pushed themselves to physical and mental limits to reach the summit of an 1800-metre mountain. With windswept dreadlocks that had never looked more bedraggled, Sam Rudolph willed his squat, solid frame, step by step. Alongside him was Stephen van der Voort, who had instantly been nicknamed 'Hoppy'.

Stephen had been born with deformed legs, and after several years of being unable to take part in any physical activity, one leg was amputated and the other received a bone graft. The operation had changed his life. Peter and Sam struggled through the snow and ice, which Sam had never seen before, and the cheerfulness of one complemented the brute strength of the other.

Sam was thirteen when he entered the twilight world of New Zealand gang life dominated by the infamous Mongrel Mob and Black Power gangs. He stole to keep himself supplied with 'happy baccy', glue and booze, spending most of his time in and out of juvenile prison until he was picked off the street by the amazing Betty Wark and went to live in Auckland's Arohanui home for Maori youth.

Sam had been there for five years, slowly learning to read and write, when Betty put his name forward for a place on Operation Raleigh. He attended one of the country's selection weekends at Papakura military camp. Sam survived the psychological, initiative and endurance tests that showed him he had qualities and capabilities hitherto unknown to him – or to anyone else. Like Peter and Dennis, he was determined to return home and assist those who had helped him break away from the vicious cycle of crime that turns children into convicts.

Meanwhile, on remote Breaksea Island, Falklands hero Simon Weston was part of the Raleigh conservation effort, trying to trap rats that threaten the rare kakapo. Simon had been with the Welsh Guards when the ship *Sir Galahad* was hit by Argentine bombs and was terribly burned on his face and hands. Nevertheless, this courageous soldier had decided 'life was for living' and volunteered as a signaller on Operation Raleigh. He was a great inspiration to the other staff and Venturers.

*

American marine biologist, Linda Walters, fresh from the Pandora expedition, was now the diving officer on Fiordland. She tells of her work in the deep clear fiords:

> The highlight of my expedition was working with scientists from the University of Canterbury. Ten of us spent two weeks collecting marine organisms throughout the fiords from a small, but well-equipped dive boat, the *Western Explorer*. Starting from Milford Sound, we worked our way south, diving at every opportunity.
>
> Waterfalls were everywhere, and with scuba gear you could get right underneath them, surrounding yourself with rainbows. The incredibly steep, ice-carved walls are as endless beneath the tideline as they are above. There is an amazing diversity of colour, plants and animals. And hidden in almost every crevice is dinner – the New Zealand crayfish, similar to Maine lobsters but minus the claws. You can catch them with your hands and they make a welcome change from dehydrated lamb and peas.
>
> The average diving depth was 21 to 33.5 metres. It was necessary to go so deep to avoid being battered by the tidal surge. At these depths, schools of spotted perch and grouper joined us and happily ate the fragments of whatever we collected.

The expedition concluded with a huge party. The Kiwi and Maori Venturers cooked the meat in the traditional way by burying it in a pit dug below the fire, and gave a rendition of the Maori war dance. In return the British replied with the Hokey-Cokey and, as the evening progressed, all nationalities produced dances that even their home countries wouldn't recognize.

Although seventy-six years old, New Zealander Alex Hyndman could still give a very respectable rendition of the Maori war dance. A radio officer, Alex and his wife, Thelma, would prove experienced and popular members of the crew of *Sir Walter Raleigh* for her forthcoming 12,000-nautical-mile voyage from Australia to Britain. The gleaming white ship had played her role magnificently and brought great credit to Hull, the English maritime city which gave her to us. Of course, the land-based expeditions would continue, and the lovely brigantine *Zebu* would provide many more exciting sea adventures, but our flagship's job was done; *Sir Walter Raleigh* was coming home.

110

CHAPTER TEN

Oceans, Seas and Sagas

Fremantle, Australia, January 1987

Sir Walter Raleigh, resplendent in a new coat of paint, swept majestically into Fremantle Harbour. Along the quays, boats were gathering for the world's greatest yacht race, the America's Cup.

Charlie Daniel and Clive Barrow, working with Rod Bartholomew, had organized the visit which would promote Operation Raleigh and help the efforts of our Australian committee. Long-time supporter Bill Henderson and his company, Pier 21, were backing us too. The ship's deck was an elegant vantage point from which to view the battle for the treasured trophy.

The starting gun of the America's Cup also signalled the imminent start of *Sir Walter Raleigh*'s voyage home. Political events in Sri Lanka, the Persian Gulf and India had necessitated drastic changes in the sea-going programme and the ship would come home a year early.

For the run home, Tommy Smith handed over to his friend Captain John Fisher, Scottish-born but long of Adelaide. Adrian Turner, the Purser, who had sailed from London aboard *Zebu* at the beginning of Raleigh, was one of the many former Venturers in the crew.

Steaming out of Fremantle Harbour on a hot, dry day in March, the ship's horn sounded a final thank you and farewell to Australia. Ahead were the infamous Roaring Forties.

The fronts thundered across the south of the Indian Ocean from Cape Horn with nothing to stop them. Notorious for its storms, grey beards and freak waves, the Roaring Forties has escorted many a fine ship to Davy Jones' deep-sea locker. *Sir Walter Raleigh* did not plan to join them. As if in defiance of the sea, the ceremonial ship's bell in the Prince of

Wales bar rang itself vigorously as the good ship pitched and rolled and the portholes were submerged for long, tense minutes.

Unable to make any headway as the Roaring Forties raged, Captain John Fisher decided to heave-to. Engine revs were kept at a level just high enough to maintain steerage into the 60-knot wind. The ship began to enjoy herself and took the storm's worst in her stride. In fact *Sir Walter Raleigh* seemed to revel in the gale, having spent many years fishing in turbulent Arctic waters.

If the ship was at home in the gale, some of the newer crew members wished they were well and truly home and back on land. The inevitable *mal de mer* plagued many and Felicity Bowden, the ship's secretary and a deck trainee, spent the first week crawling along the alleyways or curled up in a kitten-like ball at the end of her bunk. Even Steve Johnson, one of the US navy's seconded engineers, found it hard to keep his feet: his last ship had been the USS *Enterprise*, about a hundred times bigger than *Raleigh*. Later, Chief Engineer Jim Mellor admitted that the three days in the Forties were the only time he had ever been frightened during his long career at sea.

'We set our course south-west back into warmer waters so that we could carry out science projects,' wrote Adrian Turner in his log. One project was to identify and chart the distribution of all seabirds encountered from Fremantle to the Cape of Good Hope. David Eades, the Australian ornithologist leading the project, wanted to establish a correlation between the species in colder waters and those in waters of the sub-tropical convergence zone, an up-welling of tropical water in the Indian Ocean.

First, however, we had to find the zone. The search for it meant that accurate sea-water temperatures and salinity readings had to be taken round the clock. It was character-building stuff to crawl out of a bunk at 3.30 a.m. to haul a bucketful of water onto the freezing deck.

Another project was collecting sub-tropical and sub-Antarctic sea-weeds and phytoplankton that happily co-habit in this unique area. The information would be invaluable, since no study had been made here before.

112

Amsterdam Island, 1 April 1987

Radio expert Nick Perrott provided our passport to the French island of Amsterdam. Somehow our formal request to visit this lovely spot had been lost in the red tape of London and Paris and it was only as a result of his making radio contact that we were given permission to anchor.

The two days spent in the lee of the island provided a welcome change from the buffeting of previous weeks. Diving teams surveyed the shoreline, collecting seaweed and frolicking with the hundreds of southern fur seals that inhabit the island waters, under the disapproving glare of sedate elephant seals. The huge creatures lay like logs on the rocks. A favourite pastime was to try to jump across as many basking seals as possible. The hefty mammals seemed utterly relaxed about our antics, a good thing since they weigh about 2 tonnes and can rear up 3 metres.

From Amsterdam Island the ship headed north-west into more calm weather as she sped to Cape Town via the rugged island of St Helena, Napoleon's island prison. The purpose of the stop at the island was to pave the way for *Zebu*'s visit in 1988. This accomplished, the crew enjoyed the hospitality of the islanders, all very friendly and proud to be British. The main settlement, Jamestown, looks like a quaint Cornish fishing port, and the crew visited the homes of the great French emperor and saw his first burial place. His body was later exhumed and returned to France.

Sierra Leone, May 1987

The next course was set for Freetown, Sierra Leone, a six-day passage through the doldrums and across the Equator. Naval custom demands a celebration whenever the Equator is crossed, and the crew did the tradition proud as we steamed over the hot and sultry line. The humidity was stifling once we arrived in the West African port and night brought no respite from temperatures that never dropped below 37°C.

Sierra Leone, a corruption of the original Portuguese name Serra Lyoa, or Lion Mountain, was celebrating the bicentenary of the colony, established by freed African slaves in 1787. Sponsored by the English abolitionist Granville Sharp and others, the settlement made treaties with the neighbouring chiefs and prospered. One of the prominent anti-slavery philanthropists who sent the ship of slaves was from Hull. That link was what brought my old stablemate Richard Snailham, Operation Raleigh's historian and experienced expeditioner, to Freetown.

'My assignment in West Africa encompassed three separate jobs,' says Richard. 'I felt a bit like Cerberus, the mythical three-headed dog.' He continued:

> Wearing one hat, I lived on board the flagship during the visit to Freetown and was Raleigh's representative. Wearing another, I was a roving public relations officer for the city of Hull, rigging up a link with Radio Humberside and snapping pictures of Freetown's Lord Mayor and councillors.
>
> My third hat was more of a topee. John Blashford-Snell asked me to join him on a short reconnaissance into the interior to investigate the potential for future expeditions.
>
> In the bowels of the ship, in what he calls the 'Black Hole', John keeps several changes of expedition gear. He has to be prepared for the icy blasts of Tasmania, the relentless rain of Puerto Montt or, as here in Freetown, the brassy heat of Africa. Diving into the Black Hole, he came triumphantly up the companionway clutching a safari suit, a pith helmet and a bottle of J. & B.

Over the next few days we crossed the palm-covered plains, drove through forests of brilliant, flamboyant trees and boated up the Pamuna River where the locals pan for gold. It was an exhausting but rewarding recce, aided by the local British American Tobacco Company.

'On the way back,' wrote Richard Snailham, 'John fell asleep in the jeep, waking only when we rattled over the Rokel River bridge. Opening one eye he asked the driver, "Are you sure there are no lost cities up here?" and then dozed off again.'

Tenerife, 20 May 1987

Facing the sunset, *Sir Walter Raleigh* left Freetown for Tenerife, a sea passage fraught with dangers of a different kind: pirates. We had been warned that these ocean-going robbers had fast, armed boats and patrolled the waters off West Africa. The mate checked the ship's armoury, just in case we became a target.

Finally the crew spotted the towering cliffs of Santa Cruz de Tenerife, and ten days later set out in the Avon inflatables in the high seas to welcome a fleet of tall ships. They were sailing to Sydney to join Australia's birthday party, re-enacting the voyage which brought the first British to the continent.

The rendezvous of the two expeditions also meant the meeting of many old friends, like Captain Mike Kichenside. Many of the tall ships' crew had been on Operation Raleigh or its predecessor, Operation Drake, or In the Footsteps of Scott Expedition. Next stop, Gibraltar, then Lisbon and home.

Home and Hull, June 1987

All available hands were needed to prepare the ship for her homecoming. Needle guns and chipping hammers removed the passage rust and the decks and railings gleamed. Primer and paint were splashed on top, the sponsors' exhibition stands renovated and the photographs of expeditions mounted on the walls of the deck.

On the afternoon of 19 June, *Sir Walter Raleigh*, as freshly painted and powdered as her sixteenth-century namesake, sailed into the inner harbour of St Helier, Jersey and to a huge welcome at the pier. Then on to Guernsey, through the North Sea to Lowestoft and finally, the Humber estuary.

In three years the grand ship had done 43,143 nautical miles and made 117 ports of call without one serious breakdown, quite an achievement for any twenty-two-year-old, and a great tribute to those who maintained her. The anchor was weighed for the last time on 30 June at 7.30 a.m. The ship made upstream to the dock basin of Hull where HRH The Duke of Gloucester, a member of the Scientific Exploration Society, waited to welcome her home.

The Hull City Council and hundreds of friends, families, ex-Venturers and CHQ staff were on the quayside, waving and shouting congratulations. As *Sir Walter Raleigh* sailed majestically into the dock, British Aerospace jets wheeled and dived overhead and the twin cannons boomed a final salute. It was a salute to His Royal Highness, to the people of Humberside and to the enterprise that is Raleigh. *Sir Walter* had come home.

London

CHQ had undergone significant changes since its start. In 1986 we were well within our budget, but the shortfall of overseas Venturers, especially from America where we were still virtually unknown, was having a serious effect on our income. Even with the utmost economy, we faced a deficit somewhere in the future unless steps were taken, and quickly. Tony Nowell, a cheery and highly efficient businessman, was retiring from Guinness. As a chartered accountant, he was well qualified for the dual jobs of Chairman of our executive committee and commercial director.

Others came to our support as well: Derek Chidell, husband of our society's newsletter editor, and a man of considerable commercial experience; Harbourne Stephen, former managing director of the *Daily Telegraph*; and Colonel Geoffrey Dicker who joined as treasurer. Sir Jack Hayward, one of our most generous supporters, also came aboard.

From the Scientific Exploration Society we had Philip Harrison as honorary secretary, and Ruth Cartwright who had run the Procurement and Sponsorship Department for Operation Drake. I had hoped that Patrick Brook, my chum from days of shot and shell in Oman, would lead an expedition in that country. The Gulf War and the Sultan's sinking oil revenues sank that idea as well, but Patrick agreed to help us by directing the vital Inner City scheme.

People have always been Raleigh's chief strength, staff and Venturers alike. If I was not to be completely tied to CHQ, I would have to appoint a Chief-of-Staff. Into the job came Lieutenant-Colonel Geoffrey Straw, a smiling but tough former commanding officer of the Royal Fusiliers who proved a great success. Finally, Royal Marine Major Peter Leicester joined the ranks and took over the international division to bring in more Venturers from overseas.

Raleigh was going from strength to strength. On the international side more young people were learning of the expedition, aided in America by Atlantic Richfield, in Canada by Dr Joe McGinnis, in Jordan by King Hussein, in Saudi Arabia by Prince Faisal and in France by Mme Liliane Naigard. The Italians were sending many more Venturers and here at home British Airways had backed their first Venturers from within the company, having sponsored individuals every year in the past.

Also in Britain, Roberta Howlett pressed forward with the Inner City Scheme and, with the help of London's Markham Group, had increased the number of Venturers sponsored by their employers. Roberta also organized post-expedition activities for returned Venturers and every day we heard tales of our young leaders doing valuable tasks within their home community.

I was especially impressed to meet Paul Mason in Birmingham. Complete with punk-rocker hairstyle and safety pins, he is now a counsellor in a drug abuse clinic. I'd last seen him as a skinhead in Costa Rica.

Harry Cook and his PR team at CHQ did an amazing job and the press were eager for stories of the latest adventures. With so many countries and so much variety, however, there is ample scope for confusion. Recently, an artist commissioned to do a painting for Operation Raleigh, chose to portray the Venturers heading off through the Atacama Desert – on their camels. It was a splendid work and he was invited to show it to the Chilean Ambassador. The diplomat looked at the Raleigh representation and shook his head, puzzled. 'I am sorry to tell you, but there are no camels in Chile,' he said sadly. Deep in the jungle, the story was relayed to me by radio. I sent the painter a signal saying: 'Wrong desert, delete camels, insert llamas.'

There were no camels in Japan either, but there were certainly plenty of bears and bats, snakes and scorpions. The young people taking part in the expeditions in Japan would sail between the southernmost tropical islands and traverse the remote and icy ridges of Hokkaido. In between, they would trek from temple to temple and raft down white water rivers. Most important, however, the Venturers would touch part of a great culture new to all – including the young Japanese themselves.

117

CHAPTER ELEVEN

Bats, Bears and
Sabani Boats

(*Japan Leader*: Major Tony Walton, TD RA)

Okinawa, Japan, 12 June 1987

They said it couldn't be done. In the old days traders and fishermen had risked their lives to row from the southern islands to the markets in Okinawa, but it hadn't been done for fifty years. These ancient routes followed the Black Current for 300 nautical miles. The ladder of volcanic islands leading to Okinawa provided some shelter for the fishermen's wooden canoes, known as *sabanis*, but there were also vast stretches of open sea with only the sharks for company.

Operation Raleigh decided to have a go.

One month and 300 nautical miles after setting off from the island Iriomote, the crew of thirteen Venturers lifted their oars in triumph. Press boats and naval cutters escorted them into port at Okinawa. The quayside was crammed with well-wishers, television and radio crews and representatives from the company which sponsored Raleigh in Japan, Nippon Denso. Tony Walton, expedition leader, and Earl Miyamoto, project leader, were as jubilant as the crew. Tony looked at his watch and shook his head in amazement. It was precisely 12.55 on that hot June day. The boat was one hour late.

Iriomote, a tiny tropical island ringed by coral reefs, was the home base for various scientific and community projects in southern Japan as well as the training ground for the *sabani* crew. Just off the northern tip of Taiwan, the diamond-shaped dot in the ocean is unknown to most

Japanese mainlanders and light-years away from the frantic bustle of the big cities. Jumping off the fishing boat that had brought them to the island, the Venturers waded ashore, carrying their packs shoulder high. Ahead stretched a sandy beach framed by mangroves and palms. Robinson Crusoe would be green with envy, thought Par Sorme, the nineteen-year-old champion figure skater from Sweden. But no Man Friday appeared; the only footprints on the beach were those of crabs and lizards.

It quickly became apparent that the crabs and lizards resented our intrusion. So did the frogs, rats, white ants, spiders, leeches and the 20-centimetre-long poisonous centipedes. The sea gave us a chilly reception too. It teemed with sea urchins and Moray eels, highly poisonous cone shells and crown-of-thorns starfish. Hostile perhaps, but neighbours which made Iriomote a diver's paradise. Just off the bay white-tips and hammerheads circled hungrily. Our most notable island adversary, however, made itself known as soon as the Venturers began to clear a campsite: the habu.

Iriomote is one of only two Japanese islands which is home to the habu. Those on less intimate terms with the deadly snake refer to it respectfully as the Sakishima viper. I had heard of it two years ago when, with Ken-san, a wild-boar hunter and fisherman, I had explored Iriomote for a possible Raleigh base camp. 'Make plenty of noise,' Ken-san had said. 'The habu will attack if you surprise him.' I did my best to imitate an articulated lorry crashing through the undergrowth.

Since then the habus had had a baby boom. The island was thick with them and warning cries of 'Habu!' rang out frequently as the group set up their tents and built a shelter against the lashing rains. The snakes, centipedes and spiders thought the thatched shelter a big improvement on the rain-soaked jungle and promptly moved in. The frogs loved the drainage channels around the tents and filled the miniature moats with eggs which brought more habus, eager for a free lunch, and millions of mosquitoes. It was an interesting ecocycle for distant observers, less so for those closer to hand.

Only the Venturers seemed to wish the rains would end. The Vango tents leaked badly in the constant tropical downpour and the Venturers were sure that fins had begun to sprout. 'I can't wait to get to sea,' said crew member Kevin Fee from New Zealand. 'It's bound to be drier.'

119

As the rainy season finally drew to a close, *sabani* training began in earnest. Up at six, the crew began the day with a power workout, a sprint up and down the long beach, followed by a swim in the bay against the current. After a Japanese breakfast of noodles and eggs, they paddled the canoe for two hours: twenty strokes at full speed, twenty at three-quarter power, then twenty at half power. After lunch came the endurance workout, paddling at three-quarter power up and down the Iriomote bay until they could hardly lift the wooden paddles. In the process they discovered some of the boat's shortcomings: she was not rigged to run close to the wind; she couldn't tack, only jibe; and, since there was no keel, she tended to sideslip unless the wind was directly astern, which was rare. In rough weather waves broke over the sides and the Venturers found themselves paddling the air as the little boat rocked up and down.

Named *Kamadoma*, Raleigh's craft had originally been used for shark fishing. About 10 metres long, she had room for six rowing two abreast and one at the tiller. With her heavy bottom, high stern and thick cedar planks coated with shark oil, *Kamadoma* was no beauty, but she was a professional. We hadn't helped her looks by reinforcing her bow and stern with fibreglass and adding a double outrigger: without it she was guaranteed to capsize. In fact, capsizing was a built-in feature of *sabanis*; during a typhoon fishermen capsized on purpose and sheltered under their boats, preferring the threat of sharks to the anger of the storm.

Earl watched the crew become increasingly confident – and increasingly fit. Any day now the *sabani* would fly. But the damp and motley crew still wondered whether they had the stamina for a 300-mile expedition. There were tiny Yoko Matsuo nicknamed Maggot, who could get seasick in a *sake* cup; Sting (alias Keith John Lewis Ray), whose prize collection of tropical rashes made sitting on the hard benches agony; Fritz Vogel, half Maori, whose good looks had young Japanese girls everywhere convinced that he was a pop star; and K. T. Lavender, tall and blonde, who looked distractingly good in her *sabani* swimsuit. There were Catherine Lewis; Anja Ball; and Jez Daniels, ex-merchant navy who sported a diamond in his nose; Sandra Middleton-Jones; and Peter Heifetz, an American biochemist. Finally, to complete the team, there were Kevin Fee, whom the others chose as leader; Ryurji Noda; and two staff members, quietly spoken Duncan Brown and Michio Watanabe, an ex-Venturer.

'We were a diverse group to say the least and from totally different backgrounds,' says Peter. 'I think we were all a bit surprised that we got along so well. If we hadn't, though, we wouldn't have made it.'

Well before the departure of the *sabani*, the land-based projects on Iriomote were underway. Bats and cats were of special interest as Venturers charted the flight paths of bats bearing names only scientists could bestow, like the old world leaf-nosed bat and the lesser horseshoe bat, and studied the habits of a recently discovered species of wildcat.

There have always been rumours of large wildcats on Iriomote and there still are. Locals say they are as big as leopards, although none have been photographed. Only twenty years ago a new species of wildcat, the Yamaneko or mountain cat, was discovered on this remote island. Unknown to the rest of the world, it has lived in the primeval forests of Iriomote for millions of years.

Almost untouched by the Ice Age, Japan harbours a number of these 'living fossils'. Another is the giant salamander which lives in the rivers of western Honshu. Surprisingly, people inhabit only about 3 per cent of Japan's land area; the rest of the country comprises dense forest and mountains or is totally inaccessible. There may well be many more unknown and strange creatures continuing the same rhythms of life as their prehistoric ancestors.

The Yamaneko hunts at night. The Venturers adopted its habits, sleeping during the day and rising at sunset. They found tracks and the remains of exotic feasts – lizards, prawns, white-breasted water hens and fruit bats – but the cat remained an unseen phantom of the jungle. Then, one night, their luck changed.

For four hours Sarah Chapman, Sara Hartley, Par Sorme and Charles Rieckhoff had sat silently in the jungle. They marvelled at the ease with which Nori Sakaguchi, who had studied the creature for half a dozen years, could sit immobile in spite of the huge cockroaches which scuttled over his legs. Attempting to record the cat's weight, they had tied a chicken onto a scale and set up a tent for the long vigil ahead. The night noises seemed incredibly loud, crabs digging in the sand, frogs squeaking and mosquitoes buzzing like fighter planes. Every sound was amplified; they could even hear the waves crashing on the coral reef.

Suddenly a black shadow slid across the ground. The cat stepped into the light, balancing at each step as if on a tightrope. He sniffed the air. Then, with the movement of a dancer and the instinct of a killer, he bit the head cleanly off the chicken and disappeared into the night.

Charles realized he had been holding his breath and let it out in a rush. He looked with astonishment at Sara Hartley who, mesmerized by the apparition, was slowly eating a handful of nuts. Soon the cat returned and ripped the chicken to pieces.

These scientists sometimes gathered information in strange and mysterious ways, thought Doug Whitty, the lanky farmer's son from Ontario. But often it's just plain common sense. For example, to capture bats without injuring the frail creatures, you simply tied a fishing net to the mouth of their cave and waited for them to wake up and go hunting, usually at about 8 p.m. Then, to study their nocturnal flight paths, you gently prised the bats from their bonds and stuck a luminous strip onto their stomachs. Hey presto. The night was full of moving lights.

Turtle surveys presented a different problem. Sea turtles, like salmon, return to their birthplace to lay their eggs. Different species of turtle have different timetables, however. In the island chain around Iriomote, the green sea turtle nests in early May, while the loggerhead and the rare hawksbill turtles favour June.

The turtle project, led by Professor Kamesaki of Kyoto University, aimed to establish the nesting patterns of the various species. First the Venturers measured the width of the flipper marks in the sand to determine the turtle's age. Next, they recorded the temperature of the nest. Incredibly, if the temperature was below 28°C all the young would be male, and if above they would be female. Finally, they packed ten eggs from each nest in damp sand and backpacked the weighty bundle to camp. Once hatched, tagged and released, the marked baby turtles would provide invaluable research information.

First, however, the nests had to be found. The water in the damp sand and in the eggs themselves would be substantial, Doug reckoned. On the farm in Canada he had often used a divining rod to locate underground drains. Perhaps divining would work on turtle nests. The Japanese professor laughed heartily at the suggestion. Undeterred, Doug got hold of a wire clothes hanger and broke it in two. Venturer Nick Corbin tried first. Suddenly, halfway down the beach, the wires crossed. The Venturers dug furiously and found a clutch of eggs.

Doug handed the wires to the Professor. It was a hot, clear evening and the sun was going down. Rays of red and orange reflected off the sea, filling the horizon with colour. Walking along the beach, arms out-stretched, Professor Kamesaki looked up with a puzzled expression. The rods in his hands had suddenly crossed.

'We flailed away but found only damp sand,' recalled the Canadian. But a metre away the rods crossed again over a patch of vines covered with tiny violet flowers. There was no tell-tale mound and no indication of a nest. This time the Professor helped to dig. There in the sand was a large cluster of hawksbill eggs. Convinced at last, the Japanese scientist looked at the rods with new-found respect. As the moon slowly rose over the East China Sea, he continued down the beach, holding the wires before him, divining for turtle eggs.

Shiretoko Peninsula, Hokkaido, 13 April 1987

At the other end of Japan on the northernmost island of Hokkaido, Ven-turers were strapping on their crampons and preparing to face an entirely different challenge. On Monday, 13 April they set off to traverse the infamous wedge of land that juts eastwards into the sea of Okhotsk: the Shiretoko.

Hokkaido is Japan's last frontier. About the same size and latitude as the American state of Maine, Hokkaido is the only remaining outpost of the Ainu people, and its Siberian beauty is home to the arctic fox, Steller's sea eagle, the Yezo bear and freshwater fish so large they feed on rats. In the course of the next seventeen days the young climbers would meet them all; they would also become the first *gaigin*, or foreigners, in history to traverse the Shiretoko.

The 64-kilometre strip of icy wasteland is a killer. A party of Ger-mans had died in their attempt to cross it some years before, and their bones have only recently been discovered. Last year a Japanese had nearly come to an unpleasant end when he was attacked by a bear and badly mauled. The members of the Raleigh expedition all lived to tell the tale; even so the Shiretoko still took its toll.

Although other Venturers spent many days as part of the attack team, and every one of the thirty-five members of the Hokkaido expedition carried up rations and equipment, only three young men completed the entire traverse: Allan Macfarlane, a clerk with the Halifax Building Society in Glasgow who had no mountaineering experience; Kevin Wilson, another British Venturer who was a highly skilled and experienced climber; and slight, wiry Gen Terayama who runs a climbing club in Supporo, Japan. The expedition was fortunate to have the back-up of skilled mountain guides and two of Japan's most famous mountaineers, Mr Kawagoe and Mr Echigoya, who had scaled the peaks of the Himalayas.

After a crash course in climbing ice walls and administering first aid, the expedition set off. 'I was very apprehensive of what lay ahead,' wrote Allan in his log. He had good cause to be. They soon met their first and highest peak: Unabetsu. 'It was very very tough and I could have given up many times,' Allan recalls, 'but I pushed one foot in front of the other through the snow until the summit.'

The steep, icy descent was even harder. Crampons were essential and the group made a fixed-rope descent. It was a taste of what lay ahead. The days were long and hard and, on mornings when it wasn't snowing, alpine starts at 4.30 a.m. were essential. Once the sun softened the snow, the climbers would sink in hip deep even with snow shoes. At night the temperature dropped to 15° below zero and terrifying gale-force winds could reach 144 kilometres an hour.

'At the end of one twelve-hour day, we had to build an ice wall to shelter the tents from the gale,' recalled Doug Hacking. 'And one night we woke to a howling storm that sent driving rain through the inner tent wall.' The force of the wind literally moved the tents several metres, and the members of the support group were never more welcome than when, in the middle of the night, they climbed the ridge and helped move the tents in white-out conditions so severe that one could hardly see half a metre ahead.

That night the Shiretoko nearly claimed Doug's life. The young people had learned how to use their ice axes during gales to pin down the tents more securely. On this occasion the savage wind pulled one of the sharp, heavy axes free from the ground and sent it smashing through the tent, missing Doug's head by centimetres.

Amid accounts of the beauty of the surroundings, journal entries give an indication of the toughness of the traverse. 'Today I really felt like packing it in,' wrote Allan, several days into the climb. 'My whole body ached, the climb was hard, the food poor and the bent branches under the snow created dangerous air pockets which we constantly fell into.'

The support groups often had an even harder job, having to carry their own survival kit as well as food and fuel up the mountains for resupplies. A week into the expedition, Felicity 'Fliss' Greenland was up at 3.30 a.m. with nurse Sharon Newbury and Venturers Jo Thomas and Euan Rellie. They set off in the dark.

'I hadn't realized how tired I was. I cried all the way up the steep slope,' wrote strawberry-blonde cartographer Fliss candidly. 'When we finally met up with the attack team, I expected a more enthusiastic reception. I had wanted them to make my tiredness seem worthwhile. Thinking about it later, I realized they were too tired to show that they were glad.'

It was on another supply run that Fliss saw the bear. Following the country wisdom of Hokkaido, the Venturers had tied brass bells onto their rucksacks to warn bears of their approach. Climbing an open bamboo slope, the group stopped on the side of a ridge to radio the attack team. Fliss was looking up at the pine-clad hills when suddenly a massive brown bear crossed the path ahead. The youngsters had seen the scars of claw marks high up in the birch trees: even the nimblest would have a hard time escaping a hungry Yezo bear, but this 2.4-metre animal simply turned and disappeared into the forest.

After seventeen days the Venturers on the ridge spotted the sight they longed for, the spit of land edged on both sides by ocean that marked the tip of the peninsula. It was 29 April and, although two days later than they had planned, the climbers would camp that night on the beach. Their jubilation was premature, for the Shiretoko had not finished with them yet.

There had been several near misses but few casualties along the way. Paul Capper and Todd Young had suffered knee injuries and Mark Roberts had slashed his calf with his own crampon badly enough to pull him out of the traverse. It was a sad irony that the only major injury happened on the beach once the gruelling traverse was over and that it happened to Kevin Wilson who had survived blizzards, bears and howling gales.

With New Zealander Mike O'Brien, who had spent eleven days on the trek, Kevin was having fun climbing around the beach cliffs when he felt the rock he was holding come away in his hand. Falling backwards through space, Kevin's well-honed instincts took over. He managed to twist in mid-air and, amazingly, landed on his feet at the base of the 7-metre cliff. Had he fallen onto his back, he would have been smashed on the sharp rocks. As it was, he suffered severe and prolonged back injury but later made a complete recovery.

Once again the Shiretoko had tried to keep the *gaigin* who had conquered her. Once again she had failed. But I reckoned that each of the Venturers on her mountains had lost one of their nine lives.

Tokai Trail, Honshu, April 1987

It was cherry blossom time. On the large, sickle-shaped island of Honshu, centred between tropical Iriomote and the freezing wastelands of Hokkaido, two groups of Venturers began their long trek northwards from Osaka to Mount Fuji or Fuji-san, as the sacred, snowcapped cone is called. Although they had encountered many adventures along the Tokai trail, nothing had prepared them for what they now faced.

Dangling upside down 90 metres above the ground, Ben Gibson had no one to talk to but himself.

'Something is very wrong here,' he said loudly. The thin rope harness bit into his shoulders. Shutting his eyes, Ben felt himself fall into space.

'Will you respect your parents?' The voice of the Japanese monk seemed to ricochet off the cliff.

'Yes!'

Again the sickening lurch.

'Will you respect society?'

126

'Yes!'

Another drop.

'Will you complete *shugendo* training?'

'Yes!' croaked Ben for the third time. If the monk released the rope, Ben would fall to his death. Instead, to his immense relief, the white-robed monk pulled Ben back onto the ledge. He had passed the test. He had joined Operation Raleigh for adventure, thought Ben, but this was ridiculous.

'This' was part of *shugendo* training, part of the education of the Buddhist monks here in the Yoshino mountains of Honshu. A part of Buddhist discipline of which few Westerners are aware, its objectives are to train the mind and body, and to teach patience, obedience and acceptance of the unknown.

It lasted nine long days. Up at 3.30 every morning, the Venturers tramped to the temple in darkness behind the eighty-year-old priest, chanting sutras as they walked. 'Form is emptiness, emptiness is form,' repeated John Warr, from Malta. Inside the dark temple the elderly monk sounded the bell to alert the sky god of their presence, the loud reverberations shattering the silence.

Living on a vegetarian diet which consisted mostly of rice, the Venturers shared the monks' prayers and silences as well as their food. It was good to meet the English-speaking priest, Dalch, who could explain some of the meaning behind *shugendo*, because here in the mountains the vast cultural differences between East and West were felt most strongly, compounded by the communication barrier. The Japanese Venturers valiantly doubled as translators, but for many members of the expedition, Japanese and *gaigin* alike, not knowing the purpose of their actions was hardest of all.

Tracy Young, a blue-eyed Canadian from Ontario, felt the lack of communication acutely. She was not alone. Sometimes the *shugendo* training was held in sacred sites forbidden to women, as Ben Gibson's cliff-hanging test had been. At other times, following the white-robed monks, Tracy found herself on a narrow ledge, where the only way up was to climb heavy chains embedded in the rock.

Shugendo training was only one part of the trek along the steep Tokai trail. The two groups of Venturers, walking different parts of the trail, broke off from time to time to go caving, work on a construction project or learn traditional Japanese crafts. In the evenings masters of Japanese archery taught the Venturers their ancient skill. Other Venturers practised the arts of karate and kendo, the sword-fighting of the Samurai.

As always, there were some memorable fiascos. One, the attempt to build a traditional vine-and-log raft and navigate the Kiso River, will always be remembered by Scot Rognvald (Rogn) Livingstone and his companions. 'At the first river lock, the massive craft, so painstakingly constructed, was transformed into a million matchsticks!' recalls the kilted Venturer.

Such interludes over, they returned to the Tokai trail. Tracy, Ben, Rognvald and the others would spend over a month on the trek, heading north-east through the Yoshino mountains to Mount Fuji. A distance of 600 kilometres covered in thirty-two days, walking up and down 1000-metre peaks in heat, rain and snow.

The going was hard and the days were long. Far too long, thought Tony Walton when he found the Venturers exhausted and patching up their blisters at the end of a twelve-hour day. Tony called a halt at Kyoto so that they could visit the city, and ordered camp to be made every day by sundown. Along the trail, temples offered shelter for the night, or sleeping bags were unrolled beneath the flowering cherry trees. Finally, the steep, winding Tokai trail lay behind them. Before them loomed Fuji.

All parts of the expedition came together at Mount Fuji. The Venturers climbed the perfect volcanic cone at night, reaching the top of Japan's tallest and most sacred mountain as the first rays of dawn struck the sky. It was a fitting farewell to the land of the rising sun.

If the perfect symmetry of Fuji resembles the work of a careful sculptor, the Tibetan ranges are roughly drawn, snow-capped waves, forever frozen at their crest. This, indeed, is the 'rooftop of the world', and we were heading for the highest peak in China. The challenges of the Himalayas lay ahead; the Jade Venture was about to begin.

CHAPTER TWELVE

Journey to
'The Abode of God'

(*Tibet Climbing Leader:* Lieutenant-Colonel Henry Day, RE)

Mount Xixabangma, Tibet, 18 October 1987

It was bitterly cold and pitch black inside our little tent. Emma's breathing was laboured and rapid. I was having difficulty breathing too. Is it the altitude? I wondered, but we had been above 4800 metres for several weeks and were fully acclimatized.

Reluctantly pulling my arm from the warm sleeping bag, I rolled down my glove and glanced at the faint luminous dial of my wristwatch. It was 3.30 a.m. Funny, I thought, it's very quiet outside – no wind. My shoulder touched the tent wall: it was solid. Not just frozen stiff as usual, but as solid as concrete. I remembered that it had been snowing lightly as we turned in. Now we were virtually entombed.

'We've got to get out. Get dressed quickly!' I shouted.

'Oh, Father, why must you always do things at three o'clock in the morning?' came my daughter's sleepy reply.

There was no time to be lost. Pulling on thick socks, overtrousers, boots, balaclava and overgloves, I turned to the entrance. The tent door was frozen solid too and it took several strong pulls to open the zip. A wall of snow cascaded inwards. Now we heard the wind, and digging through the snow with our mess tins, cleared a way to fresh air.

My torch beam reflected off the horizontal snow, driven by the fury of the storm. Nearby I heard cries and laughter, but in the blizzard I could see nothing. Suddenly in a brilliant blue flash of lightning, I saw that the girls' tent had collapsed. With amazing good humour they staggered to the more robust army mess shelter.

Meanwhile, Emma and I had cleared the snow from our tent to prevent the alloy frame from breaking under its burden. Elsewhere in base camp everyone dug to save tents and stores, whilst on the slopes of the mountain, the climbers kept a wary vigil for the ever-present threat of avalanche.

Camp Two was totally buried and the precious ITN video camera and much of our best film were lost. At 6300 metres, four mountaineers were marooned for three days. Our advance science camp was cut off on a distant glacier.

More dramas lay ahead. The Scientific Exploration Society's Tibet expedition to Mount Xixabangma had all started when another Sapper, Lieutenant-Colonel Henry Day, and I planned a mountaineering expedition for Operation Raleigh. Tibet was an obvious choice. Sharing borders with Bhutan, Burma, India and Nepal, it is a mysterious land of awesome mountains, deserts and lakes. For centuries Tibet has been shrouded in secrecy and closed to outsiders, but by 1984 the 'Roof of the World' was opened to foreigners and we obtained permission to mount a climbing and scientific project on Mount Xixabangma. At 8046 metres, it is the world's thirteenth highest mountain. It is also the greatest Himalayan peak within China, of which Tibet is part.

We planned to set out in September 1987, at the end of the monsoon, when there is normally little snow below 4800 metres. Our team of thirty-four was drawn from four countries. Two tough and resourceful American ladies, nurse Paula Urschel and executive Pamela Stephany from the Bank of Boston, were members of previous Operation Raleigh expeditions. The British contingent consisted of soldiers, scientists and climbers, some of whom were also Raleigh veterans. Imperial Chemical Industries (ICI) became our major commercial sponsor and sent a young executive, Ivan Hui, from their Hong Kong office. Speaking Mandarin, he was to prove a valuable member of the expedition. The Swires Group, who own Cathay Pacific Airways, backed us too, and sponsored Chung Kin Man, an experienced Hong Kong mountaineer, and another asset on the language front. Through the efforts of our chief scientist, Dr Henry Osmaston, the Chinese Academy of Science agreed to provide two scientists. An interpreter, liaison officer and Tibetan driver also joined us from the Chinese Mountaineering Association. One of our goals was the encouragement of Himalayan mountaineering, and Henry Day selected ten young aspirants to join his team and gain experience of climbing at higher altitudes.

The science group also included three young research assistants who had recently graduated from Bristol University, plus a newly qualified nurse, my twenty-three-year-old daughter, Emma. By the time we took to the field, Jade Venture was not one of the Raleigh expeditions, but it shared Raleigh's aims and challenges. As patrons we had our good friends, General Sir John Mogg and Eric Hotung. Indeed, it was Eric's generosity that made it all possible.

No one could pronounce Xixabangma (Shisha-bangma), so we code-named it Jade Venture. On 11 September we began our long trek from Kathmandu to Tibet. The heavy monsoon had caused serious landslides along the Friendship Highway linking Nepal to China, and the road was impassable by vehicle for some 32 kilometres before the Chinese border.

Most of us acclimatized to the altitude by marching northwards over the mountains. Lance-Corporals John House and Jim Kimber with 178 porters carried 4 tonnes of stores up the valley of the Bhote Kosi. I met them winding their way over the landslides. Each man bore a large box with the label 'Jade Venture' and an ICI logo.

Filing up a narrow mountain path, we came upon some American tourists who watched the procession with interest.

'Tell me, sir,' said an elderly gentleman. 'What's ICKY?'

'ICKY?' I replied, somewhat puzzled.

'Yeah, I.C.I. on each box.'

I quickly explained that ICI manufactures, amongst other things, fertilizers and explosives.

'Looks as if you've enough to fertilize the whole of China, then blow it up,' retorted the American.

At that point John House walked past carrying a steam lance which is used to drill holes for taking scientific measurements in glaciers. The evil-looking lance bears a strong resemblance to a weapon from *Star Wars*. On it the words 'Made by British Aerospace', who also manufacture missiles, were clearly visible. To contribute to the confusion, John wore a T-shirt inscribed 'JADE VENTURE – THE EMPIRE STRIKES BACK'.

'I get it,' the American winked. 'The CIA has companies like ICKY. Good luck to you, young fellow.'

Perspiration poured off us as we continued the climb up the high, steep slopes, picking off tenacious leeches that dropped from every tree, bush and shrub. It was a fit, lean group which finally reached Tibet.

Tibet, 18 September 1987

The climbing and scientific groups had got to Tibet at about the same time. However, once across the border there were more landslides and, at Zhangmu, we had a lucky escape, being narrowly missed by a rock fall. No sooner had we traversed a slope when boulders the size of houses crashed down the mountain. Thirteen people had already been killed at the same spot.

We now understand why our Chinese interpreter, Wei Jian Kong, kept telling us to 'Hully! Hully!'

Gratefully we clambered aboard a sturdy lorry, which, in spite of its obsolete design, was to prove a reliable runner in the weeks ahead. Glad to be off our feet, we happily endured the drizzle as the open truck wound its way through the precipitous gorges once known to the caravan traders as 'The Gates of Hell'.

Far below us the rapids of the River Po roared a greeting as the cold, white water tumbled from the great glaciers of the Himalayas to the plains of India. Our destination was the little town of Nyalam. Old stone buildings and tin sheds provided a backdrop to the partly built hotel at the junction of two rivers. Now at 3750 metres, we puffed and panted as we set up our camp in the icy wind.

From here Henry Day would start his climbers on the 28-kilometre march to their base at 5000 metres. After long negotiations, a train of yaks was assembled to carry the stores, and later even diminutive donkeys were used. These sturdy little animals were so small that the specially made yak-boxes were often dragged off them if the donkeys passed too close to outlying rocks.

*

Above: Operation Raleigh Venturers were the first foreigners ever to participate in the Hari boat race on Ishegaki. *Below:* Venturers aboard their hand-built raft on the River Kiso, Japan – the first time the river had been rafted by foreigners. The raft broke up seconds after this photograph was taken.

Left: David Bennett from Sheffield working with a Japanese venturer in the Rause National Park on Hokaido, Japan.

Below: The Jade Venture science and support group crossing from Nepal into China.

Right: Pamela Stephany from the USA wi[th] her yak en route to Mt Xixabangma.

Below right: The strange footprints found by Dr Henry Osmaston on the northern slopes of Mt Xixabangma.

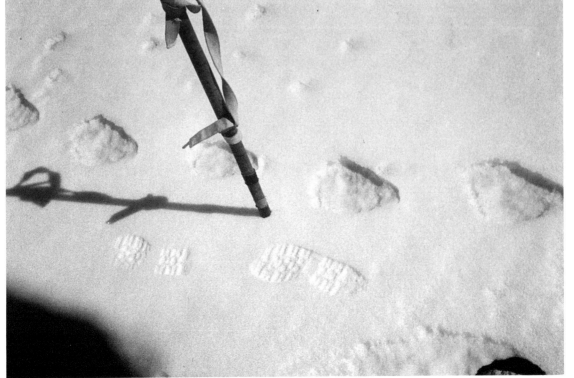

Above: Yaks bringing in the winter fodder north of Mt Xixabangma in Tibet.

Opposite: The bleak high valley of the Po river in Tibet.

Below: After the blizzard at Jade Venture's base camp in Tibet.

Above: British Venturer Dawn Muir on a glacier at the foothills of the Himalayas, in the Kohistan region of Pakistan.

Right: Venturers working in the heat and dust on the Aliabad Road in northern Pakistan.

Below: A footbridge over the River Indus in northern Pakistan.

Waving off the climbers, the academic team turned their attention to the job ahead. It was, to say the least, ambitious. With our Tibetan driver, Basna, and his faithful old truck, we set out to investigate the archaeology, botany, ecology, geology and zoology on the northern side of the mountain. We still felt the effect of altitude, but the scenery made us equally breathless. Army composite rations yielding 4000 calories a day kept our energy levels high.

On our way up the mountain we paused at a small monastery some 9 kilometres north of Nyalam. A serious young monk ushered us into a low-ceilinged cave which, some 900 years before, had housed one of Tibet's best-loved religious masters, the poet Milarepa. Like many Tibetan monasteries, it was destroyed during the 1966 Cultural Revolution but has since been rebuilt with Chinese Government funds.

Dr John Davies, an old Raleigh hand, advised me on our altitude stops and at 4260 metres we paused at the village of Yalan. A low hill ahead was crowned with ruins. 'Ah, a lost city,' joked Pamela Stephany. We camped by the road and were soon surrounded by grubby, grinning children.

Scanning the pictures in my wildlife books, the children claimed to have seen wolves, bears, wild goats, blue sheep, snow leopards and even the Yeti. Our diminutive guests departed as the sun dropped behind the hills and the temperature followed suit.

The next day we explored and mapped the ruins of what appeared to be a fortified monastery. The massive walls had suffered fearful destruction about which the villagers knew nothing, except that it had happened long ago. Checking historical records, we guessed the monastery had been a victim of King Langdarme who tried unsuccessfully to eradicate Buddhism some 1100 years ago. Relatively little is known of Tibetan archaeology, however, and our observations on this and other sites await expert examination.

The Lalung Leh pass at 5100 metres marks the limit of the South Asian monsoon. At the top we had breathtaking views of the snowclad Himalayan range. Next we passed into a wasteland of dry, gravelly hills and soon came to the barren Tibetan plateau. A vast landscape of windswept grasslands and desert stretched between snowcapped mountains.

Settlements in the region are few and far between. The inhabitants of this rugged land are self-reliant nomads. Their homes are sturdy tents,

133

Venturers on a difficult track in northern Pakistan.

warmed by stoves, and herds of goats, sheep and yaks surround the camps. At Lake Paiku we saw convoys of yaks, like troops of tanks, advancing across the arid plateau. The lead beasts flew red flags, religious rather than political symbols.

On the plain were wild asses, gazelles, woolly hares and what appeared to be a fierce crossbreed of wolf and dog. Moving about the region, our studies continued in an area where few foreigners have been.

The sun shone and at midday the temperature usually reached 21°C. Henry Osmaston, who at sixty-five was one of the fittest of the team, and Jonathan Cook, a young geologist, even managed a swim in the chilly waters.

Henry and the research assistants took several yaks and moved to the remote Dasuo glacier that flows north from Xixabangma. At 6100 metres they discovered fantastic ice pyramids over 45 metres high, standing in rows like huge dragons' teeth. These strange formations are only found on the north side of the Himalayas and the Karakoram mountains and these were the largest Henry had ever seen.

He also discovered some extraordinary, and as yet totally unexplained, footprints in the snow. Unlike those of a bear, and closer to a human foot, the prints disappeared into the vastness of Tibet. There was no sign of the creature that had made them, but the scientist captured the intriguing tracks on film.

We returned to Nyalam, pausing *en route* to let Jonathan dig out a fossil rib from the roadside on the Lalung Leh pass. Henry estimated it to be 5 million years old, probably deposited when the Himalayas were a mere 900 metres high.

We also needed yaks for the next part of the expedition up the south-eastern side of Xixabangma. Overnight their price doubled! Clearly, they must be the most profitable cattle in the world.

Although yaks appear large, clumsy creatures, they move with surprising grace, trotting quickly on their dainty hoofs up the narrow trails, their flowing hair waving in the breeze. Said to be the most efficient, all-purpose animal in the world, they provide their owners with butter, meat and milk, as well as wool, clothes and tentage. Their dung dries quickly in the sun and is used as fuel and building material. To this litany of praise it must be added that they can be ill-tempered and obstinate. I noted the caution with which their handlers approached their sharply pointed horns. In our train were also several dzo. A cross between the yak and domestic cattle, the dzo is smaller but certainly carries the same load as its big brother.

As we plodded up a gently sloping valley, the pace was that of a pleasant, easy walk, giving us time to enjoy the magnificent scenery and observe our surroundings. The whistles of the herdsmen steering their beasts became for us the strange music of the mountains. In the early afternoon we reached a major obstacle. A huge moraine rose 450 metres above a fast-flowing river. We were already over 4260 metres high and, in the thin air, it took us an hour of puffing up an ill-defined path to reach the cairn, bedecked with prayer flags, at the top.

Beyond the crest lay the intermediate base and we camped amongst piles of ration boxes – the emergency store. Next day, after a steady climb through boulder fields, we reached Henry Day's main base, with its yellow tents nestling among the rocks in the shadow of the mountain. At 5000 metres and only some 8 kilometres from the summit, this was to be our home too.

East Face, Xixabangma, 17 October 1987

Luke Hughes and Stephen Venables were already part way up the virgin east face of Xixabangma that rose at a 65-degree angle from the glacier below. Meanwhile, John Davies, our senior medical officer, and I used the lightweight Avon inflatable to begin a hydrographic survey of the clear, cold lake at 5167 metres above sea level.

'You'll be dead in a couple of minutes if you fall in,' said John cheerfully as we launched the craft. Later we discovered that we had unwittingly established the world altitude record for rowing a boat!

Everything was going rather well. The climbers were making good progress and Jonathan's geological specimens and Claire's plant collection were increasing rapidly. Meanwhile, Marion Roberts' sharp eyes had spotted several clusters of blood-red garnets. The rest of us concentrated on studying the wildlife, including the tiny tailless rodents that we fondly called Tibetan mice.

It was on one of our mouse hunts that I came across a different quarry. The dark figure of a man standing in a snow-filled gully too dangerous to descend but only some 550 metres away. 'Must be a Yeti,' we joked. But as he didn't move in the four hours we were there, we decided that the 'Yeti' was a rock. I took some pictures of it with my telephoto lens for good measure, just to show how easy it is to think you have seen the abominable snowman.

Our only link with the outside world, the BBC, brought news of a hurricane in Britain, but our minds were on our own weather as ominous dark clouds swept up from Nepal. As dusk fell the temperature registered $-20°C$. The first flakes of snow began to swirl about the tents. Later that night the storm struck and raged for the next thirty-six hours.

The deep snow, shortage of fuel and the fact that no yaks could possibly reach us, soon changed the expedition into something of a survival exercise. The mountaineers evacuated most of their camps and Henry Osmaston's party had an epic escape from their glacier in what was, by now, a full-scale blizzard. They were lucky to reach base camp with only mild frostbite.

To make matters worse, a petrol stove exploded in our mess tent and Annabel Huxley, a member of the science group, and I were only saved from serious burns by the rapid action of Paula and Emma, who hurled us, flaming, into a snowdrift. Our demi-paradise had become a freezing hell. Eventually the storm passed and, as the sun shone, temperatures rose again. However, we now had to contend with a 1.8-metre blanket of soft snow. We'd have given much for a pair of skis.

As the sun swung past, we trudged along a high ridge now tipped with a razor edge of blown snow. Claire, weighing only 47 kilos, was carrying a 32-kilo pack. She would never abandon the botanical specimens. I've seldom met such an uncomplaining, resolute person.

A French climber coming up from Nyalam warned us that another storm was predicted. We radioed this news to Henry Day and wondered how on earth they would get out in even more snow. Near intermediate base we again met a leading Polish climber, Wojtek Kurtyka, and his friend, Halina Sickaj, whom we had first encountered in Nyalam. These marvellous people shared their 93° proof mountain tea, a greatly appreciated brew.

I listened to the BBC and the news of the stock market crashing a world away, and then stepped outside to gaze one last time at the moonlit landscape. Scanning the mountain face before me I saw something move. It looked like a couple of foxes, but at dawn Wojtek showed me fresh wolf tracks.

Finally reaching the town, we learned of the tragedy caused by the blizzard. People had frozen to death in buses trapped in the high passes on the Lhasa road; villagers had died of hypothermia; and several expeditions had lost men in avalanches. A group of Tibetans watching us hobble in shook their heads in amazement that we had survived our stay on Gosainthan, the Sanskrit name for Xixabangma. It means 'The Abode of God'.

Now we had only to reach Kathmandu. The road along which we had driven forty days before was blocked in a hundred places by landslides and the 32-kilometre walk through the 'Gates of Hell' was littered with mud, rocks, trees and tangled telephone wires. It was after dark when Wei Jian Kong and I, our frostnipped feet hurting like hell, stumbled into a hut on the outskirts of Zhangmu. There we found Emma and Jonathan, who provided a welcome dish of noodles. Refreshed, we traversed the worst landslide of all, guided by a drunken Tibetan and a fading pencil torch.

'If we could see where we were going, I don't think we'd do this,' I remarked to Jonathan as we scrambled over the loose rubble and around cascading waterfalls.

After a night in a dormitory at the local hotel, we crossed the frontier into Nepal. Disappointed tourists waited in vain for permission to enter Tibet, for following the Lhasa riots, foreigners were banned once more. I wondered how long the unrest would last. My thoughts were transformed into action by the roar of a nearby explosion that sent rocks flying around us. Our newly acquired Nepalese porters dropped the baggage and fled for their lives, whilst we sheltered beneath our packs and prayed that the Chinese Army engineers would cease blasting.

Another long march and a few lifts later we reached Kathmandu, where my old friends, Jim and Belinda Edwards, took us in and provided a wonderful feast. I needed it. I had lost 12 kilos!

*

On the mountain Henry Day's team had gone back up the east face. Stephen and Luke came tantalizingly close to the summit but were turned back at 7600 metres by strong winds. The team had spent the night out in temperatures of −35°C in a snow cave – without sleeping bags. Although the summit remained unconquered, the climbers did complete a new route up the eastern face and had succeeded in climbing the 7300-metre summit of Pungpa Ri.

It had been an epic expedition in itself, and a testing journey out again. The yaks never did reach the base camp and all our heavy equipment was cached in the hope that it might be collected the following spring. The successes in both mountaineering and science, and the close liaison with the Chinese Academy of Science, bode well for future cooperation. Miraculously, everyone got home safely, although several had frostbite. Before joining the Raleigh expedition in Pakistan, I paused in Hong Kong to thank ICI and Swires.

Of special interest were the pictures I'd taken of the 'Yeti', but, although they showed all the features round about in sharp focus, the centre of each frame was empty. The distinct black figure we'd all seen and joked about had disappeared. Strange things do happen at high altitude in 'The Abode of God'.

CHAPTER THIRTEEN

The Snows of Shangri-la

(*Pakistan Leader:* Lieutenant-Colonel David Bromhead, LVO Royal Regiment of Wales)

Northern Areas, Pakistan, 9 October 1987

It was early October. The monsoons were over but the bearded elders of the remote mountain village of Dubair, high in the Karakoram mountains of north-western Pakistan, shook their heads and glanced at the skies. In the tiny roadside stalls selling apples and pomegranates, villagers felt a change in the air and hastily headed for home.

The clouds gathered above the ragged peaks of the world's highest mountain ranges. First softly, then with increasing force, the rains began again. Only this time it was different. This time the skies opened in anger, pouring hail onto the mud and brick houses clinging to the cliffs above the River Indus. For ninety-two hours rain and lightning lashed the rocky outcrops. High winds sent the slender trees crashing to the ground.

Below Dubair the bloated Indus sped through the gorge, carrying trees and boulders in its path. Called the 'Lion River', it rises in Tibet and winds through the vast mountain ranges of the Karakorams and Himalayas to the Arabian Sea. Now the river lived up to its name, roaring through the Hunza Valley, which some call Shangri-la.

Finally, the mountains could take no more. The sound of thunder was almost lost in the crash of breaking rock. Ledges broke free and fell from great heights, bringing down boulders in vast avalanches. The rivers of stone ripped up the terraced fields and slashed through Dubair to join the Indus.

Fourteen days later it was over. In Dubair six people had died and seven houses had been swept into the river. The famous Karakoram

Highway linking Pakistan with China, an engineering feat 804 kilometres long, was ruptured in fifty-six places. The highway was the lifeline between Operation Raleigh's remote mountain camps and essential food supplies. The same weather had trapped me on Tibet's highest mountain, Xixabangma, 1280 kilometres to the east.

Brigadier Jan Nadir Khan listened to the early reports of the massive avalanches. He was President of the Adventure Foundation (Pakistan), an organization whose objectives are very similar to Operation Raleigh's, and which coordinated our expedition in Pakistan. An engineer, Jan Khan had helped to build the Karakoram Highway. It had taken twenty years and claimed the lives of over 400 men. He knew better than anyone that the damage to the highway, the old Silk Route of Marco Polo's time, would take days, and perhaps weeks, to repair.

The three Operation Raleigh camps were isolated both from each other and from the Brigadier's command post in Abbottabad. Although late at night, he began a new battle plan for Raleigh. A few hours later he rang Islamabad. Nadeem Anwar answered.

The handsome young secretary of the Adventure Foundation, Nadeem, had worked tirelessly to set up the expedition with his father. The conversation was brief, but it told Anwar what he needed to know to help save the situation: the resupply jeep had successfully arrived at the expedition sites a day before the monsoon. At least there was food and fuel. In addition, Pakistan's air chief, a patron of the Adventure Foundation, would loan us a C130 Hercules to airlift two groups to the Hunza Valley in the Northern Areas. Although, once over the slides, the Venturers would be cut off from the world, they could at least begin their projects. Operation Raleigh Pakistan was back in business.

'*Inshallah*,' replied Nadeem thankfully. 'As Allah wills.' The Brigadier had discussed the new plan with expedition leader David Bromhead and deputy leader Lieutenant-Colonel Zia Hussain Kizilbash. Together they had evaluated the benefits and risks. The greatest threat was not the monsoon; it was illness or injury.

Allah's will was to test all our resources. It was a Friday – the special day of prayer and worship for Muslims and a day when no one was at their desk – that the crisis struck. Predictably, disaster came in threes.

'Mayday, Mayday,' the voice crackled over the airwaves. 'This is radio control, Rawalpindi Army Aviation Command, calling Gilgit Helisquad. One of the Venturers has almost lost his manhood.'

This remarkable message was broadcast for all to hear. Although the 'Mayday' call was serious, Brigadier Jan Khan chuckled when he heard it. He knew that in this politically sensitive corner of Pakistan, surrounded by India, China and Soviet-controlled Afghanistan, foreign intelligence officers were listening to all communications, unsure as to what this strange 'Operation Raleigh' was, and how this collection of colonels and brigadiers were involved.

It all began with Basit Khan. The 1.8-metre tall, massively built Venturer had a pedigree of courage. His grandfather, Lieutenant-Colonel Durrani, had received the George Cross, and his father, Pakistan's chief test pilot, is also the pilot for the President of Pakistan. On Thursday evening, 15 October, Basit doubled up in pain. Venturer Kim Rowswell and expedition nurse Fiona Dolan suspected acute appendicitis. They were at Passu, 2400 metres above sea level, surrounded by massive glaciers and mountains. The next radio communication with David Bromhead at Aliabad, 45 kilometres away, was not scheduled until seven the following morning and only Aliabad's radio could reach the Brigadier hundreds of kilometres to the south. Even if an evacuation could be arranged quickly, tomorrow might be too late, thought Fiona grimly.

Between the Raleigh camps at Passu and Aliabad stretched the ruptured Karakoram Highway. In parts the road had fallen away entirely, leaving a yawning gap down to the Indus. In other places the highway was buried under boulders or flooded by glacial streams. Even walking in daylight between the two camps would be difficult, thought Andy Terry, one of the leaders at Passu. Could anyone run the long distance, and at night?

At two in the morning Andy Terry and the group leader, Maqbool Abbas, decided to wake the two men who might save Basit's life: Guy Duke, a twenty-three-year-old ornithologist and staff member, and Howard Winston, a fell runner from England's Lake District. Both were ready in minutes. The night was bitterly cold. As the Suzuki, which would take them as far as the first landslide, pulled up, another Venturer, Shabir Naqvi, jumped in. He would accompany the driver back. A firm Raleigh rule is always to travel in pairs.

The second disaster struck 3.2 kilometres before they reached the slide. A power cable had fallen during the monsoon and the wires caught the wheels of the Suzuki. The car lurched and overturned, stopping centimetres short of a sheer drop to the river 30 metres below. This time the Lion River had lost its prey, but Shabir was thrown violently against the gearstick, causing severe injury to what the Mayday call delicately referred to as his 'manhood'. Shabir's own words – in Urdu or in English – are unprintable.

Three disasters: one illness, one injury and an overturned vehicle. And time was running out. Guy dashed back for help while Howard gave what first aid he could. As soon as the vehicle arrived to rescue the rescuers, the two runners set off at speed. The sooner they could radio a message to the Brigadier, the sooner a helicopter could be dispatched to Passu. 'Even an hour could make all the difference,' Fiona had said. In addition, the expedition doctor, Farooq Akhtar, was at the Aliabad camp with David and Zia, a team which could swing into action as soon as the runners arrived – if they did arrive.

Like all nightmares, this one came to an end. Guy and Howard had run over 40 kilometres at high altitude in the moonlight, navigating fallen rocks and precipitous gorges. Later, Howard would lose all his toenails from the pounding they took against the rocks. For hours the two runners kept up the fast and easy pace of athletes. Only 10 kilometres from Aliabad, Guy's knee locked and Howard continued alone. He reached the camp at 6.30 a.m. and collapsed, just as Andy Terry's SOS message came in. Dr Farooq rushed to the exhausted Venturer.

'I'm fine, thanks,' grinned Howard from his prone position. 'But I could use a little breakfast.'

Heroes are made of pretty stern stuff. After a breakfast of dal (lentils) and chapattis, Howard went rock-climbing with a group of Venturers in Aliabad. Then he slept for forty-eight hours straight. While he and Guy rested from their mountain run, Dr Farooq made the long journey back to his patients in Passu. Within hours they were whisked to hospital by helicopter. Basit quickly recovered and Shabir's manhood, to everyone's profound relief, remained intact. Tested to the limit, Operation Raleigh was, as the Brigadier said, 'still very much in business'.

*

A land endowed with so much natural beauty, the North-west Frontier has a multitude of other treasures. Foremost among them are its people. The Ismailis of the Hunza Valley, followers of His Highness, The Aga Khan, are renowned for their longevity. Several of the men in Aliabad claimed to be at least a hundred.

Now it was autumn. The harvested fruit trees turned gold and red, the colours of the rubies, garnets and topazes found near the Venturers' camp. Sue Farrington, a former personal assistant who had trotted around the globe with me for years, was ultimately responsible for this expedition. Researching a book on British cemeteries in Pakistan, she had broached the idea of a Raleigh Pakistan phase to Brigadier Jan Khan. Later she had worked out some of the details with retired British Indian Army officer Tony Chadburn, whose knowledge of the region and its people was invaluable. It was wonderful that Sue was able to be with us in Hunza.

With David Bromhead, Zia, Quartermaster Sergeant Martin Jones and some of the Venturers, Sue and I let greed take over as we searched for calcite fragments studded with rubies and jade. Not Bond Street treasure, perhaps, but at some time in the future these sparkling pieces of stone might prove important to Pakistan.

The geologists among us thought less about sapphires and more about slate. The grey slate buttressing these still-growing mountains provided a passport to the past. For weeks the Venturers had been working with Dr Baqri, the energetic geology director of the Museum of Natural History in Islamabad, and with Dr Mahmood Raza, a Yale University Ph.D., curator of the earth sciences division.

'This is the collision point of the Eurasian and Indian plates,' explained Mahmood Raza. 'The same things are happening now that occurred 20 million years ago. This part of Pakistan is a time machine – geology of the past and geology in formation. It's like walking back into history.'

Rakaposhi Base Camp, 25 October 1987

It was still dark in the Hunza Valley when the Venturers struggled out of their sleeping bags and into their warmest clothes. The icy moon

143

reflected off the ground frost and turned the tents to silver. Tariq Saad Siddiqui, a Pakistani naval officer and a co-leader of the group at Aliabad, cheerful even at 5 a.m., was already dressed in a heavy down anorak and trousers; a thick white scarf was wrapped round his head like a helmet. Behind him loomed the faint outline of Rakaposhi, the fourth highest mountain on earth. Tariq knew Rakaposhi well. He knew too the cold and difficult ascent the Venturers faced so late in the year.

Mark Blatchly was to lead the reconnaissance group up the difficult north face of Rakaposhi to the base camp of the 7787- metre peak. There they would spend the night in temperatures diving to $-30°$C. Mark, who had worked for National Westminster Bank, his sponsor, since he was sixteen, and another British Venturer, Pollyanna Kellett, planned to stay on the icy ridge for a second night while the rest of the group went down to bring up their own teams in staggered ascents.

This was the heart of the world's greatest concentration of high peaks, the confluence of the three massive ranges of the Himalayas, the Karakorams and the Hindu Kush. Uncharted glaciers blanketed over 256 square kilometres, a country known only to the snow leopard and mountain goat.

Quickly the Venturers ate a breakfast of chapattis and hot, sweet tea. Each would carry a 17.4-kilo pack, holding rations, a stove, sleeping bag and half of a two-man Vango tent for survival. Robert Grinstead, John Williamson, Gus McGrath and the others hoisted their packs and set off behind Pollyanna and Tariq as the first rays of the sun hit the serrated peaks. The October sun goes down behind Rakaposhi at 3.15 in the after- noon, Tariq had told the Venturers, and its warming rays would not strike their tents until ten o'clock the following morning.

Eager to see Gilgit, a market village where one can buy anything from sleeping bags to silver bangles, the other Venturers in the Aliabad camp were awake with the Rakaposhi climbers. They had planned a less stren- uous expedition: to the Aga Khan polo fields. It was 1 November, the beginning of a week-long celebration in the Hunza Valley, marking the birth of Pakistan in 1947. Polo, as much of a national sport as cricket, was one of the highlights of the celebration. In Gilgit it is still played in its earliest, and roughest, form.

Perched on the stone wall of the polo grounds, Catherine Beurle, an Australian, and Suhail Kayani from Pakistan, looked around them. Even here, snowcapped Rakaposhi dominated the sky. High on her flanks, the group of Raleigh climbers would be setting up camp. The two Venturers jumped as the drums loudly announced the arrival of the polo teams.

'No rules whatsoever,' said Colonel Zia as the horses took off at a full gallop. A handsome white horse slipped and fell on the soft ground. Its rider landed heavily. Several more went down shortly after. Deaths are not uncommon in this game that mimics war.

As the sun slipped behind the Karakorams, the climbers on Rakaposhi felt the sudden chill of sundown. It would be dark for the next eighteen hours.

'Tea ready yet?' asked Simon Parrish hopefully, looking balefully at the frozen parathas and cold curry that would be supper.

Mark Blatchly shone his torch on the lump of ice slowly melting over the primus. 'Not long now,' he replied. 'Another hour or two.'

In this land of late dawns and early sunsets live some of the world's rarest creatures. Hawks, falcons and eagles slice dizzy arcs above the narrow valleys. Below them graze the wild Markhor goat and the ibex, Marco Polo and Urial sheep, and the Himalayan black bear. It is also the hunting ground of the snow leopard.

For David Mallon, a thirty-nine-year-old zoologist from Manchester, the snow leopard had become an obsession. He had searched for the big cat for over a dozen years in India, Mongolia, Nepal and Kashmir: now he hoped to find his quarry in Pakistan. On the same day that Mark and Pollyanna were leading their group up Rakaposhi, and others were cheering on the polo teams in Gilgit, David Mallon and eleven Venturers reached the 4800-metre summit of the Khunjerab pass, the edge of China. Snow leopard country.

There had been a fresh fall of snow the night before. Jane Newson, a teacher from Wales, and Dave Edwards from Indiana, walked slowly, looking for tracks of hare, fox, wolf and pika, the Himalayan guinea pig. For Darren Rollens, a Venturer from the Bahamas, seeing snow for the first time made the search for the snow leopard even more of a thrill. Spotting an unusual mound of gravel and shale at the foot of a cliff, David Mallon called the rest over. 'The leopard was here,' he said softly. 'And not very long ago.'

The search was on in earnest. The group spent five days near the pass, building a windbreak to protect them from the icy winds which blew down the valley. The nights were clear and a brilliant moon filled the sky. Sitting around the fire after supper, Jane looked around the vast expanse of mountains and plains. Somewhere out there the leopard is watching us, she thought.

The leopard stayed well out of sight, however, moving higher into the mountains where the spiral-horned Markhor goats grazed. Dave Edwards and Andy ('McPhee') Kerr decided to climb a 'small' peak – a mere 4800 metres – to look for tracks. Both were experienced mountaineers and eager to have one last chance of seeing the snow leopard. They would have to return to Aliabad before long.

On that day they became just a little careless and David was unlucky. By the time he came off the mountain his feet were white and frozen. Jane tried to massage the blood back into his toes, but it was too late. They turned black and swollen, and became very painful.

'First-degree frostbite,' pronounced Dr Cronk. 'We can save your toes, but you won't be doing any more climbing for a very long time.'

'You can never take the mountains for granted,' Tariq had always warned. 'They will not give you a second chance.'

'What makes love like a tiger and winks?' asked Mark Woodgate, Tariq's deputy leader. None of the ribald replies were right. Answering his own joke, Mark laughed, looked directly at his audience and gave an exaggerated wink. From then on, he was called Tiger.

The Brigadier had asked the Venturers to map the routes of their long treks for the Adventure Foundation. Tiger's group started near Gilgit and walked up the valley to the Shandur pass. Although the nights were freezing, during the day the hot sun beat down on the valley floor, pushing the temperature well into the high thirties.

Even in this heat, the Venturers respected the customs of the country and wore long-sleeved shirts and trousers. They were hot and tired. The sight before them had to be a mirage: a deep turquoise lake bordered with willows, set like a jewel in between snowcapped pinnacles: the perfect place to make an early camp.

The combination of the beautiful Lake Bahachhat and the intense heat proved too much for Tiger. He whipped the orange flysheet off his tent and set to work, lashing logs together to make a board and inflating two survival bags. Canadian Venturer Marie-Josée ('M.J.') Leblanc, an engineering student, decided he must have sunstroke. Then she grinned. Tiger was making a windsurfer. Quickly she helped tie on the tent fly for a sail and the survival bags for outriggers. For once, ignoring custom, Tiger stripped down to his red boxer shorts and set sail for a distant island. As a fresh breeze whipped the glacial lake, a cheer rose from the onlookers. The only windsurfer in the Hindu Kush sailed serenely out to the middle of the lake, then slowly sank into the freezing water.

The trekkers had tougher moments. The group led by Ahmed Maqsood and Dr David Cronk had its share of problems. For a start, some of the packs which the Venturers carried would have made the strongest porter move to the seaside. There was the heat, but one expected that, and the group adapted by making alpine starts in the cool pre-dawn. Then, too, there were the flies, blisters, diarrhoea and cramps, dehydration, electric storms and, for all but the local Venturers, the high altitude problem. But they took that in their stride. What they hadn't reckoned on were snipers and explosions.

In the beginning, though, the altitude sapped their strength. At the first pass, the 4267-metre Niat Gali, it began to tell. 'At times it was all I could do to concentrate and set my body into gear,' wrote Yvonne Elston, the tall, slim Venturer from Cambridgeshire. 'Plod, plod, plod. Breathe. Count to ten. Rest for ten. Want to stop but I can't.'

And after that it got steeper.

Already acclimatized, some of the Pakistani Venturers fared better. Seventeen-year-old Mohammad Nasir took everyone under his wing and became the self-appointed camp manager. The fittest helped the others with their packs.

The group fought its way up scree slopes, with boulders balanced so delicately that the slightest pressure sent them crashing. They climbed through snow, across open plains and barren desert, giving wide berth to hawk-faced nomads carrying automatic Kalashnikov rifles. One day David Bromhead looked up from the steep path to see a man lining him up in his sights. Feeling as if he had stumbled into a Western, David hit the dust as several rounds were unleashed. Nineteen years before, David and I had survived two epic battles on the Blue Nile in the mountains of Ethiopia. Our eventual escape was largely due to his fast reactions – but that's another tale.

It was the following evening that Jane Newson would never forget. Lily Munirullah, washing in a glacier pool, heard the screams and dressed in a flash. The niece of the Brigadier, a schoolteacher and hot-air balloonist, she had agreed to join the expedition as staff, and to accompany Parvin Marri, the only female Pakistani participant. Running towards the screams, it looked to Lily as though the entire camp was on fire. Jane had bent down to light the kerosene stove. As she did so, the fumes from an open meths bottle ignited.

The explosion knocked people off their feet. For Jane, everything seemed to happen in slow motion, but Maqsood reacted with lightning speed. Shielding her eyes with his hands, he pushed her into the nearest tent, forcing her face into the wet earth. Her hair was alight and the tent burst into flames. While Maqsood struggled with the resisting girl, Trish and the others smothered the tent fire and Tim Yates drenched the flaming bottle of meths.

Over the next few days Jane's face blistered and turned black with the dust she couldn't wash off. But her eyesight was unharmed and there would be no scar, thanks to Maqsood's instant reflexes and David Cronk's medical skill.

Aliabad, 3 November 1987

Mr Baig strode angrily through the apricot orchards. 'I am going to write to Prince Charles,' he muttered to anyone willing to listen. 'He has sent me girls to do a job for men.'

Three months later, when I came to the Hunza Valley from Tibet, Mr Baig told me he would write another letter to our Patron: 'I'm going to say thank you for sending us such fine, strong girls who helped us to build our road.'

I was glad but not surprised. Amongst the girls were some superb athletes and mountaineers, like Helena Flynne, a qualified mountain leader, and Kathy Bainbridge, who plans to join the first British women's expedition to Gasherbrum 2, here in the Karakorams in 1989.

By any standard, the road-building project in the Hunza Valley was a great success. The new link road from the high fields would enable farmers to get their crops to market. It had been started by the outstanding Aga Khan Rural Support Programme, which invited us to help. Up at 5 a.m. to get a head start on the hot sun, the Venturers lugged axes, crowbars, picks and shovels up to the terraces.

It would be hard to imagine a lovelier place, thought Rehmat Kareem, a Venturer from nearby Gilgit. Even the villagers called the Hunza river valley, studded with poplars and apricot trees and encircled by mountains, Shangri-la. Kareem wedged a granite rock under the boulder. Beside him, Jani Rollins from Salt Lake City, covered from top to toe in a powdery veil of dust, leaned on the crowbar.

The group looked like an international chain gang. Most wore *shalwar-kamiz*, the attractive national dress of Pakistan, consisting of trousers and a long-sleeved overshirt, but they had chosen patterns that would make the King's Road sit up and take notice. The mixture of languages was equally exotic. Aymar du Chatenet chatted to M.J. in French; Yukari and Azmat had their own mix of Urdu, English and Japanese; and Elspeth Matheson's soft Scottish inflection mingled with New Zealand and Australian accents. By the end of the expedition, not one but two link roads had been built, each wide enough for a tractor and far smoother than the Silk Route still etched in the mountains.

At the opening ceremony, garlanded with chrysanthemums and dusted with flour for luck, I cut the wide red tape across the new road and thanked the Adventure Foundation, the Aga Khan Rural Support Programme and the villagers, Venturers and Raleigh supporters everywhere.

The chairman of the village project held up his hand, thanking us in turn. 'We have seen many foreigners pass by, but for the first time in the history of Hunza, you have stopped to work with us.'

It had indeed been hard work, but a greater pleasure.

OPERATION RALEIGH
COUNCIL AND EXECUTIVE

PATRON
His Royal Highness The Prince of Wales KG KT GCB

HONORARY PRESIDENT
Walter H. Annenberg KBE

HONORARY VICE-PRESIDENT
General Sir John Mogg GCB CBE DSO DL

OPERATION RALEIGH ADVISORY COUNCIL

CHAIRMAN
Vice-Admiral Sir Gerard Mansfield KBE CVO

R. A. Simon Ames
Fiona, Countess of Arran
J. J. D. (Paddy) Ashdown MP
B. David Barton FCA (Honorary Treasurer)
The Lord Beaverbrook
David C. Blamey
Colonel John Blashford-Snell MBE DSc (Hon) FRSGS (Chief Executive)
David Chipp
The Lord Clinton JP DL
Admiral Ralph W. Cousins
Alban Davies
Roger Davies
Dame Mary Donaldson GBE
John Dunn
James Gatward
Lieutenant-Colonel Sir Martin Gilliat GCVO MBE

150

John C. Groves
Eric Hotung
The Lord Mayor of Hull
David Kay
P. David King
Admiral of the Fleet The Lord Lewin KG KCB MVO DCS
Major-General Morgan Llewellyn OBE
Roger Lyons
Ron Murrell
Peter Prior CBE DL
Lieutenant-General Sir David Ramsbotham KCB CBE MA
The Lord Redesdale
George Robertson MP
Sir Harry Secombe CBE
Dr Andrew Sinclair
Sir James Spicer MP
Major Wandy Swales TD FRGS
Stephen L. Sutton MS DPhil FRES
Maurice C. R. Taylor
General Sir Harry Tuzo GCB OBE MC
Wm John Wall
Major-General Michael Walsh CB DSO
Dr Peter Wilcox (Special Adviser)
Jimmy Young CBE

SCIENTIFIC EXPLORATION SOCIETY COUNCIL

David Barton FCA
David C. Blamey DSc (Hon)
Colonel John Blashford-Snell MBE FRSGS (Chairman)
Mrs Ruth Cartwright FRGS
Colonel Geoffrey Dicker CBE TD DL FCA
Archie Futrell III
Rupert Grey LL B
Philip Harrison FRGS
Vice-Admiral Sir Gerard Mansfield KBE CVO
Andrew W. Mitchell BSc FRGS
Tony Nowell OBE FCA
Professor Chris Robinson

151

Mrs Ann Smith
Richard Snailham MA FRGS
Harbourne Stephen CBE DSO DFC
Dr Jane Wilson

CHAIRMAN OF OPERATION RALEIGH EXECUTIVE AND COMMERCIAL DIRECTOR

Tony Nowell OBE

CHIEF OF STAFF

Lieutenant-Colonel Geoffrey Straw OBE

HONORARY ACCOUNTANTS

Ernst & Whinney

HONORARY AUDITORS

Peat Marwick McLintock

HONORARY LAWYERS

Birkbeck Montagu

OPERATION RALEIGH EXECUTIVE

Colonel John Blashford-Snell MBE DSc (Hon) FRSGS
Anthony Bowring
Mrs Ruth Cartwright FRGS
Roger Chapman MBE FRGS
Ken Cherrett
Squadron Leader Derek Chidell MBE
Captain Harry Cook RN (Retd)

153

STAFF AT OPERATION RALEIGH CHQ,
1986-7

The Power House, Alpha Place, Flood Street, London SW3 5SZ

Our thanks to everyone for all their hard work.

EXECUTIVE OFFICE
John Blashford-Snell
Geoffrey Straw
Tony Nowell
Sue Farrington
Lucy Thompson
Nadia Brydon
Sally McGowan-Scanlon
Annabel Swales
Sue Holmes
William Swales
Sonia Aziz

PRESS OFFICE
Captain Harry Cook RN (Director)
Frances Chidell
Catherine Barr
Sarah Wilson
Peta Lock
Catherine Charley
Susie Long-Innes

RESEARCH OFFICE
Eibleis Fanning (Deputy Director)
Nicholas Payne
Jolomi Alagoa
Dina Wheatcroft

UK DIVISION
Roberta Howlett (Director)
Ingrid Juhanson
Gary Edwards
June Best
David Gifford
Eric Crofts
Cecilia Neville
Lorna Black
Rupert Good
Sue Clark
Steve Hide
Philip Wells
Edward Collins
Grant McPherson
Wilf Owen
Max Speedy
Bob Fitzgerald
Sidney Mabbott
Coralie Critchley
Katherine Malley

INTERNATIONAL DIVISION
Peter Leicester (Director)
Malcolm Hyatt
Anthony Agar
Hans Jaecker

Jane Pares
Boo Everard
Katherine Crookshank

FINANCE
Neil Purvis (Director)
David Murray
Sandy Neville
Nick Perrott
Penny Knocker
Charles Brown

PICTURE LIBRARY
Christopher Sainsbury
Sue Lloyd
Robert Young
Robin Kelk
Christine Frisch
Annette Price

INNER CITIES
Patrick Brook (Director)
John Allen
Pam Hartshorne

SUPPORT
Dick Festorazzi (Director)
Iain Harper
Claudia Lake
Louise Fothergill
John Parsloe
Miles East
Anthony Bowring
Jennifer Watts
Keith Somerville-Jones

PLANS
Roger Chapman (Director)
Harriet Ford
Mary Corbett
Peter Ormerod
Pippa Lack
Sandra Stinchcombe
John Symons
Simon Headington
Naomi Shindle
Mark Hannaford

MOVEMENTS
Gerald Oliver

OPERATIONS AND
COMMUNICATIONS
Felicity Bowden
Sue Lawless
Joanna Shelbourne

ART
Ley Kenyon

FILMS
Belinda Allen

CHQ MEDICAL OFFICER
Lindsey Ellis

LIST OF SPONSORS

The following list of companies and individuals who have given sponsorship to Operation Raleigh has been compiled from the records available to us as at the end of January 1988. We apologize for any errors or omissions which may have occurred. Corrections can be made by contacting Operation Raleigh, Alpha Place, Flood Street, London SW3 5SZ.

Operation Raleigh would like to give special thanks to the many people and companies who gave so generously to help individual Venturers and who are far too numerous to be mentioned here.

UK SPONSORS

3M HEALTH CARE LTD
A. & F. PEARS LTD
A. GALLENKAMP & CO. LTD
A.B. OPTIMUS LTD
ABC INTERNATIONAL
ABC NEWS INTERCONTINENTAL INC.
A.C. CANOE PRODUCTS LTD
ACTA PTY
AEG TELEFUNKEN UK LTD
A. E. H. SALVESEN'S CHARITA-BLE TRUST
AEI CABLES LTD
AGA NAVIGATION AIDS LTD
A. M. HARRIS LTD
A. McKENZIE CHARITABLE TRUST
A.P. VALVES LTD
A. W. GALE CHARITABLE TRUST
ABBEY NATIONAL BUILDING SOCIETY
ABBEY RENT-A-CAR (1980) LTD
ABBEYDALE TRUST
ABBOTT & BUTTERS LTD
ABBOTT LABORATORIES LTD
ABBOTTS PACKAGING
ABELA MANAGEMENT SERVICES SA
ACHESON COLLOIDS LTD
ACORN COMPUTERS LTD
ACORN SOFTWARE LTD
ACTION SPORTS
ADAMSON, F.
ADAMSON CHRONISTER

VALVES INC.
ADDIS LTD
ADDISON-WESLEY PUBLISHING
ADVANCE ACOUSTICS LTD
AEROPARTS ENGINEERING CO. LTD
AFRICAN MEDICAL RESEARCH FOUNDATION
AGFA GEVAERT LTD
AGIP STA
AIR FLORIDA (EUROPE)
AIR NEW ZEALAND (UK) LTD
AIR PRODUCTS LTD
AIRBORNE INDUSTRIES LTD
AIRCALL PLC
AIREY & WHEELER LTD
ALAN & SHEILA DIAMOND TRUST
ALBANY LIFE ASSURANCE
ALBERT BAXTER LTD
ALFA LAVAL COMPANY LTD
ALFRED McALPINE LTD
ALFRED PREEDY & SONS LTD
ALICE (STANCOIL) LTD
ALLAN COBHAM ENGINEERING LTD
ALLAN GENERATORS LTD
ALLAN, LESLIE
ALLCORD LTD
ALLEN & HANBURY LTD
ALLIANCE FREEZING CO.
ALLIED CARPET STORES LTD
ALLIED FISHER SCIENTIFIC
ALLIED HAMBRO FINANCIAL

MANAGEMENT
ALLIED LYONS PLC
ALLIED MILLS LTD
ALSFORD CHARITABLE TRUST
ALTUS BUSINESS SYSTEMS LTD
AMERICAN TOURISTER LTD
AMOCO UK LTD
AMOXIL BRAND EXECUTIVE
ANCHOR FOODS LTD
ANCHOR MARINE PRODUCTS
ANDREW, CHALMERS & MITCHELL LTD
ANDREW, JOHNSON, KNUDSON LTD
ANDREWS INDUSTRIAL EQUIP-MENT LTD
ANFIELD FOUNDATION
ANGLIA CANNERS LTD
ANGLISS, PHYLLIS
ANGLO-PERUVIAN SOCIETY
ANN, DR T. K.
ANNENBERG, WALTER, KBE
ANSETT
ANTHONY HORNBY CHARIT-ABLE TRUST
ANTHONY JAMES STUDIO
ANTLER LUGGAGE
ANTLER OF PALL MALL
APOLLO INDUSTRIAL & GENERAL
APPROVED PRESCRIPTION SERVICES LTD
AQUA HYDRAULICS LTD
AQUAFINE (UK) LTD

156

LIST OF SPONSORS

AQUALAC (SPRING WATERS)
LTD
AQUAMAN (UK) LTD
ARC GROUP
ARCO (UK) LTD
ARGOS DISTRIBUTORS LTD
ARMCO FINANCIAL SERVICES
ARMITAGE SHANKS & CO. LTD
ARMOUR PHARMACEUTICAL
LTD
ARMSTRONG MOTOR CYCLES
LTD
ARMSTRONG PATENTS CO. LTD
ARNETTS BAKERY
ARNOLD LAVER & CO. LTD
ARRAN, LADY
ARTFLOW STUDIOS
ARTIST HOME SUPPLIES
ARUN PRODUCTS
ASC LTD
ASHLAND WORLDWIDE INC.
ASSOCIATED BISCUITS LTD
ASSOCIATED BRITISH FOODS
LTD
ASSOCIATED BRITISH PORTS
ASSOCIATED CONTAINERS
ASSOCIATED FISHERIES
ASSOCIATED LEAD MANUFAC-
TURERS
ASSOCIATED LEAD MANUFAC-
TURERS
ASSOCIATED STEAMSHIP
AGENCY
ATHENA PRODUCTIONS
ATKINSON & PRICKETT LTD
ATLAS COPCO (GB) LTD
ATLAS PENCILS
AUDIO & DESIGN CALREC LTD
AUDIO VISUAL EDUCATIONAL
SYSTEMS CO.
AURORA PLC
AUSTRALIAN AIRLINES
AUSTRALIAN CITY PROPERTIES
LTD
AUTOMATED MARINE PROPUL-
SION
AUTOMOBILE ASSOCIATION
AVM FERROGRAPH
AVON INFLATABLES LTD
AVON RUBBER CO. PLC
AWDREY, WYLES & BAILEY
AYALA DESIGN & BUILDING
LTD
AYTON, H.

B. COOKE & SON LTD
B. DANBY & CO. LTD
B. A. BEADLE & CO. LTD
BAT CO. (HONG KONG) LTD
BICC PLC
BRS SOUTHERN LTD
BAILHACHE & BAILHACHE
BALL, V.

BALTIC EXCHANGE
BAMA INTERNATIONAL LTD
BANGOR DEPARTMENT OF EDU-
CATION
BANK OF SCOTLAND
BANK LINE, THE
BANTEX STATIONERY LTD
BARCLAYS BANK INTERNA-
TIONAL LTD
BARCLAYS BANK PLC
BARCLAYS LIFE ASSURANCE CO.
LTD
BARDS SMOKED SALMON LTD
BARNARD, A. T. & B.
BARNARDOS DISTRIBUTION
BARNES & MULLINS LTD
BARNEY'S PR
BARROW CADBURY TRUST
BART SPICES
BARTLETT CHEMICALS INC.
BASIL SHIPPAM CHARITABLE
TRUST
BASKETMAKERS COMPANY
BASS CHARRINGTON PLC
BASS EXPORT LTD
BASS, G.
BASS PLC
BATCHELORS FOODS LTD
BATLEY GS PARENTS ASSOCIA-
TION
BAUSCH & LOMB UK LTD
BAXTERS OF SPEYSIDE LTD
BAYER (UK) LTD
BAYLY, VICE-ADMIRAL
SIR PATRICK
BBC JOURNALIST TRAINING
BBC PUBLICATIONS
BEATRICE LAING TRUST
BEATTIE-EDWARDS, TOM
BEAUCHAMP CRADICK ASSOCI-
ATES
BEAVERBROOK FOUNDATION
BEDFORD CHARITY, THE
BEECHAM RESEARCH
LABORATORIES
BEJAM FREEZER FOOD
CENTRES LTD
BELIZE CONNECTION, THE
BELLWAY MARINE
BELLWAY PLC
BENCARD
BENDER & CASSEL LTD
BENHAM CHARITABLE SETTLE-
MENT
BENN BROTHERS
BENNS INFORMATION SERVICES
BENTLEY, R.
BERGEN & BALL
BERGHAUS LTD
BERK PHARMACEUTICALS LTD
BERNARD, COUNTESS GRETA
BERNARD PIGGOT TRUST
BERNARD SUNLEY FOUNDA-
TION

BERNI, FRANK
BEROL LTD
BESCO BARON LTD
BETTESHANGER COLLIERY
BHANJI, ABDUL
BILL MOORE PRODUCTS
BILLINGSGATE TRADERS LTD
BINATONE INTERNATIONAL
LTD
BIRDS EYE WALLS LTD
BIRKBECK MONTAGU
BLACK, LORNA
BLACK & DECKER LTD
BLACK & EDGINGTON HIRE LTD
BLACK & WHITE
BLACKBURN RURAL
INDUSTRIES
BLACKBURNS ALUMINIUM LTD
BLACKMORE, SON & CO.
BLAKE & SONS (GOSPORT) LTD
BLAIR ADAM HOUSE
BLUE CIRCLE INDUSTRIES PLC
BLUE COACH TOURS LTD
BLUE CRACK TOURS LTD
BLUNDELL PERMOGLAZE LTD
BLYTHE SAPPERS, THE
BMS (COOKWARE) LTD
BOEHRINGER INGELHEIM LTD
BOOKS FOR STUDENTS LTD
BOOTS CO. PLC
BORODIN COMMUNICATIONS
GROUP LTD, THE
BOSTIC LTD
BOURNVILLE WORKS CHARITA-
BLE CO. LTD
BOVRIL LTD
BOWATER SCOTT CO. PLC
BOWMAN, JAMES & SONS
BOWRING, ANTHONY
BOWRING CHARITIES FOUNDA-
TION
BOWYERS (WILTSHIRE) LTD
BOXFOLDIE CO. LTD
BOYD STEAMSHIP CORPORA-
TION
BP CHEMICALS LTD
BP OIL INTERNATIONAL LTD
BPCC DESIGN & PRINT LTD
BRADBURY, T. I.
BREWERS COMPANY
BRIDGEHEAD TRUST
BRISTOL PNEUMATIC LTD
BRISTOL UNIFORMS LTD
BRITANNIA ARROW HOLDINGS
PLC
BRITISH AEROSPACE PLC
BRITISH AIRPORTS AUTHORITY
BRITISH AIRWAYS
BRITISH ALCAN ALUMINIUM
LTD
BRITISH AMERICAN OPTICAL
CO. LTD
BRITISH AMERICAN TOBACCO
CO. LTD

157

BRITISH ARKADY COMPANY
LTD
BRITISH ASSOCIATION OF
INDUSTRIAL EDITORS LTD
BRITISH BAKERIES LTD
BRITISH BROADCASTING COR-
PORATION
BRITISH CALEDONIA (HONG
KONG)
BRITISH CALEDONIAN AIRWAYS
LTD
BRITISH CAR AUCTIONS
BRITISH CENTRAL ELECTRI-
CITY CO. LTD
BRITISH COAL
BRITISH FISH CANNERS LTD
BRITISH GAS PLC
BRITISH HOME STORES
BRITISH MARKET, THE
BRITISH MICRO
BRITISH NATIONAL INSURANCE
CO. LTD
BRITISH NATIONAL LIFE ASSUR-
ANCE CO.
BRITISH NUCLEAR FUELS LTD
BRITISH OIL PLC
BRITISH OLIVETTI LTD
BRITISH OXYGEN CHEMICALS
LTD
BRITISH RAILWAYS BOARD
BRITISH RED CROSS SOCIETY
BRITISH ROAD SERVICES
BRITISH SALT LTD
BRITISH SHIPBUILDERS
BRITISH STEEL CORPORATION
BRITISH SUB AQUA CLUB
BRITISH TELECOM INTERNA-
TIONAL
BRITISH VICE-CONSUL
HOUSTON
BRITISH VIGGO
BRITISH VINEGARS LTD
BRITOOL LTD
BRITTEN, MAJ.-GEN. R. W. J., CB
MC
BRITVIC LTD
BRIXTON ESTATE PLC
BROCADES (GREAT BRITAIN)
LTD
BROCKLEBANK, CUNARD
BROTHER INDUSTRIES LTD
BROUGHTON, NICK
BRS (SOUTHERN) LTD
BRYANT BROADCAST & DATA
COMMUNICATIONS
BSC PLATES
BUCHANON, C. R. M.
BUCKLAND PRESS GROUP LTD
BUDGET RENT-A-CAR
BUITONI CATERING PRODUCTS
BULLOCK, BRAITHWAITE & CO.
LTD
BURMAH CASTROL LTD
BURTON CHARITABLE TRUST

BUTLIN, LADY SHEILA
BUTLINS PLC
BUTTER DANE UK LTD
BYRNE, J. C.

C. & A. ROCKES CHARITABLE
TRUST
C. & J. CLARKE LTD
C. SHIPPAM & CO. LTD
C. B. NORTH LTD
C. L. ASSOCIATES
C. L. CADBURY TRUST
C. T. BATCHELOR & SON
CADBURY SCHWEPPES CHARI-
TABLE TRUST
CADBURY SCHWEPPES LTD
CADOGAN TATE LTD
CALDBECK INTERNATIONAL
LTD
CALDECOTE, ROBIN
CALLNON, DENNIS
CALMIC MEDICAL DIVISION
CALOR GAS LTD
CALOUSTE GULBENKIAN FOUN-
DATION
CAMBERWELL SCHOOL OF ARTS
& CRAFTS
CAMBRIDGE TUTORS EDUCA-
TIONAL TRUST
CANADA DRY RAWLINGS LTD
CANADIAN PACIFIC AIRLINES
CANNON INDUSTRIES LTD
CANON UK LTD
CAPE BOARDS & PANELS LTD
CAPE INDUSTRIES PLC
CAPITAL RADIO
CAPPER PASS & SON LTD
CAPPS QUICK PRINT
CARAVAN CLUB
CARAVEL MANUFACTURING
LTD
CARESS-POLE, RICHARD
CARIBBEAN PAINT MANUFAC-
TURING CO. LTD
CARLSBERG BREWERY LTD
CARNATION FOODS CO. LTD
CARNEGIE DUNFERMLINE
TRUST
CAROLINA SKIFFS INC.
CARPENTERS SHIPPING
CARPETS INTERNATIONAL LTD
CARSTON ELECTRONICS LTD
CARTWRIGHT & BUTLER
CASELLA LONDON LTD
CASSENE
CASTLE & COOKE FOOD SALES
CO.
CASTLE HILL HOSPITAL
CASTLEFIELDS
CATHOLIC WOMEN'S LEAGUE
OF JERSEY - SAMARES
BRANCH
CAYMAN AIR
CEE VEE ENGINEERING LTD

CENTRA GRAPHICS
CENTRAL ELECTRICITY GENER-
ATING BOARD
CENTRONIC DATA COMPUTERS
(UK) LTD
CETAPRINT
CHAMBERS & FARGUS
CHAPMAN ENVELOPES
CHAPMAN FOUNDATION, THE
CHAPTER HOUSE
CHARLES BARKER CITY LTD
CHARLES F. THACKRAY LTD
CHARLES FRANK LTD
CHARLES HENRY FOYLE TRUST
CHARRINGTON CATERING
CHARTERHOUSE BANK (JERSEY)
LTD
CHASE MANHATTAN BANK
CHATSWORTH LTD
CHAUCER FOODS LTD
CHESHIRE COUNTY COUNCIL,
HALTON DISTRICT
CHEVRON OVERSEAS PETRO-
LEUM LTD
CHILETABACOS
CHILTERN FOODS LTD
CHILTON SURGICAL LTD
CHINA TRADE
CHLORIDE EUROPE/DEFENCE
MARKETING UNIT
CHLORIDE GROUP LTD
CHLORIDE MOTIVE POWER
CHLORIDE STANDBY SYSTEMS
CHRISTIAN & NIELSEN LTD
CHRISTIAN SALVESON LTD
CHRISTIES LTD
CHRISTOPHER LAING FOUNDA-
TION
CHROMACOPY
CHUBB FIRE SECURITY LTD
CHUBB LOCK CO.
CIBA GEIGY
CIBA LABORATORIES
CINE EUROPE LTD
CIRIO CO. LTD, THE
CITIBANK
CITICORP INSURANCE BROKERS
LTD
CITRA SOFT DRINKS LTD
CITY OF BIRMINGHAM
CITY OF COVENTRY
CITY OF HULL
CITY OF PLYMOUTH
CITY OF SALFORD
CLANBRASSIL TRUST CO. LTD
CLARK INDUSTRIES LTD
CLEGHORN WARING & CO. LTD
CLENAGLASS ELECTRIC LTD
CLINICAL SOCIETY OF BATH
CLINIQUE LABORATORIES LTD
CLINTON, LORD
CLOCKMAKERS COMPANY
CLOTHTEC LTD
CLOTHWORKERS FOUNDATION

CLYDESDALE BANK PLC
COALITE GROUP PLC
COATES & CO. (PLYMOUTH)
  LTD
COHEN, FREDDIE
COLE, DAVID
COLEMAN UK
COLEMANS OF NORWICH
COLLINS, E.
COLORSIX LABORATORIES
COLOUR PROCESSING
  LABORATORIES
COLT CAR CO. LTD
COMET GROUP PLC
COMMERCIAL CONTAINER
  TRANSPORT
COMPAGNIE GENERAL MARI-
  TIME
COMPAIR INDUSTRIAL LTD
COMPAIR REAVELL LTD
COMPASS MARITIME
COMPUTER CONCEPTS
CONOCO (UK) LTD
CONSERVATIVE CENTRAL
  OFFICE
CONSOLIDATED GOLD FIELDS
  PLC
CONTINENTAL GRAIN CO.
CONTINENTAL SCRAP METAL
  LTD
COOPER, A. R. V.
COOPER, G. C.
COOPERATIVE WHOLESALE
  SOCIETY LTD
COOPERS & LYBRAND
COPE ALLMAN PLASTICS LTD
CORDELL NORTHWOOD LTD
CORK, BAYS & FISHER LTD
CORNES, M.
CORNWALL MINING SERVICES
COSTAIN PROCESS LTD
COTSWOLD CAMPING
COUNTY OF SOUTH
  GLAMORGAN
COURAGE BREWERIES
COURAGE TRUST
COURTAULDS LTD
COVENTRY BUILDING SOCIETY
COZEN-HARDY, LORD
CPC (UK) LTD
CRANE PACKAGING LTD
CRAYONNE LTD
CRESSWELL, D. J.
CREWSAVER MARINE EQUIP-
  MENT LTD
CRISTIN, ADVOCATE R. H.
CROCKER, WILLIAM & CHARLES
CROOKES PRODUCTS LTD
CROWN HOUSE ENGINEERING
  LTD
CRYPTO PEERLESS LTD
CULPEPER LTD
CUMMINS ENGINE CO. LTD
CYB LTD

DAILY TELEGRAPH
DAIRY CREST FOODS
DALE, K. W., OBE TD CENG
  RCIBS
DALGETY PLC
DALIDEA TRUST
DANIEL J. EDELMAN LTD
DANISH AGRICULTURAL PRO-
  DUCERS
DARTINGTON FARM FOODS
  LTD
DASHWOOD BREWER &
  PHILIPPS LTD
DAVID PINDER & PARTNERS
DAVIES, ALLEN
DAVY & CO. (LONDON) LTD
DAWNFRESH SEAFOODS LTD
DCL FOOD GROUP
DDD (SECURITY SYSTEMS) LTD
DE SAVARY, PETER
DEAK & CO. LTD
DEAK-PERARA
DEAN & CHAPTER OF
  WESTMINSTER
DEB CHEMICAL PROPRIETARIES
  LTD
DECCA RADAR LTD
DELMAR CHARITABLE TRUST
DELOITTE, HASKINS & SELLS
DELTA AIRLINES
DELTA GROUP PLC
DENCO LTD
DENNIS CURRY CHARITABLE
  TRUST
DENT DAVIS ASSOCIATES LTD
DENTSPLY LTD
DEPARTMENT FOR NATIONAL
  SAVINGS
DEPARTMENT OF EDUCATION,
  NORTHERN IRELAND
DEPARTMENT OF EDUCATION &
  SCIENCE
DEPARTMENT OF THE ENVI-
  RONMENT
DEUTZ ENGINES LTD
DEVONAIR RADIO LTD
DEXION LTD
DHL INTERNATIONAL (UK) LTD
DIBRO LTD
DICKS, R. S.
DIVEMEX LTD
DIXONS PHOTOGRAPHIC LTD
DONALD BROWN (BROWNALL)
  LTD
DONOVAN, D.
DOROTHY HOLMES CHARIT-
  ABLE TRUST
DOUGLAS MARTIN TRUST
DOWLING SEWING MACHINES
  LTD
DOWSETT ENGINEERING &
  CONSTRUCTION LTD
DRAEGER SAFETY LTD
DRAKE, T. R.

DRAPERS CO., THE
DREWETT, HARRY
DRG PLASTICS
DUCKHAM, ALEXANDER & CO.
  LTD
DUDLEY COX CHARITABLE
  TRUST
DUFFIN, L. G.
DUGARD, J. R.
DUKE, MAJ.-GEN. SIR GERALD
DULVERTON TRUST, THE
DUNCAN FLOCKHART & CO.
  LTD
DUNLOP FOOTWEAR LTD
DUNLOP INDUSTRIAL & PRO-
  TECTIVE
DUNLOP MARINE SAFETY
  PRODUCTS
DUNNETTS (BIRMINGHAM) LTD
DURAPIPE LTD
DURHAM CHEMICAL DISTRIBU-
  TORS
DUTTON, J. R.
DUTTON, TONY
DYERS LEAZE LACOCK
DYLON INTERNATIONAL LTD

E. LEITZ INSTRUMENTS LTD
E. D. CADBURY CHARITABLE
  TRUST
E. L. RATHBONE CHARITABLE
  TRUST
E. P. BARRUS LTD
EARLE, A.
EAST RIDING FARM PRODUCTS
  LTD
EASTERBROOK ALLCORD & CO.
  LTD
ECHO-TOOL
EDDYSTONE RADIO LTD
EDELRID (UK) LTD
EDEN VALE
EDUCATIONAL MAILING SERV-
  ICES
EDWARD STAMFORD LTD
EDWARDS, TOM BEATTIE
EGA LTD
ELBAR-PINEFIELD LTD
ELBATAINER (UK) LTD
ELDER DEMPSTER LINES LTD
ELECTRICITY COUNCIL
ELECTRO COPY & HULL
  DRAWING
ELECTRO FURNACE PRODUCTS
  LTD
ELECTROLUX LTD
ELEY IMPERIAL METAL
  INDUSTRIES LTD
ELI LILLY & CO. LTD
ELIDA GIBBS LTD
ELLINGER, HEATH, WESTERN &
  CO.
ELLIS & EVERARD CHEMICALS
  LTD

ELLIS BOOKER LTD
ELLIS FOUNDATION
ELWYN HARPER DIVING EQUIP-
MENT
EMMOTT FOUNDATION LTD,
THE
EMPIRE STORES
EMTRAD LTD
ENEX INTERNATIONAL LTD
ENGLISH ABRASIVES LTD
ENGLISH CHINA CLAYS PLC
ENGLISH CLAWS
ENSIGN FLAG CO. LTD
ENVIRODOOR MARKUS LTD
EQUITY & LAW CHARITY
ERCOL FURNITURE LTD
ERNST & WHINNEY
ESCHMANN BROTHERS &
WALSH LTD
ESSEX, DAVID
ETHICON
EUROPOWER HYDRAULICS LTD
EVER READY LTD
EXPRESS DAIRIES
EXTON GOLD LTD

F. E. WRIGHT (UK) LTD
F. J. PARSONS & CO. LTD
F. R. SCOTT LTD
F. S. TURNER & CO.
FABER PREST HOLDINGS PLC
FAIRCLOUGH BUILDINGS LTD
FAIRCLOUGH CONSTRUCTION
GROUP
FALMOUTH DOCKS OIL
EXPLORATION
FARLEYS HEALTH PRODUCTS
LTD
FARMITALIA CARLO ERBA LTD
FARRINGTON, SIR HENRY
FENNER INTERNATIONAL LTD
FENWICK, KATIE
FENWICK LTD
FIDELITY INTERNATIONAL (CI)
LTD
FILM EDGE NUMBERING
FINDLATER, MACKIE, TODD &
CO. LTD
FISCO PRODUCTS LTD
FISH TRADER, THE
FISHER, M. H.
FISHMONGERS COMPANY
FISONS CHARITABLE TRUST
FISONS PHARMACEUTICALS
LTD
FITZMAURICE HOUSE LTD
FLAG TRAVEL LTD
FLYING TIGERS LTD
FOOD BROKERS LTD
FOOTPRINT TOOLS LTD
FOOTWEAR LTD
FORBO (UK) LTD
FORD MOTOR CO. LTD
FORD (UK) LTD

FORESTRALL LTD
FOSTER & BRAITHWAITE
FOULDS & SONS
FOUNTAIN DRINKS
FOUNTAINHEAD PUBLICITY &
ADVERTISING
FOX FAMILY
FOX'S BISCUITS
FRANK SMYTHSON LTD
FRANK W. JOEL LTD
FRANKFURTER ALLGEMEINE
FRASER, I. D.
FREDERICK OLIVER LTD
FREEPORT ADVERTISING &
PRINTING LTD
FREEPORT CASES LTD
FREEPORT HARBOUR CO. LTD
FREIGHTLINERS
FRENCH FLINT
FROZEN QUALITY LTD
FUJI PHOTO FILM (UK) LTD
FURNESS WITHEY (SHIPPING)
LTD

G. & A. E. SLINGSBY LTD
G. & M. POWER PLANT & CO.
G. ORANGE & CO. LTD
G. H. ZEAL LTD
G. K. MATHEWS & ASSOCIATES
LTD
G. M. MORRISON CHARITABLE
TRUST
G. S. PLAUT CHARITABLE
TRUST
G. S. VOASE LTD
GT MANAGEMENT
G. W. BIGGS & SON LTD
G. W. LATUS
G. W. SPARROW & SONS
GALLAGHER LTD
GANDARA PANAMA SA
GARUDA INDONESIAN AIRLINES
GAS & EQUIPMENT LTD
GASKELL, B. H.
GATEWAY FOODMARKETS LTD
GAULT DEVELOPMENTS LTD
GEIMUPLAST
GENESIS PR LTD
GEOFFREY ROBERTS ASSOCI-
ATES
GEOGRAPHICAL MAGAZINE
GEORGE DREXLER OFREX
FOUNDATION
GEORGE HAMMOND LTD
GEORGE PRICE ENGINEERING
GEORGE TROY & SONS LTD
GEORGE WIMPEY CHARITABLE
TRUST
GERRARD INDUSTRIES LTD
GESTETNER HOLDINGS PLC
GESTETNER INTERNATIONAL
LTD
GESTETNER (UK) LTD
GILL CHARITABLE TRUST

GILMAN & CO. LTD
GLAXO LABORATORIES LTD
GLEN REELS LTD
GLOAG, MATTHEW & SON LTD
GLOBE ENGINEERING LTD
GLOUCESTERSHIRE COUNTY
COUNCIL
GLOUCESTERSHIRE QUEEN'S
SILVER JUBILEE TRUST
GODINGTON CHARITABLE
TRUST, THE
GOLD ARROW MACHINE
GOLDCROSS PHARMACEUTICALS
GOLDEN WONDER LTD
GOLLEY, SLATER & ROW
GOODYEAR PACKAGING
GOODYEAR TYRE & RUBBER CO.
GOURMET FROZEN FOODS
EXPORT CO.
GOVETT, HOARE
GRAHAM POULTER PUBLIC
RELATIONS
GRAINGER, L. C.
GRAMPIAN TV
GRANADA FOUNDATION
GRANADA TV RENTAL
GRAND BAHAMA BAKERY LTD
GRAND METROPOLITAN PLC
GRANNET COMMUNICATIONS
LTD
GRANTHAM YORK TRUST
GREAT BRITAIN SASAKAWA
FOUNDATION
GREEN, B. E.
GREENHAM TRADING LTD
GREIG, MIDDLETON & COM-
PANY
GROCER, THE
GROSVENOR ESTATES
GROUP III INC.
GROUT & COMPANY
GUENOC WINERY
GUEST, KEEN & NETTLEFOLDS
PLC
GUINNESS PLC
GUNTER CHARITABLE TRUST
GWENT COUNTY COUNCIL

H. & A. KENDRICK
H. & T. MARLOW LTD
H. CLARKSON & CO.
H. FINE & SON LTD
H. MOELLER LTD
H. J. HEINZ CO. LTD
HMS *RALEIGH*
HP FOODS LTD
H. P. BULMERS LTD
HACKING, LOIE G.
HALDANE FOODS LTD
HALIFAX BUILDING SOCIETY
HALL & WOODHOUSE LTD
HALL'S BARTON ROPERY CO. LTD
HALLEY'S COMET SOCIETY
HALTRAC LTD

HAMMERSMITH & FULHAM
COUNCIL
HAMPTON SCHOOL
HAMWORTHY ENGINEERING
LTD
HANSCO LTD
HANSON TRUST PLC
HARLANDS OF HULL LTD
HARRIS, E. J.
HARRIS QUEENSWAY GROUP
PLC
HARRISON COWLEY PUBLIC
RELATIONS
HARRODS LTD
HAVERHILL MEAT PRODUCTS
HAWLEY GROUP PLC
HAX LTD
HAYWARD, SIR JACK
HAZLEWOOD FOODS PLC
HEALTH AID
HEART OF VARIETY LTD, THE
HEAT-O-VENT ELECTRIC LTD
HEDGES & BUTLER
HELIX LTD
HEMPEL'S MARINE PAINTS LTD
HENDRY BROTHERS (LONDON)
LTD
HENRI-LLOYD LTD
HENSMAM
HERBERT SLATER LTD
HERBERT SMITH & CO. LTD
HERON POWER PRODUCTS LTD
HERON SUZUKI (GB) LTD
HERTZ RENT-A-CAR LTD
HETTICH LTD
HEWLETT PACKARD LTD
HEYGATES LTD
HIATT & CO.
HICKSON'S TIMBER PRODUCTS
LTD
HIGHLAND SPRING LTD
HILTON COLOUR LTD
HIND, PROF. J. ANTHONY
HITCHINGS, RUSSELL
HK COMMERCIAL BROADCAST-
ING CO.
HOBBS, H.
HODGE SEPARATORS LTD
HOECHST (UK) LTD
HOGG ROBINSON CARGO LTD
HOGG ROBINSON CHARITABLE
TRUST
HOGG ROBINSON TRAVEL LTD
HOLIDAY INN
HOLLAND & HOLLAND LTD
HOLMES TANNERS LIMITED
HOME DEPOT
HONDA (UK) LTD
HONEYWELL BULL LTD
HONGKONG BANK FOUNDA-
TION
HONG KONG TELEPHONE CO.
LTD
HOTEL DE FRANCE (JERSEY)

HOTUNG, ERIC E.
HOWARD LEOPOLD DAVIS
SCHOLARSHIPS TRUST
HP FOODS LTD
HPL CONTAINERS LTD
HRH THE PRINCE OF WALES
HUBBARD-READER GROUP LTD
HULL CITY AFC PLC
HULL CITY COUNCIL
HULL FISHING VESSEL OWNERS
HULL TELEPHONE COMPANY
HUMBER FREEZER TRAWLER
OWNERS CO. LTD
HUMBERSIDE FOOD
MACHINERY LTD
HUMBERSIDE WELDING
SUPPLIES
HUNTING GROUP
HUNTLEY & PALMER FOODS
PLC
HUSQVARNA FOREST & GARDEN
HUTTON & CO. LTD
HYDROGRAPHIC DEPARTMENT
HYETT ADAMS LTD

IBM (UK) LTD
ICI LTD
ICI PHARMACEUTICALS PLC
ICI VISQUEEN POLYTHENE FILM
IMI YORKSHIRE FITTINGS LTD
ITT CONSUMER PRODUCTS (UK)
LTD
ITT JABSCO LTD
ITV
IBERIA INTERNATIONAL AIR-
LINES
IBSONMAIN LTD
ICE'N'EASY SEAFOODS
IDEAL STANDARD LTD
IDLEWILD TRUST
ILSA SHARP EDITORIAL
SERVICES
IMPALLOY LTD
IMPERIAL BREWING & LEISURE
LTD
IMPERIAL BUSINESS EQUIP-
MENT
IMPERIAL LIFE ASSURANCE CO.
OF CANADA
IMPERIAL PROFESSIONAL
COATING
INFORMATION SERVICES LTD
INSTITUTE OF FREIGHT
FORWARDERS
INSTITUTE OF MARKETING
INTERCONTINENTAL HOTELS
INTERNATIONAL DISTILLERS &
VINTNERS LTD
INTERNATIONAL LABS LTD
INTERNATIONAL PAINTS
(YACHT DIV.)
INTERNATIONAL SIGNAL &
CONTROL GROUP PLC
INTERNATIONAL YOUTH YEAR -

JERSEY COMMITTEE
INVERESK
INVERFORTH CHARITABLE
TRUST
IRONMONGERS HALL
IVOR INNES PHOTOGRAPHY

J. & M. DOLMETSCH LTD
J. GRESHAM & CO. LTD
J. KNAGGS & CO. LTD
J. LYONS & CO. LTD
J. MARR & SON LTD
J. MEREDITH BUSINESS EQUIP-
MENT
J. YOULE & CO. LTD
J. A. MARSHALL & CO. LTD
J. A. PYE'S CHARITABLE TRUST
J.B.S. ASSOCIATES LTD
J. D. POTTER LTD
J. H. FENNER & CO. LTD
J. J. VICKERS & SONS
J. T. SCOTNEY LTD
J. W. AGER & SONS LTD
J.W. AUTOMARINE
JACOBS & PARTNERS
JAEGAR HOLDINGS LTD
JAEGER, TELEX-VERLAG
JAGUAR CARS LTD
JAMES, CATHERINE & LADY
GRACE
JAMES, COLIN
JAMES BURROUGH PLC
JAMES, FREDERICK & ETHEL
ANNE MEASURES CHARITY
JAMES HAMILTON LTD
JAMES MOGGRIDGE WINES
JAMES NEILL HOLDINGS LTD
JANE HODGE FOUNDATION
JANE'S DEFENCE WEEKLY
JANSSEN PHARMACEUTICALS
LTD
JAPAN AIRLINES CO. LTD
JARDINE GLANVILLE INSUR-
ANCE BROKERS
JAVERETTE
JAYBEAM SA
JEBSEN & CO. LTD
JEHAN, DUDLEY
JENKINS & CATTELL LTD
JENKINS, MICHAEL RHYS
JENKS BROKERAGE/SHORTS
SPICES
JERSEY ELECTRICITY CO. LTD
JERSEY ROUND TABLE
JERSEY SOCIETY IN LONDON
JESSOPS OF LEICESTER LTD
JEYES LTD
JOE BROWN SHOP
JOHN BARTHOLOMEW & SON
LTD
JOHN BULL LTD
JOHN BURGESS & SONS LTD
JOHN F. CORLYON FURNITURE
LTD

161

JOHN FINLAN PLC
JOHN PLUMER & PARTNERS LTD
JOHN RIDGEWAY SCHOOL OF
 ADVENTURE
JOHN TAWS LTD
JOHN TRELAWNY LTD
JOHN WEST FOODS LTD
JOHN WRIGHT & SONS
JOHNSON & JOHNSON LTD
JOHNSON, RICHARD & ASSOCI-
 ATES
JOHNSON WAX
JOHNSONS OF HENDON LTD
JOHNSTON'S CONSTRUCTION
 CO.
JOICEY TRUST
JONES & BROTHER LTD
JONES, C.
JOSEPH, N. G.
JOSEPH WALKER
JULIANAS DISCOTHEQUES
JUSTERINI & BROOKS LTD

K SHOEMAKERS LTD
KHD GREAT BRITAIN LTD
KALAMAZEL TRUST
KANGOL LTD
KARRIMOR INTERNATIONAL
 LTD
KAY & CO. LTD
KEELERS LTD
KEIO PLAZA INTERCONTINEN-
 TAL
KELLOGGS OF GREAT BRITAIN
 LTD
KELVIN HUGHES CHARTS &
 MARITIME SUPPLIES LTD
KEMPNER CORPORATION
KENCO COFFEE CO. LTD
KENCO TYPHOO CATERING
 SERVICES
KENDALL COMPANY, THE
KENNETH WILSON HOLDINGS
 LTD
KENREY ELECTRONICS LTD
KENYON, LEY
KERR STEAMSHIP CO. INC.
KILLGERM CHEMICALS LTD
KING TOUR CO
KINGS TOWN ENGRAVING CO.
 LTD
KIRBY LAING FOUNDATION
KIRBY WARWICK PHARMACEU-
 TICALS
KLARK-TEKNIK
KLEINWORT BENSON (JERSEY)
 LTD
KLEINWORT CHARITABLE
 TRUST, SIR CYRIL
KNOWLEDGE-INDEX
KNOWSLEY BOROUGH COUNCIL
KODAK LTD
KOMPASS PUBLISHERS LTD
KOREL, GEORGE PTS EX RAF

KROY (EUROPE) LTD
KRUPP ATLAS ELECTRONIC
 (UK) LTD

L. E. PRITCHITT & CO. LTD
L. E. WEST & CO.
LA MOTTE GARAGES LTD
LAING INDUSTRIAL ENGINEER-
 ING & CONSTRUCTION LTD
LAING PROPERTIES
LAINGS CHARITABLE TRUST
LAMPORT & HOLT LINE
LANCER INDUSTRIES LTD
LANDORE METAL PRODUCTS
LAND-ROVER LTD
LANE, FOX & PARTNERS
LANIGAN, STUART
LANSDOWNE CLUB
LANSING BAGNALL LTD
LAXTON, J. R.
LAZARD BROS & CO.
LE BRUNS BAKERY LTD
LE VOUGEUR FAMILY
LEA & PERRINS LTD
LEAFE & HAWKES LTD
LEDERLE LABORATORIES
LEE, WING TAT
LEE COOPER GROUP PLC
LEE HYSAN ESTATE CO. LTD
LEEDS & HOLBECK BUILDING
 SOCIETY
LEGAL & GENERAL GROUP PLC
LEOPOLD DE ROTHSCHILD
 TRUST
LEROCO EXPORTS LTD
LESLIE & GODWIN CHARITABLE
 TRUST
LESLIE BISHOP & CO.
LESSER BUILDING SYSTEMS
 LTD
LETRASET, ESSELTE
LEVER BROS LTD
LEVERHULME, THE VISCOUNT
LEX SERVICES PLC
LEYLAND PAINT & WALLPAPER
 PLC
LIFEGUARD EQUIPMENT LTD
LIGHT ALLOY LTD
LIGHTHOUSE CLUB, THE
LILO LEISURE PRODUCTS LTD
LINC INTERNATIONAL COMMU-
 NICATIONS
LION FOODS LTD
LIONS CLUB OF JERSEY
LIPHA PHARMACEUTICALS LTD
LIPTON EXPORT LTD
LIQABUE PANAMA
LITTLE SHIP CLUB
LITTLEMORE SCIENTIFIC
 ENGINEERING
LIVERPOOL FOOTBALL CLUB
LLOYD HUGHES ASSOCIATES
LLOYDS BANK PLC
LLOYDS CHARITIES TRUST

LLOYDS GRANTS SUB-
 COMMITTEE
LLOYDS OF LONDON PRESS LTD
LLOYDS REGISTER OF
 SHIPPING
LOCKWOODS LTD
LOFTHOUSE OF FLEETWOOD
 LTD
LOM FOOD SERVICES
LONDON BOROUGH OF
 HACKNEY
LONDON BOROUGH OF
 HARINGEY
LONDON BOROUGH OF
 WANDSWORTH
LONDON CHAMBER OF
 COMMERCE
LONDON ELECTRICITY BOARD
LONDON LAW TRUST
LONDON SCOTTISH MARINE
 OIL CO.
LONDON UNDERGROUND LTD
LONDON WINDSURFING
 CENTRE
LONRHO PLC
LUCAS AEROSPACE
LUCAS, P. A.
LUISI, HECTOR E.
LYON EQUIPMENT

M. HARLAND & SON LTD
M. E. G. MOORE LTD
M.E.L. LTD
M. G. DUFF LTD
M.R. WINES
M.T. COOK AIRLINE
MACADIE, COLIN
MACARTHYS SURGICAL LTD
MACDOUGALL, J. L.
MACKENSON-SANDBACH, IAN
MACRAE, D. A.
MAERSK CO. LTD
MAGDALEN HOSPITAL TRUST
MALAYSIAN AIRLINE SYSTEM
MALCOLM WEST PLANT HIRE
 LTD
MALLINSON-DENNY LTD
MANCHESTER CITY COUNCIL
MANDARIN HOTEL (JAKARTA)
 LTD
MANLEY RADCLIFFE LTD
MANNESMANN TALLY LTD
MANNING, B. J.
MANPOWER SERVICES COMMIS-
 SION
MANPOWER WORK CONTRAC-
 TORS
MARCONI INTERNATIONAL
 MARINE CO. LTD
MARCONI RADAR SYSTEMS LTD
MARCONI SECURE RADIO
 SYSTEMS
MARCONI SPACE SYSTEMS
MARFLEET REFINING CO. LTD

MARINE POWER INTERNA-
TIONAL
MARINE PROJECTS (PLYMOUTH)
MARINE SOCIETY
MARK AMY LTD
MARK C. BROWN & SON LTD
MARK PRODUCING COMPANY
LTD
MARLBOROUGH COMMUNICA-
TIONS LTD
MARS CONFECTIONERY COM-
PANY
MARTINDALE PROTECTION LTD
MASS TRANSIT RAILWAY COR-
PORATION
MATTESONS MEATS LTD
MATTESSONS WALL'S LTD
MATTHEW, R.
MATTHEW HALL ENGINEERING
LTD
MATTHEWS BUTCHERS LTD
MAY & BAKER PHARMACEUTI-
CALS
MAYFIELD BROS LTD
McCAIN INTERNATIONAL LTD
McCALLUM, S.
McCANN-ERICKSON
McKELLER WATTS
McKENNA, R. A.
MEAT PROMOTION EXECUTIVE
MEDIA PROJECT DEVELOP-
MENTS
MELBA TRADING CO. LTD
MELSON WINGATE LTD
MENDHAM ENGINEERS LTD
MEPR MICRODATA SYSTEMS
LTD
MERCERS LIVERY COMPANY
MERCHANT TAYLORS SCHOOL
MERCURY MARINE
MERIEUX (UK) LTD
MERRYDOWN WINE PLC
MERSEY FREIGHT SERVICE
MERSEYSIDE COUNTY COUNCIL
MERSEYSIDE TASK FORCE
METAL BOX PLC
METEOROLOGICAL OFFICE
METIER MANAGEMENT SERV-
ICES LTD
METROPOLITAN BOROUGH OF
BOLTON
METROPOLITAN BOROUGH OF
SEFTON
METROPOLITAN POLICE
OFFICE
MICROVITEC PLC
MIDDLESEX MEMORIAL TRUST
MIDLAND & SCOTTISH MARINE
INVESTMENTS
MIDLAND DIVING EQUIPMENT
MIDLAND EDUCATION CO. LTD
MIDSHIP MARINE INC.
MIKE PAGE OFFICE SUPPLIES
MILK MARKETING BOARD

MILLER, CURWEN
MILSON, J. S.
MIMAC
MIMS
MINIGRIP (LONDON) LTD
MINISTRY OF DEFENCE
MIRACLE TECHNOLOGY (UK)
LTD
MK ELECTRIC LTD
MOBIL OIL CO.
MODERN HOTELS GROUP
MOËT ET CHANDON
MOLYSLIP HOLDINGS LTD
MONO PUMPS LTD
MONTAGUE L. MEYER (HULL)
LTD
MOODY FOUNDATION
MOORE, A. E.
MOORE, G.
MOORE PARAGON (UK) LTD
MOORE STREET MANAGEMENT
MOORES & ROWLAND
MORANE PLASTIC CO. LTD
MORGAN CRUCIBLE COMPANY
FUND
MORNING FOODS LTD
MORTON, ALISTAIR
MOSELEY, J.
MOSS, BARRY & TREVOR
MOTOROLA INC.
MOY-PARK LTD
MULTILINK

NABISCO BRANDS LTD
NABISCO GROUP LTD
NAIRN FLOORS LTD
NAMMACK DIRECTOR
NAPP LABORATORIES
NATIONAL CAR PARKS LTD
NATIONAL COAL BOARD
NATIONAL SAVINGS BANK
NATIONAL WESTMINSTER BANK
NATIONWIDE BUILDING
SOCIETY
NEEDLERS PLC
NEILL TOOLS LTD
NESTLÉ CO. LTD
NETLON LTD
NEW CHESHIRE SALT WORKS
LTD
NEW COURT CHARITABLE
TRUST
NEW GUARANTEE TRUST OF
JERSEY, THE
NEW MOORGATE TRUST FUND,
THE
NEW STRAITS TIMES
NEW ZEALAND MEAT PROMO-
TIONS
NEWAGE ENGINEERS LTD
NEWCASTLE-UPON-TYNE COUN-
CIL FOR VOLUNTARY SERVICE
NEWS GROUP NEWSPAPER LTD
NICHOLAS LABORATORIES LTD

NIGEL GIFFORD LTD
NIMROD & GLAVEN TRUST
NIPPON EXPRESS CO. LTD
NIPPONDENSO CO. LTD
NOBLE, E.
NOEL, C. P.
NORDIA
NORMAN FAMILY CHARITABLE
TRUST
NORMAN WALKER LTD
NORTECH SERVICES LTD
NORTH BRITISH MARINE
GROUP LTD
NORTH FACE (SCOTLAND) LTD
NORTH SEA MEDICAL CENTRE
NORTH STAFFS & SOUTH
CHESHIRE BROADCASTING
LTD
NORTHERN FOODS LTD
NORTHERN ROCK BUILDING
SOCIETY
NORTHERN SINK SUPPLIES LTD
NORTHWOOD COLOUR CENTRE
LTD
NORTON, JOHN AND JANE
NORTON, ROSE, BOTTERELL &
ROCHE
NSS NEWSAGENTS PLC

OAKLEY, PATRICIA
OCCIDENTAL INTERNATIONAL
OIL
OCE COPIERS
OCEAN PUBLICATIONS
OFFICE & ELECTRONIC
MACHINES LTD
OFFICE WORLD
OLDHAM, B.
OLDHAM BATTERIES LTD
OLDHAM METROPOLITAN
BOROUGH
OMELEY TRUST
OPTICAL & TEXTILE LTD
OPTREX LTD
ORION INSURANCE
ORTIZ-PATINO, SEÑOR
OSRAM
OULTON BROAD CALOR
CENTRE
OVERSEAS COMMODITIES LTD
OVERSEAS CONTAINERS LTD
OVERSEAS TRADING CORPORA-
TION
OVERSEAS WOMEN'S CLUB
OXFORD EXHAUST SYSTEMS
OZALID (UK) LTD

P. WILLOUGHBY LTD
P.D. PLASTICS LTD
P.F. CHARITABLE TRUST
P. H. HOLT TRUST
P.M. PARTNERSHIP
PACIFIC STEAM NAVIGATION
CO.

163

PADDINGTON CHARITABLE
  ESTATES
PAINS WESSEX SCHEMULY LTD
PALLOT GLASS LTD
PAN-AMERICAN WORLD AIR-
  WAYS
PANAMA MARINE SAFETY &
  SUPPLY
PANASONIC TECHNICS (UK)
  LTD
PARK ADVERTISING & MARKET-
  ING
PARKE-DAVIES RESEARCH
  LABORATORIES
PARSONS BROTHERS LTD
PARTORIA ENGINEERING LTD
PASTA FOODS LTD
PASSION PICTURES LTD
PATAY PUMPS
PATERSON PRODUCTS LTD
PAUL CADBURY TRUST
PAYNE CHARITY
PEC PHOTOGRAPHIC ELECTRI-
  CAL CO.
PEERLESS PLASTICS PACKAG-
  ING
PELLING & CROSS LTD
PELTZ FOOD CORPORATION
PENDEFORD METAL LTD
PERKINS ENGINES LTD
PEROLIN MARINE CO. LTD
PERSTORP WARERITE LTD
PETER BLOOMFIELD CO. LTD
PHAROS MARINE LTD
PHILIP GEORGE & SON
PHILIP KINGSLEY PRODUCTS
PHILIPS ELECTRONICS LTD
PHILIPS (HONG KONG) LTD
PHILLIPS SERVICE
PHONOTAS GROUP LTD
PHOTOGRAPHIC ELECTRICAL
  CO. LTD
PILKINGTON BROTHERS LTD
PILKINGTON FIBREGLASS LTD
PILKINGTON GLASS LTD
PILKINGTON LTD
PILKINGTONS CHARITABLE
  SETTLEMENT
PITNEY BOWES PLC
PLESSEY ELECTRONIC SYSTEMS
  LTD
PLESSEY MILITARY COMMUNI-
  CATIONS
PLYMOUTH CITY COUNCIL
PLYSU CONTAINERS LTD
POGO PRODUCING CO.
POLYTECHNIC MARINE
POND-JONES, P. H.
POORE, J.
PORTER BROTHERS
PORTER CHADBURN PLASTICS
  LTD
PORTEX
PORTH 84 LTD

POSGATE, J. S.
POST OFFICE, THE
POTTER CLARKE LTD
POWELL, T. W.
POWER TOOL HIRE
POWERSPORT INTERNATIONAL
  LTD
PRENTICE-HALL
  INTERNATIONAL
PRESTIGE GROUP LTD
PRICE, D. A. C.
PRICES PATENT CANDLE CO.
  LTD
PRIESTMAN BROS LTD
PRIMECUT FOODS LTD
PRINT TRADE SERVICES
PRINTRITE (UK) LTD
PRITCHARD, CHRISTINE
PROCESS CONTROL CO.
PROCTER & GAMBLE LTD
PRODUCT SUPPORT GRAPHICS
PRUDENTIAL ASSURANCE CO.
  LTD
PUNCH PUBLICATION LTD
PUSSERS NAVY RUM
PYE TELECOMMUNICATIONS
  LTD
PYRAMID COMMUNICATIONS
  LTD
PYSER LTD

QANTAS AIRWAYS
QUEENSWAY GROUP PLC

R. & E. COORDINATION
R. CURTISS & SONS LTD
R.F.D. GROUP PLC
R. GAULT DEVELOPMENTS LTD
R.S. COMPONENTS LTD
RABONE CHESTERMAN LTD
RACAL ACOUSTICS LTD
RACAL DECCA MARINE NAVIGA-
  TION
RACAL MARINE RADAR LTD
RACAL TACTICOM LTD
RADIATION TECHNOLOGY INC.
RAINFORD TRUST
RANK FILM LABORATORIES LTD
RANK FOUNDATION
RANK HOVIS McDOUGALL LTD
RANK PULLIN CONTROLS
RANK XEROX (UK) LTD
RAPIDEX OF LONDON
RAYNER ESSENCE GROUP LTD
RAYSON, BOB
READER'S DIGEST ASSOCIATION
READY MIXED CONCRETE
REAVELL (COMPRESSED AIR)
  LTD
RECKITT & COLEMAN PHARMA-
  CEUTICALS
RECKITT HOUSEHOLD
  PRODUCTS
RECORD RIDGEWAY TOOLS LTD

REDIFFUSION CONSUMER
  ELECTRONICS LTD
REED CORRUGATED CASES LTD
REED INTERNATIONAL PLC
REED PUBLISHING LTD
REEVES, IAN
REID, JOHN
REMPLOY
RENAULT (UK) LTD
RENTOKIL LTD
REYNOLDS, H. E.
RHYS-JENKINS, MICHAEL
RICHARD CADBURY CHARIT-
  ABLE TRUST
RICHARD DUNSTON LTD
RICHARD SIZER LTD
RICHARDSON SHEFFIELD LTD
RICHMOND & RIGG PHOTO-
  GRAPHY
RIDLEY INTERNATIONAL LTD
RIKER LABORATORIES
RIORDAN, R. M.
RIPLEY & CO. LTD
ROBERT BRUCE FITZMAURICE
  LTD
ROBERT WILLIAMSON DESIGN
ROBERT WILSON & SONS
ROBERTSON, MIKE
ROBERTSON, BRIGADIER S.
ROBERTSON NESS TRUST
ROBINSON, MAJOR P.
ROBINSON HANNON LTD
ROCHE PRODUCTS LTD
ROCKWARE
RON COOK ENGINEERING
RORER HEALTH CARE LTD
ROSE & CO. (HULL) LTD
ROSES, DAVID AUSTIN
ROSS FOODS LTD
ROTARY CLUB OF BINGLEY
ROTARY CLUB OF DROITWICH
ROTARY CLUB OF JERSEY
ROTHLEY TRUST, THE
ROTHSCHILD & SON
ROTUNDA LTD
ROUSELL LABORATORIES LTD
ROWAN-BENTALL CHARITY
  TRUST
ROWBOTHAM CHARITABLE
  TRUST
ROWNTREE MACKINTOSH PLC
ROYAL BANK OF CANADA
ROYAL BANK OF SCOTLAND
  PLC
ROYAL BOROUGH OF KENSING-
  TON & CHELSEA
ROYAL BRITISH LEGION, THE
ROYAL GEOGRAPHIC SOCIETY
ROYAL JORDANIAN AIRLINES
ROYAL JUBILEE TRUST
ROYAL NAVAL RESERVE
  OFFICERS
ROYAL NEW ZEALAND NAVY
ROYAL SOVEREIGN LTD

ROYAL TRUST (CANADA)
ROYALE PRINT LTD
RUDGE, VIC
RUSCADOR LTD
RUSSELL & McIVER LTD
RYCOTE MIC SHIELDS
RYVITA COMPANY, THE

ST ANDREWS DOCK SURGERY
ST GEORGE'S DAY CLUB
ST IVEL LTD
ST JOHN AMBULANCE BRIGADE
ST MICHAEL'S MOUNT CHARI-
  TABLE FOUNDATION
SMC CORPORATION
SAATCHI & SAATCHI
SABRE INTERNATIONAL
  PRODUCTS
SAFETY AIR SERVICES
SAGE FOODS
SALAAM, HANY
SALTER INDUSTRIAL MEASURE-
  MENT LTD
SAMARES INVESTMENTS
SAMUEL BANNER & CO. LTD
SAMUELSON GROUP PLC
SAMUELSON LIGHTING LTD
SANDVIK (UK) LTD
SANDWELL METROPOLITAN
  BOROUGH COUNCIL
SANTA FÉ (UK) LTD
SARGOM INTERNATIONAL LTD
SAVE & PROSPER EDUCATIONAL
  TRUST
SAVE & PROSPER INTERNA-
  TIONAL
SAVOY HOTELS PLC
SCAFLON LTD
SCHERING CHEMICALS LTD
SCHERING HEALTH CARE LTD
SCHERWOOD MEDICAL
  INDUSTRIES LTD
SCHOOL OF ELECTRICAL &
  MECHANICAL ENGINEERING
SCHOOL OF SIGNALS
SCHRODER CHARITABLE TRUST
SCHWARTZ SPICES LTD
SCOTFRESH LTD
SCOUTS
SCUBAPRO (UK) LTD
SEA CONTAINERS LTD
SEA TRUST, COMMITTEE OF
  THE
SEA WEATHER MARINE
  SERVICES
SECCOMBE, JONNY
SECOL LTD
SECURICOR LTD
SECURITY SERVICES PLC
SEDGEMOOR DISTRICT
  COUNCIL
SEFTON EXPLORATION ASSOCI-
  ATION
SEGAL & SONS LTD

SEIKO TIME
SELFRIDGE HOTEL
SELLERS, G
SELTEC AUTOMATION LTD
SERVIS DOMESTIC APPLIANCES
  LTD
SETON PRODUCTS LTD
SEVEN SEAS HEALTH CARE LTD
SFIA
SHANDWICK PR CO. LTD
SHAW FOUNDATION
SHELL EXPLORATION & PRO-
  DUCTION LTD
SHELL INTERNATIONAL
SHELL TANKERS (UK) LTD
SHELL UK
SHERWOOD MEDICAL
  INDUSTRIES
SHIPPHAM & CO. LTD
SHIPPING CORPS OF NEW
  ZEALAND
SHORTS SPICES
SHOWERINGS LTD
SIEMENS LTD
SIERRA LEONE NATIONAL SHIP-
  PING CO.
SIGNS & LABELS LTD
SILLETT, D. F.
SILVA COMPASSES (UK) LTD
SILVER REED (UK) LTD
SILVER SPRINGS HOTEL
SIMON ROSEDOWNS LTD
SIMPSON LAWRENCE LTD
SIMPSON MARINE
  REFRIGERATOR SYSTEMS
SIMPSON READY FOODS LTD
SIR GEORGE MARTIN TRUST
SIR JAMES KNOTT TRUST
SIR JAMES RECKITT CHARITY
SIR JOHN PRIESTMAN CHARITY
  TRUST
SIR JULES THORN CHARITABLE
  TRUST
SIXTY MINUTES
SKCF
SKELLERUP INDUSTRIES
SKETCHLEY PLC
SKI WHIZZ
SKY PHOTOGRAPHIC SERVICES
  LTD
SMALL, ADRIAN
SMALL CRAFT DELIVERIES LTD
SMEDLEYS LTD
SMITH, E. A.
SMITH, JOHN, CBE JP DL
SMITH & NEPHEW LTD
SMITH CHARITABLE TRUST
SMITH'S CONTAINERS LTD
SMITHS FLOUR MILLS
SMITHS INDUSTRIES LTD
SNOWDON MOULDING
SOCIETY OF MANUFACTURERS
  AND TRADERS
SOL TENCO LTD

SONY BROADCAST LTD
SONY CORPORATION OF HONG
  KONG
SONY MAGNETIC PRODUCTION
  LTD
SONY (UK) LTD
SOROPTIMISTS INTERNA-
  TIONAL OF JERSEY
SOUTH MIDLANDS COMMUNI-
  CATIONS
SOUTHERN-EVANS (HUMBER)
  LTD
SOUTHERN PORT SERVICES
SPEAR & JACKSON TOOLS LTD
SPEEDBIRD AVIATION
SPENDER AUDIO SYSTEMS LTD
SPILLERS INTERNATIONAL LTD
SPOKESMAN COMMUNICA-
  TIONS LTD
SPOONER, A. W.
SPRINGFIELD FIRE ARMS LTD
SSC & B LINTAS
SSVC
STAEDTLER (UK) LTD
STANHOPE-PALMERS CHARITY
STANLEY TOOLS LTD
STARNA LTD
STARTIN, C. D.
STATES OF JERSEY EDUCATION
  COMMITTEE, THE
STEADFAST TOOLS LTD
STELRAD GROUP LTD
STERLING HEALTH
STERLING HYDRAULICS LTD
STERRY, PETER
STEVE JAMES LTD
STEVENSON, DONALD
STEWART WRIGHTSON
  CHARITY TRUST
STIEFEL LABORATORIES LTD
STORNO LTD
STOTT & SMITH GROUP LTD
STRAPEX (UK) LTD
STRATFORD, H. M.
STRUMECH ENGINEERING LTD
STRUTHERS & CARTER LTD
STUART PHARMACEUTICALS
STYLO PLC
SUB-SEA SERVICES
SUBMEX
SUBSPEK INSPECTION CONSUL-
  TANTS
SUE HAMMERSON CHARITABLE
  TRUST
SUN, THE
SUPERFLIX LTD
SUPREME PLASTICS LTD
SUZUKI (GB) CARS LTD
SVENSKA ICI
SWANN-NORTON LTD
SWINTEX LTD
SWISS BANK CORPORATION
SWS FILTRATION LTD SYSTEM
SYMINGTON'S & CO.

165

T. CADBURY TRUST
TI RALEIGH INDUSTRIES
TANDBERG LTD
TANGANYIKA HOLDINGS
TANNOY LTD
TANQUERY GORDON & CO. LTD
TARMAC
TASCO SALES
TATE & LYLE PLC
TATTERSALLS LTD
TAYLOR OF HADFIELD, LORD
TAYLOR WOODROW GROUP
TEA COUNCIL
TEAR FUND
TECHNOMATIC LTD
TEK CHEMICALS INTERNA-
TIONAL LTD
TELEDATA LTD
TEMPCO UNION LTD
TEMPLE, MAJ. E.
TENNECO EUROPE INC.
TENNENT CALEDONIAN
BREWERIES
TESCO STORES HOLDING
TEXACO LTD
THANET ELECTRONICS LTD
THATCHER, DENIS
THETFORD MOULDED PRO-
DUCTS LTD
THOMAS & JAMES HARRISON
LTD
THOMAS BATY & SONS
THOMAS HILL ENGINEERING
(HULL) LTD
THOMAS HUDSON BENEVO-
LENT TRUST
THOMAS MASON CHARITABLE
TRUST
THOMAS TUNNOCK LTD
THOMAS WALKER & SON LTD
THOMPSON, LLOYD & EWART
THOMPSON, LUCY JANE
THOMPSON, LYNDA
THOMPSON MEDICAL CO.
THORN/EMI FERGUSON LTD
THORN EMI PLC
THORN EMI VIDEO FACILITIES
THORNGATE TRUST
TILDA RICE LTD
TIMES BOOKS
TIRFOR LTD
TOLLMAN-HUNDLEY HOTELS
TOPHAM, KEITH
TOSHIBA (UK) LTD
TOUZEL, MICHAEL
TOWER HOTEL
TOWNE CEA (SHIP RIGGERS)
LTD
TRADE & TRAVEL PUBLICA-
TIONS
TRANSART GROUP LTD
TRANS AUSTRALIA AIRLINES
TRAVENOL LABORATORIES LTD
TRIATOM LTD

TROLL SAFETY EQUIPMENT
LTD
TROY, MARY
TRUSTEE SAVINGS BANK
TRUSTHOUSE FORTE LTD
TSB CHANNEL ISLANDS LTD
TSB LIFE LTD
TSB TRUST CO. LTD
TUDOR TRUST, THE
TULANE UNIVERSITY
TUPPERWARE CO.
TUTOR SAFETY PRODUCTS LTD
TVS TV CENTRE
TWINING CO. LTD
TWO COUNTIES RADIO
TWYDALE TURKEYS LTD
TYNE GANGWAY CO. LTD
TYPOGRAPHICS LTD

ULSTER TV PLC
UNDERWATER INSTRUMENTA-
TION
UNICORN CLUB
UNIGATE DAIRIES LTD
UNIGATE FOODS LTD
UNILEVER EXPORT LTD
UNILEVER PLC
UNION INTERNATIONAL PLC
UNIPART
UNITED BISCUITS LTD
UNITED NEWSPAPERS LTD
UNITED SCIENTIFIC HOLDINGS
UNITOR SHIP SERVICES
UNWIN GRAIN LTD

V.W. PRODUCTS CHEMICALS
LTD
VALIN PRODUCTS
VAN DEN BERGHS & JURGENS
LTD
VAN LEER (UK) LTD
VANGO (SCOTLAND) LTD
VARIG BRAZILIAN AIRLINES
VDU INSTALLATIONS LTD
VECTOR INTERNATIONAL LTD
VENTECH LTD
VERBATIM LTD
VERNON, BRIGADIER H. R. W.
VERNON CARUS LTD
VERNON EAST PR CO. LTD
VESTEY, E. J.
VESTEY, LORD
VIASA AIRWAYS
VICKERS PLC
VICKERS SHIPBUILDING &
ENGINEERING LTD
VIDEO-FILM PRODUCTIONS LTD
VIDEOTEL MARINE INTERNA-
TIONAL LTD
VIEWPLAN LTD
VIKING LIFE SAVING EQUIP-
MENT
VIRGIN GROUP
VISCOSE CLOSURES LTD

VOLKSWAGEN MARKETING
VOLVO PENTA (UK) LTD

W. A. HANDLEY CHARITABLE
TRUST
W.B. PHARMACEUTICALS LTD
W. H. GROVES & FAMILY LTD
W. H. SMITH & SON LTD
W. O. STREET FOUNDATION
W. R. GRACE LTD
WACKER CHEMICALS LTD
WADMAN, J.
WADDINGTON GAMES LTD
WAGNER, PAULINE
WAITAKI LONDON LTD
WAITROSE
WALDMANN (UK)
WALKER, DOUGLAS
WANDSWORTH COUNCIL
WARNER LAMBERT HEALTH
CARE
WATER WEIGHTS
WATES FOUNDATION, THE
WCB MAILBOX LTD
WEBB & BOWER
WEDD, DURLACHER,
MORDAUNT & CO.
WEDGWOOD HOTEL WARE
WEEKS TRAILERS LTD
WEIR, ANDREW & CO. LTD
WELBECK LABORATORY
WELCONSTRUCT
WELLCOME FOUNDATION
WELTON FOUNDATION
WELTONHURST LTD
WEST GLAMORGAN COUNTY
COUNCIL
WESTLAND PLC
WESTMINSTER CHAMBER OF
COMMERCE
WESTMINSTER CITY COUNCIL
WESTMINSTER DREDGING CO.
LTD
WESTON HYDE PRODUCTS LTD
WHARTON WILLIAMS TAYLOR
WHATMAN LTD
WHEELS RENTALS LTD
WHELPTON, T. J.
WHITE WATER SPORTS
WHITE'S ELECTRONICS (UK) LTD
WHITTINGHAM & PORTER LTD
WHITWORTHS HOLDINGS LTD
WIG & PEN CLUB
WIGGINS TEAPE GROUP LTD
WIGMORE MEDICAL EQUIP-
MENT SUPPLIES
WILD HEERBRUGG (UK) LTD
WILFRED & CONSTANCE CAVE
FOUNDATION
WILKIN & SONS LTD
WILKINS, RICHARD
WILKINSON BROTHERS
WILKINSON HOME & GARDEN
DIVISION

166

LIST OF SPONSORS

WILKINSON SWORD LTD
WILLIAM BROADY & SON LTD
WILLIAM DAWSON PLC
WILLIAM GRANT & SONS LTD
WILLIAM MALLINSON & SON
LTD
WILLIAM PAGE CO. LTD
WILLIAM PEARSON LTD
WILLIAMS & GLYNS BANK
WILLIAMSON TEA HOLDING
PLC
WILLIS & BATES LTD
WILLIS COMPUTER SUPPLIES
LTD
WILSON'S OF SCOTLAND
WINCANTON GROUP LTD
WINCHESTER UK
WIRRAL BOROUGH COUNCIL
WITTINGTON INVESTMENTS
LTD

WOGEN ANNIVERSARY TRUST
WOLVERHAMPTON METROPO-
LITAN BOROUGH COUNCIL
WOOD'S TIMBER CO. LTD
WOODHOUSE, DRAKE & CAREY
LTD
WOODWARD SCHOOLS (MID
DIV.) LTD
WOOLWICH EQUITABLE BUILD-
ING SOC.
WORDPLEX LTD
WORLD TRADE CENTRE
WORSHIPFUL COMPANY OF
ACCOUNTANTS
WORSHIPFUL COMPANY OF
ACTUARIES
WORSHIPFUL COMPANY OF
BAKERS
WORSHIPFUL COMPANY OF
BUTCHERS

WORSHIPFUL COMPANY OF
GARDENERS
WORSHIPFUL COMPANY OF
SHIPWRIGHTS
WYETH LABORATORIES

YAESU MUSEN CO. LTD
YMCA
YORKSHIRE DRY DOCK CO. LTD
YORKSHIRE IMPERIAL FITTINGS
YORKSHIRE MARINE CONTAIN-
ERS LTD
YORKSHIRE PLANT (HUMBER) LTD
YORKSHIRE POST
YORKSHIRE TV LTD
YOUNG, GRAHAM

ZIEF, ARNOLD
ZOELLNER & CO.
ZONAL LTD

USA SPONSORS

9TH & 9TH MARKET & CAFÉ
A & A BUSINESS MACHINES
A. E. FINLEY & ASSOCIATES INC.
A. J. FLETCHER EDUCATIONAL
AND OPERA FOUNDATION
INC.
ADVOCATE MESSENGER
AGENCY ONE
AKHENATON INC.
AKIN, GRUMP, STRAUSS, HAUER
& FELD
AKT DEVELOPMENTS
ALBEMARLE SAVINGS AND
LOAN
ALBRIGHTS MILL
ALEXANDER INTERNATIONAL
ALEXANDER P. THORPE FOUN-
DATION
ALFALFA OMEGA EXPRESS
ALLENTON REALTY
ALVIN H. BUTZ, INC.
AMERICAN CYANAMID COM-
PANY
AMERICAN INTERNATIONAL
SCHOOL IN CARACAS
AMERICA'S
QUADRACENTENNIAL CORP.
AMF HATTERAS YACHTS INC.
ANDEL ENGINEERING CO.
ANDERSON, MOSS, RUSSO &
GRIEVERS
ANDREW JACKSON AREA
SCHOOLS
ARCHER DANIELS MIDLAND CO.
ARCO CORP.
ARMSTRONG, BRINKLEY, ELAM
& KNOTT
ART C. KLEIN CONSTRUCTION
INC.

ASHEVILLE CITIZEN-TIMES
PUBLISHING
ASHVILLE KIWANIS CHARITIES
INC.
ATLANTIC HIGHLANDS LIONS
CLUB
ATLANTIC HIGHLANDS PUBLIC
LIBRARY ASSOCIATION
ATLANTIC PUBLISHING CO. OF
TABOR CITY
ATLANTIC SERVICES OF
CHARLESTON
ATR WIRE AND CABLE CO.
AWAI, EUNICE L.
AYERS & MADDUX INC.
AZUSA PACIFIC UNIVERSITY

BAHAMA RURITAN CLUB
BAILES OLD MILL LTD
BAKER FOUNDATION INC.
BALBOA BAY CLUB
BALENTINES INC.
BANK OF BOSTON
BANK OF HAWAII
BANK OF NEW HAMPSHIRE
BANK OF THE HAMPTONS
BARBOUR'S CUT IMPORT
SERVICE INC.
BARNES MOTOR AND PARTS CO.
INC.
BARNHILL CONSTRUCTION CO.
BAXLEY'S FOOD SERVICE INC.
BAY CARBON CO. INC.
BAYLIFF INSURANCE AGENCY
BAYLOR UNIVERSITY
BAYSHORE PHARMACY
BEATRICE FOUNTAIN INC.
BEL AIR PRESBYTERIAN
CHURCH

BENDANA & CARLTON, ATTOR-
NEYS AT LAW
BENZ OIL
BISHOPS DISCRETIONARY FUND
BLACKWELL AUTO PARTS
BLUE BELL INC.
BOBBY MURRAY CHEVROLET
INC.
BODALE PRESS INC.
BOND LAUNDROMAT
BONDOUX INVESTMENT MAN-
AGEMENT
BOOZ, ALLEN & HAMILTON INC.
BOYD'S MINI MART
BRAINERD KIWANIS CLUB
BRANCH BANKING & TRUST CO.
BRAND-SCHNEIDER REAL
ESTATE
BRANDEIS UNIVERSITY
BREWER FOUNDATION
BROOK REALTY
BROOKFIELD CENTRAL HIGH
SCHOOL
BURLINGTON DISTRICT COUN-
CIL ON MINISTRIES
BURNIE BATCHELOR STUDIO
INC.
BYERLEY'S ANTIQUES

C. REECH'S PHARMACY
CALABASH WEST
CALIFORNIA COMMUNITY
FOUNDATION
CAMERON-BROWN INSURANCE
AGENCY
CAPITOL GRAPHICS INC.
CARMEL PRESBYTERIAN
CARNEAL DOWNEY CONSTRUC-
TION CO.

167

CAROL-EMM INC.
CAROLANTIC REALTY INC.
CAROLINA BIOLOGICAL SUPPLY CO.
CAROLINA CYCLING CLUB
CAROLINA POWER & LIGHT
CAROLINA READY MIXED CONCRETE CO.
CAROLINA SECURITIES CORP.
CAROLINA SKIFFS INC.
CAROLINA TELEPHONE & TELEGRAPH
CARRS QUALITY CENTERS INC.
CARTERET FAMILY PRACTICE CLINIC
CARTERET SAVINGS AND LOAN ASSOCIATION
CASO CLEANERS AND TAILORS
CASSIDY RESTAURANTS
CEDAR HILL MEMORIAL PARK INC.
CENTURY CITY ROTARY CLUB
CERNAVA INSURANCE AGENCY
CHAMELEON ARTWEAR
CHAN, JOSEPH
CHAPEL HILL NEWSPAPER
CHARLES CRONE ASSOCIATES INC.
CHARTER FEDERAL SAVINGS AND LOAN
CHAS. H. JENKINS & CO.
CHASE MANHATTAN BANK
CHATHAM VALLEY FOUNDATION INC.
CHATT KIWANIS YOUTH FAIR
CHEMICAL BANK
CHESSON AGENCY INC.
CHEVRON USA
CHICK-FIL-A INC.
CHING, JOSEPH
CHINNA, DEBRA A.
CHONG, ELIZABETH J. N. F.
CHRISTOPHER CLUB OF TIPTON, INDIANA
CHUN, DR MICHAEL S.
CITIZENS NATIONAL BANK
CITY NATIONAL BANK & TRUST
CITY OF NEW YORK
CITY OF RALEIGH
CLIFTON AND YOUNCE TIRE SERVICE
COASTAL DAIRY PRODUCTS INC.
COASTAL PLANE FREIGHT SERVICE INC.
COLITE INDUSTRIES INC.
COLLIER COBB & ASSOCIATES
COLUMBIA SAVINGS AND LOAN ASSOCIATION
COMMUNITY PROPERTIES INC.
COMPUTER SOUTH-GREENSBORO
CONGRESS OF THE US, HOUSE OF REPRESENTATIVES

CONNELL OIL CO.
COPPERVISION INC.
COSMOPOLITAN CLUB OF ELIZABETH CITY INC.
COSMOS BOOK CLUB
CRAFTSMASTER HOMES CORP.
CRAFTY COLLECTABLES

DARE COUNTY BOARD OF COUNTY COMMISSION
DART & KRAFT FOUNDATION
DEALERS WAREHOUSE CORP.
DELI UNLIMITED
DELOITTE HASKINS & SELLS
DELTA AIRLINES
DENUOMO DATSUN
DEPARTMENT OF BIOLOGY - USC
DEVOTO & CO. INC.
DHL CORP.
DIA LOGOS INTERNATIONAL
DINNER FOR THE EARTH
DIOCESE OF OKLAHOMA
DOMINO FOUNDATION
DON SMITH TRAVEL SERVICE
DOOLING & DOOLING CPA
DOUTHAT, ALICE Y.
DRAKE AWNING AND WINDOW SERVICE
DREAM VALLEY FARMS
DREYFUS, MAX AND VICTORIA
DRS BAILEY & SCHRUM, OPTOMETRISTS, PA
DUKE UNIVERSITY
DUPLIN COUNTY ARTS COUNCIL INC.
DUTCH FORK OPTIMIST CLUB
DYNAMIT NOBEL SILICON, INC.

EASTERN FUELS INC.
EASTONS INC.
EDITH POOLE AUDIO VISUAL
ELECTRONIC DATA SYSTEMS
ELIZABETH CITY GOLDEN 'K' CLUB
ELIZABETH CITY JUNIOR WOMEN'S CLUB
ELM GROVE INVESTMENTS
EMERSON ELECTRIC CO.
ENGLISH SPEAKING UNION
ENVIROTEK INC.
ERNST & WHINNEY
ETHYL CORPORATION
EVERED LINCOLN–MERCURY INC.
EXCELSIOR LODGE No. 175
EXECUTIVE WOMEN'S NETWORK
EXPLORER POST

FEAT FOUNDATION
F. H. REALTY
FAIR WINDS INC.
FAIRCHILD INDUSTRIES FOUN-

DATION INC.
FARM AUDIT BANKS
FARRIOR & SONS INC.
FEDERAL LAND BANK PCA
FELTEX CARPETS OF NEW ZEALAND
FERRARA, CHRISTOPHER
FIRST CHURCH OF CHRIST, SCIENTIST
FIRST FEDERAL BANK OF RALEIGH
FIRST HAWAIIAN BANK
FIRST NATIONAL BANK OF JOLIET
FIRST NATIONAL BANK OF LUDDOCK
FISKIN & FISKIN
FISKS CAMERA SHOP
FLOWERS BY RAMON
FORT SILL NATIONAL BANK
FOSTER, CONNER & ROBSON, PA
FRAME GALLERY
FUTRELL & HUNTER

GAILU SHOP
GARDEN VILLAGE AT COUNTY CORNER
GARDINER MAREK INSURANCE AGENCY INC.
GEC AVIONICS INC.
GENERAL FOODS CORP.
GENESEE BANK
GENESIS BICYCLES
GEORGE W. JENKINS FOUNDATION INC.
GOEBEL COLLECTORS' CLUB
GOODYEAR TIRE AND RUBBER CO.
GOOSE AND GRIDIRON SOCIETY
GRACO FOUNDATION
GRANDFATHER MOUNTAIN CORP.
GREEN TREE VILLAGE
GREENTREE FUND
GREGORY POOLE EQUIPMENT CO.
GRUBER'S GARAGE
GSSI/SPANDEX USA
GUARD CORPORATION

HACKNEY INDUSTRIES INC.
HAKAN/CORLEY AND ASSOCIATES INC.
HAMM'S DRIVE-IN
HAMPTON HOUSE GALLERY
HANCOCK BANK
HANS JOHNSON COMPANY
HARBORVIEW TOWERS INC.
HARNETT OIL CORP.
HARRIS TEETER
HARRISON OIL CORP.
HARTS SEA SHELL INC.
HATTIESBURG COCA COLA BOTTLING CO.

168

HEAT TRANSFER SALES INC.
HEIDELBERG HEIGHTS LIONS
  CLUB
HENRY HUDSON REGIONAL
  SCHOOL LIBRARY
HENRY J. & DRUE E. HEINZ
  FOUNDATION
HERNDON & ASSOC. INC.
HERNDON LUMBER &
  MILLWORK INC.
HIGSON, DOUGLAS
HILLSDALE FUND INC.
HOGAN OUTDOOR INC.
HOLIDAY COMPANIES
HOLIDAY INDUSTRIES
HOLLIE DESIGNS
HOME FEDERAL BANK
HOME SAVINGS INC.
HOMECARE FOUNDATION
HONEYWELL INC.
HONOLULU ADVERTISER, INC.
HONOLULU FEDERAL SAVINGS
HOPPER, PATRICK W.
HOUGEN FOUNDATION
HOWARD & SMITH INSURANCE
  AGENCY
HUDSON BELK DEPARTMENT
  STORES
HUNT ORGANIZATION
HUNT REALTY INVESTMENTS
HUTCHINSON & MAMELE

IBM CORP.
ICI FIBERS INC.
I.S.I. FURNITURE RENTAL CORP.
IMPERIAL ELEVATOR CO. INC.
INFANTINE BROTHERS DISPO-
  SAL CO.
INTEGON FOUNDATION INC.
INTERACT CLUB, NORTH-WEST-
  ERN LEHIGH JR & SR HIGH
  SCHOOLS
INTERFIRST BANK, DALLAS
INTERNATIONAL PAPER BOX
  MACHINE CO. INC.
INTERNATIONAL SCIENCE AND
  TECHNOLOGY INSTITUTE
  INC.
INVESTORS MANAGEMENT
  CORP.
ISHIMA, NANCY
ISLA VISTA BOOKSTORE

J & W VENDING
J. EDWARDS CO. INC.
JAMES G. K. McCLURE EDUCA-
  TIONAL AND DEVELOPMENT
  FUND INC.
JANG, HELEN L.
JAYCEE BUSINESS MACHINES
  INC.
JBS SYSTEMS INC.
JEWELS BOUTIQUE INC.

JEWISH COMMUNITY FEDERA-
  TION ENDOWMENT FUND
JEYCO PRODUCE CO. INC.
JK/GLOBE CO. INC.
JOBS FOR YOUTH/CHICAGO INC.
JOE BRAND OF AUSTIN INC.
JOFFRORY AUSTON HOME
  BROKERS
JOHN HACKNEY AGENCY INC.
JOHNSON FUNERAL HOME
JOHNSON-LAMBE CO.
JOLIET JUNIOR COLLEGE
JOSEPH BRIDGE REALTY
  TRUST II
JOY MACHINE CO.

KAR KOVER KINGS INC.
KATHIS HAIR DESIGNERS
KENNEDY & FORD INSURANCE
KERSHAW AUTO SUPPLY
KERSHAW FINANCE COMPANY
KERSHAW IGA FOODLINER
KISTLER POLE BUILDINGS
KITAGAWA, MARSHA E.
KITTY HAWK KITES
KIWANIS CLUB OF LAWTON
KIWANIS CLUB OF OZONE PARK
  INC.
KIWANIS CLUB OF PALMER
  TOWNSHIP
KIWANIS CLUB OF REDLANDS-
  MORNING
KIWANIS OF HOWARD BEACH
KLEIN ASSOCIATES INC.
KOPKA REALTY
KRAFT INC.
KUTZ INC.

L & M BOOK CO. INC.
L. B. SMITH FAMILY FOUNDA-
  TION
LACROSSE ROTARY FOUNDA-
  TION INC.
LADIES AUXILIARY TO
  CHEYENNE MOUNTAIN
LAKE WILSON BOARDING
  KENNELS INC.
LAMBERT'S CABLE SPLICING
  CO.
LANCO INDUSTRIES INC.
LARRIVA'S ACE ELECTRIC CO.
LAU, ALICE YAP
LAU, BERNADETTE J.
LAU, DENNIS L.
LAU, DIANE JOYCE
LAU, MILTON K. K.
LAWTON PUBLISHING CO.
LAWTON ROTARY CLUB
LEE, CHRISTINE C.
LEE, ERIN MARIE
LEE, JON
LEE, LORRAINE L.
LEE, PATRICIA C.
LEE, PATRICK K. M.

LEE, ROBERT
LEE, TINA
LEIGH BUSINESS FARMS INC.
LEONG, JACK Y. H.
LEONG, ROBERT S. W.
LEROY'S FISH MARKET
LETTEREX COMMUNICATIONS
  INC.
LEWIS COMMUNICATIONS
LEWISTON SUPPLY CO. INC.
LOGAN DRIVE BAPTIST
  CHURCH
LOONEY TUNES SKI ASYLUM
LUCAS TRAVEL INC.
LUNDY PACKING CO.
LUTHERAN BROTHERHOOD,
  MILWAUKEE COUNTY NORTH
  BRANCH NO. 8433
LYNCHBURG FAMILY PHYSI-
  CIANS

M & I NORTHERN BANK
MAGNUM EQUIPMENT CO.
MALAPROP'S BOOKSTORE/CAFÉ
MARIETTA WHITE WATER UNIT,
  A DIVISION OF SDC, INC.
MARK-ETTE VARIETY STORE
MARROW PITT HARDWARE CO.
  INC.
MARSH & McLENNON INC.
MARTIN, PAUL D.
MARY DUKE BIDDLE FOUNDA-
  TION
MASTIC TRUST
MAYFAIR ANIMAL HOSPITAL
MAYO KNITTING MILL INC.
McGLADREY, HENDRICKS &
  PULLEN CPA'S
MECHANICS BANK
MEDFORD MOTORS INC.
MEDICAL AND DENTAL MAN-
  AGEMENT
MEDICINE SHOPPE, PRESCRIP-
  TIONS, INC.
MELBOURNE SHOPPING CEN-
  TERS INC.
MELOY FOUNDATION
MEMPHIS PIG OUT
MERCY HOSPITAL
MEREDITH COLLEGE
METROSCAN TRAFFIC NET-
  WORK
MEXICAN AMERICAN CO.
MID SOUTH BANK AND TRUST
  CO.
MINERAL MINING CORP.
MORNING CALL
MORROW PIANO & ORGAN CO.
MOYLE, FLAIGAN, KATZ, FITZ-
  GERALD & SHEEHAN, PA
MT LEBANON COUNCIL OF
  REPUBLICAN WOMEN
MT LEBANON TOWNSHIP
  POLICE ASSOCIATION INC.

MUNRO PETROLEUM & TERMI-
NAL CORP.
MURRAY WHISNANT, ARCHI-
TECTS
MYERS PARK UNITED METHOD-
IST CHURCH

NA PALI ZODIAC PRODUCTIONS
NC AUTOMOBILE DEALERS
ASSOCIATION
NAGY, BEVERLY C.
NAKAGAWA, EARL T.
NATIONAL ASSOC. TEXAS COM-
MERCIAL BANK
NATURAL HEALTH PRODUCTS
INC.
NAYLORS INC.
NEW HAMPSHIRE CHARITABLE
FUND
NEW HAVEN SAVINGS BANK
NEWLAND EXTENSION
HOMEMAKERS CLUB
NEWLAND – PROVIDENCE
RURITAN CLUB
NEWMAN MACHINE CO.
NEWTON-NEEDHAM CHAMBER
OF COMMERCE
NEXSEN, PRUET, JACOBS & POL-
LARD
NOALMARK BROADCASTING
CORP.
NOEL MORRIS INSURANCE
AGENCY
NOGALES LIONS CLUB
NORTH CAROLINA DESIGN
FOUNDATION INC.
NORTH CAROLINA GENERAL
ASSEMBLY
NORTH CAROLINA NATIONAL
BANK
NORTH CAROLINA STATE UNI-
VERSITY
NORTH FULTON INFERTILITY
OB. GYN.
NORTH HILLS INC.
NORTHSIDE APARTMENTS INC.
NORTH-WESTERN LEIGH EDU-
CATION ASSOCIATION
NORTH-WESTERN MUTUAL LIFE
INC.
NOTTINGHAM PHARMACY
CORP.
NYCOIL COMPANY

O & R TRAILER REPAIR INC.
OBSTETRICS & GYNECOLOGY
OF ATLANTA, PC
OCCIDENTAL PETROLEUM
OFF THE WALL ENTERPRISES
INC.
OLIVE CO.
OMNI MEDICAL
ON THE SQUARE INC.
OPTIMIST CLUB OF EASTON

ORR AND RENO PA
OUTBACK INC.
OWEN'S MOTEL AND RESTAU-
RANT

PAC-FAB
PACE MEMORIAL UNITED
METHODIST CHURCH
PACIFIC AUTO GLASS INC.
PAGE HIGH SCHOOL STUDENT
COUNCIL
PAL TRAVEL AND TOURS
PAMLICO DREDGING CO.
PARK, RODNEY J.
PARK TRAVEL AGENCY
PARKER'S OF DANVILLE
PASQUOTANK COUNTY EXTEN-
SION
PASQUOTANK RURITAN CLUB
PAUL BOND BOOK CO.
PAULUCCI FAMILY FOUNDA-
TION
PAYNE & DOLAN INC.
PEL-FREEZE
PERFORMANCE BINDERY INC.
PERMANENT LABEL CO.
PERRY BROTHERS TIRE SERVICE
PHILIP POST & ASSOCIATES INC.
PHOENIX TRIMMING CO.
PIKE INDUSTRIES INC.
PILOT CLUB OFF SOUTH-EAST
LOS ANGELES
PINE HILLS TRAVEL LTD
PIONEER HI-BRED INTERNA-
TIONAL INC.
PRO DEC PRODUCTS INC.
PROGRESSIVE GROCER
PROVIDENCE COLLEGE ALUMNI
ASSOC.
PTWT INC.
PUBLIC RELATIONS

QUICKPRINT OF ROCKY
MOUNTAIN INC.
QUINTITIES INC.

RADEX
RALEIGH RADIO SOCIETY
RALEIGH KIWANIS FOUNDA-
TION INC.
RALEIGH OFFICE SUPPLY
RAMADA INNS INC.
RAN HOLDING INC.
REAL ESTATE AGENCY INC.
REDLANDS GLASS HOUSE INC.
REED NATIONAL CORP.
RENZ LANDSCAPING INC.
RESERVE WAREHOUSE CORP.
RIB ROOF INDUSTRIES INC.
RICK'S OF WISCONSIN
RIDGEWAY BAPTIST CHURCH
RJR NABISCO INC.
ROCKWELL INTERNATIONAL
CORP.

ROSARY SOCIETY OF ST JOHN'S
ROSLYN SAVINGS BANK
ROSS HARDWARE
ROSS MADDOX JEWELER
ROTARY CLUB OF BROOKFIELD
ROTARY CLUB OF CRESENT
ROTARY CLUB OF DANVILLE
ROTARY CLUB OF GREATER
STATESVILLE
ROTARY CLUB OF LONG BEACH
ROTARY CLUB OF MONTROSE
ROTARY CLUB OF MOREHEAD
ROTARY CLUB OF NOGALES
FOUNDATION INC.
ROTARY CLUB OF RALEIGH
FOUNDATION
ROTARY CLUB OF SAYVILLE
ROTARY CLUB OF THE
TARRYTOWNS INC.
ROTARY CLUB OF YUCAIPA
VALLEY
ROWAN BUSINESS FORMS INC.
RUSSO FOR CONGRESS COM-
MITTEE

SACRAMENTO BEE
SACRAMENTO REGIONAL FOUN-
DATION
SAFEGUARD BUSINESS
SYSTEMS
ST AGNES RECTORY
ST AGNES THRIFT SHOP
SAKS FIFTH AVENUE
SALISBURY INTERNATIONAL
WOMEN'S CLUB
SALISBURY JUNIOR WOMEN'S
CLUB
SALS MEAT MARKET
SALTY DOG MARINA INC.
SAMPLERS INC.
SANCHEZ ENTERPRISES INC.
SCHOOL BOARD RECOGNITION
FUND
SEA VIGIL
SECURITY BANK AND TRUST
SERR'S OF REDLANDS
SEWANEE CHAPTER OF AMERI-
CAN RED CROSS
SEWELL SUPPLY CO.
SHED INC.
SHORE FLORISTS
SIMPLE PLEASURES
SIMPSON AND UNDERWOOD
REALTORS
SINGH PONTIAC-BUICK-
CADILLAC-GMC TRUCKS INC.
SIX FORKS ANIMAL HOSPITAL
SLEEPY HOLLOW PTSA
SLOSSMAN CORP.
SMITH, BARNEY, HARRIS,
UPHAM & CO. INC.
SMITHS PHARMACY
SOCIETY OF HISPANIC PROFES-
SIONAL ENGINEERS FOUNDA-
TION

SOON, ELMO Y.
SOUTH PARK LIONS CLUB
SPARTA FOOD SYSTEMS INC.
SPECIAL CONSULTING SERV-
  ICES INC.
SPEEDO'S ONE-HOUR PHOTO
SPRINGDALE INC.
STAFFLINE INC.
STANDARD BUILDING SUPPLY
  INC.
STANDARD TILE INC.
STANLEY VIDMAR INC.
STEWARTS ANIMAL HOSPITAL
STOUT CUSTOM BICYCLES
SUFFOLK CO. ORGANIZATION
  FOR THE PROMOTION OF
  EDUCATION
SUGAR CAMP LUMBER CO. INC.
SUMMERHILL ANTIQUES
SUN BANK, NA
SUN/DAILY HERALD, BILOXI

TGS INC.
TARBORO PRINTING CO. INC.
TARBORO-EDGECOMBE ASSN
  OF MANUFACTURERS
TARHEEL CONCEPTS IN SPE-
  CIALTY ADVERTISING
TEKNOWLEDGE
TETRA TECH INC.
THARRINGTON, SMITH &
  HARGROVE
THEO. H. DAVIES & CO. LTD
THORACIC & CARDIOVASCULAR
  ASSOC.
THORNE DRUG CO.
TI-CARD INC.
TIPTON COUNTY FARM BUREAU
TIPTON TELEPHONE COMPANY
  INC.
TITLE GUARANTY & ABSTRACT
  CO. LTD
TOMBALL FEED CENTER
TOMER TRAVEL CORP.
TORTILLA FACTORY LA COCINA
  INC.
TOSHIBA AMERICA INC.
TOWER ANIMAL HOSPITAL
TRANSAMERICA CORP.
TRANSIT MIX CONCRETE CO.
TRAVEL BY COUPONS

TREASURE COVE OF OLDE
TREND SETTERS
TRI STATE ENVELOPE CORP.
TRIANGLE ANIMAL HOSPITAL
TRIESTE MUSA RAD
TRINITY EPISCOPAL CHURCH
TRUCK AND TRAILER PARTS
  INC.
TUPPERWARE
TUPPERWARE HOME PARTIES
TURNER OIL CO. OF WILSON
  INC.
TYSON FOUNDATION INC.

US LEASING
U-STORE-IT MINI WAREHOUSE
UNEV. GRAPHICS
UNION NATIONAL BANK
UNION SAVINGS BANK
UNION UNITED METHODIST
  CHURCH
UNITED AUTO WORKERS,
  LOCAL 664
UNITED METHODIST CHURCH
UNITED METHODIST WOMEN
UNITED PRESBYTERIAN WOMEN
UNITED SERVICE CO.
UNITED STATES ARMED
  FORCES
UNIVERSITY FLORIST INC.
UNIVERSITY GRAPHICS
UNIVERSITY OF NORTH
  CAROLINA
UNIVERSITY OF SOUTH
  CAROLINA
UNIVERSITY OF SOUTHERN
  MISSISSIPPI
UNIVERSITY OF TENNESSEE AT
  CHATANOOGA
UNIVERSITY PHARMACY

VAM PTS
VIKING TRAVEL
VISION QUEST
VISTA VERDE GUEST RANCH

W. B. BATEMAN & SONS
W. E. WALKER FOUNDATION
W. S. CLARK & SONS INC.
WACHOVIA BANK AND TRUST
  CO. NA

WADKIN USA
WAIKIKI AQUARIUM EMPLOYEE
  CO-OP
WAITE'S FORMAL DEN
WAKE VETERINARY HOSPITAL
  INC.
WALLACE O'NEAL DAY SCHOOL
WALSH, MANONEY AND
  PONZINI
WALSH SERVICE STATION
WARD AND SMITH, PA
WASTE ENTERPRISES INC.
WESLEYAN UNIVERSITY
WESTEND FOUNDATION INC.
WESTERN AUTO ASSOC. STORE
WESTON FORUM
WEYERHAUSER CORP.
WHEATLEY/WILLIAMS, ARCHI-
  TECTS
WHISTLING PINES MOTEL
WHITE CRYSTAL DINER
WHITE PLUMBING COMPANY
WHOLESALE SUPPLY COMPANY
  INC.
WILCOX, GAYLORD H.
WILDROSE MOUNTAINEERING
  CYCLERY
WILLIAM BATZ AND ASSOCI-
  ATES
WILLIAMS AGENCY INC.
WILLOW CLEANERS II
WILMETTE HARBOR ASSOC.
WILSON ASSOCIATES
WILSON LUNCHEON LIONS
  CLUB
WILSON PETROLEUM CO. LTD
WISINGER & COMPANY
WJRT-TV
WOODHAVEN ANIMAL CLINIC
WRENN-PHARR INC.

YE OLDE WAFFLE SHOP
YEE, WILLIAM C.
YMCA
YOUNG-NICHOS FUNERAL
  HOME
YOUR BEST LITTLE HAIR
  HOUSE

ZEMA CORPORATION
ZONTA CLUB OF SUFFOLK AREA

AUSTRALIA SPONSORS

AWA PTY LTD
AIR NORTH
AIR QUEENSLAND
AIRFLITE PTY LTD
ALL SAINTS WINES
ANALYTICAL SERVICES
ANZ BANK
ARMED FORCES FOOD

ARNOTT MOTTERAM MENZ
AUSTRALIAN AIRLINES
AUSTRALIAN ANTARCTIC DIVI-
  SION
AUSTRALIAN BROADCASTING
  COMMISSION
AUSTRALIAN GAS LIGHT COM-
  PANY

AUSTWARE GROUP
AVIS

BHP PETROLEUM
BP AUSTRALIA LTD
BARCLAYS INTERNATIONAL
  (AUST.) LTD
BELLWAY PTY LTD

BOHL, G. M.
BONDS COATES PATON LTD
BROKEN HILL PROPRIETARY
  LTD
BURNS PHILP & CO. LTD
BUSINESS & PROFESSIONAL
  WOMEN'S CLUB

CADBURY SCHWEPPES AUS-
  TRALIA LTD
CARLTON UNITED BREWERIES
  LTD
CASCADE BREWERY
CASUARINA HOME IMPROVE-
  MENTS CENTRE PTY LTD
CHANNEL 8 TV
CHILLAGOE CAVING CLUB
CITY DISPOSALS
CITY MAZDA (BRISBANE)
CLIFFS WESTERN AUSTRALIA
  MINING
COMMONWEALTH DEPART-
  MENT OF ADMINISTRATIVE
  SERVICES
CONSERVATION COMMISSION
  OF THE NORTHERN TERRI-
  TORY
COOINDA FOUR SEASONS
  HOTEL-MOTEL
CO-OP MOTORS
CROCODILE FARMS NT PTY LTD
CROSSLAND TOYOTA
CULTUS GOLD
CULTUS PACIFIC
CULTUS RESOURCES

DARWIN BAKERY
DARWIN CINEMA
DAVID SYME & CO. LTD
DEPARTMENT OF COMMUNITY
  DEVELOPMENT
DEPARTMENT OF CONSERVA-
  TION, FORESTS AND LANDS,
  VICTORIA
DEPARTMENT OF HEALTH
DEPARTMENT OF INLAND
  FISHERIES
DEPARTMENT OF PRIMARY
  PRODUCTION
DEPARTMENT OF TRANSPORT &
  WORKS

ELSEGOOD & SON
ENCROFT PTY LTD
ERNST & WHINNEY

FAIRFAX, SIR VINCENT
FARMHOUSE GALLERY
FITZROY ISLAND RESORT
FRESHA PRODUCTS
FUJI (AUSTRALIA)

G. H. COLES & CO. LTD
GESTETNER PTY LTD

GIBSON ASSOCIATES
GREYHOUND AUSTRALIA

HOBART MARINE BOARD
HUDBAY OIL

ICI AUSTRALIA LTD
ICL AUSTRALIA PTY LTD
INDEPENDENT GROCERS CO-OP
  LTD

JOHN YATES-DOVER
JOHNSON MATTHEY LTD
JUSTIN SEWARD

KATHERINE GORGE TOURIST
  ASSOCIATION
KEETLEYS TOURS PTY LTD
KRAUSS, GARY

LAKE TYERS ABORIGINAL COM-
  MUNITY
LAVAN SOLOMAN
LEGACY
LIPTONS TEA
LIQUID AIR (AUST.) LTD
LITTLE BRETON NOMINEES
LUCZYNSKI, A.

MODE
MANUFACTURERS' MUTUAL
  INSURANCE LTD
MARINE BOARD OF HOBART
MATERIAL CONTROL SYSTEMS
MATHERS SHOES
MAX'S RED VALLEY TOURS
McDONALD HAMILTON LTD
McGOWAN PRODUCE
MENELING MEATS
METZLER
MORRISON'S TOURIST SERVICES
MR T SHIRT
MULGRAVE SHIRE COUNCIL

NASHUA
NATIONAL PARKS AND WILD-
  LIFE SERVICE
NATIONAL SAFETY COUNCIL OF
  AUSTRALIA (VIC.)
NESTLÉ'S AUSTRALIA PTY LTD
NEW SOUTH WALES GOVT
  PREMIER'S DEPT
NIKON
NORTHERN TERRITORY GOV-
  ERNMENT
NT DEPT OF HEALTH & COM-
  MUNITY SERVICES
NT DEPT OF INDUSTRIES &
  DEVELOPMENT
NT DEPT OF PRIMARY PRODUC-
  TION
NT DEPT OF TRANSPORT &
  WORKS
NT EMERGENCY SERVICES

NT GOVERNMENT PRINTING
  OFFICE
NT MUSEUM OF ARTS & SCI-
  ENCE
NT POLICE FORCE

OPERATION RALEIGH NORTH-
  ERN TERRITORY COMMITTEE
OPERATION RALEIGH
  QUEENSLAND COMMITTEE
OPERATION RALEIGH TASMA-
  NIA COMMITTEE
OPERATION RALEIGH VICTORIA
  COMMITTEE
OSBORNE METALS LTD

PK KITCHENS (NT) PTY LTD
PACIFIC DUNLOP LTD
PATA NORTH AUSTRALIA
PAR AVION
PAULS (NT) PTY LTD
PAULS QUF
PERKINS SHIPPING PTY LTD
PURITY

QUEENSLAND ALUMINIUM LTD
QUEENSLAND CEMENT & LIME
QUEENSLAND DEPT OF YOUTH
QUEENSLAND EGG BOARD
QUEENSLAND FAR NORTH
  YOUTH ASSISTANCE FUND
QUEENSLAND NATIONAL PARKS
  AND WILDLIFE SERVICE
QUEENSLAND RAILFAST
QUEENSLAND STATE GOVERN-
  MENT
QUEENSLAND TOURIST AND
  TRAVEL CORP.

R & G ASSOCIATES
RANK INDUSTRIES (AUST.) LTD
ROTARY CLUB OF TOOWOOMBA
  EAST
ROTARY CLUBS OF CAIRNS
ROTARY CLUBS OF MELBOURNE
ROTARY CLUBS OF SOUTHERN
  TASMANIA
ROWE, C. K.
ROYAL AUSTRALIAN AIR FORCE
ROYAL AUSTRALIAN ARMY
ROYAL AUSTRALIAN NAVY
ROYAL FLYING DOCTOR
  SERVICE
ROYAL MELBOURNE INSTITUTE
  OF TECHNOLOGY

ST JOHN AMBULANCE SERVICE
SCIENCE ESTABLISHMENT
SHELL AUSTRALIA LTD

TAA
TGIO
TASMANIAN HYDRO-ELECTRIC
  COMMISSION

TASMANIAN NATIONAL PARKS
AND WILDLIFE SERVICE
TASMANIAN POLICE
TASMANIAN STATE GOVERN-
MENT
TELECOM AUSTRALIA
TERRITORY INSURANCE OFFICE
THORN EMI PTY LTD
TONG SING PTY LTD
TONY PURDON-STRAHAN
TRESIZE, PERCY
TULLY WHOLESALERS NT

UNDERWATER TECHNOLOGY
UNILEVER AUSTRALIA LTD
UNIVERSITY OF TASMANIA,
EDUCATION DEPT
UNIVERSITY OF TASMANIA,
ZOOLOGY DEPT

VICTORIA RIVER WAYSIDE INN
VIKING FIBREGLASS
INDUSTRIES

WESTERN AUSTRALIAN
MUSEUM

WESTPAC BANKING CORP.
WHIM CREEK
WILLIAM ANGLISS GROUP
WIMPEY, GEORGE, AUSTRALIA
PTY LTD
WIPPERMAN, A.
WORSLEY ALUMINUM LTD
WRIGHT, PAUL

YAL TROPICANA LODGE
YANCHEP SUN CITY

BAHAMAS SPONSORS

BAHAMAS GOVERNMENT, MIN-
ISTRY OF YOUTH AND SPORTS
BAHAMAS GOVERNMENT,
ROYAL BAHAMAS DEFENCE

FORCE
BAHAMAS INTERNATIONAL
TRUST CO. LTD
BANCA DELLA SUIZZERA

ITALIANA
BRITISH AMERICAN INSURANCE
CO.
HAYWARD, SIR JACK, OBE

BAHRAIN SPONSORS

BAHRAIN ROUND TABLE NO. 1
BRITISH AIRWAYS
GENERAL ORGANIZATION FOR

YOUTH AND SPORTS
QUANTAS AIRWAYS

BELIZE SPONSORS

AIKMAN, HON. DERECK
AIRPORT CAMP
ASHCROFT, MICHAEL
BATTYS BUS COMPANY
BELIZE DEFENCE FORCE
BOAT GRACIELA
BOAT ISLA MIA
BOWEN, BARRY
BOYTON, MARY
BRANCHE, W.
BREEZE, BOB
BRITISH HIGH COMMISSION
CALDER, S.
CORNER, THE
CRAIG, W.
CRAWFORD, RUDOLPH
CROSBY, JOHN
DUNCAN, ANGUS

ELLIMAN, K.
EWING, MR
FAUX, SHELMADINE
FLOWERS, H.
GOLDSON, HON. PHILIP
HALL, N.
HARRIS, BARBARA
HELP THE AGED
HUTCHINSON, J. B.
HYDE, J. V.
INGRAM, S.
JAX, JOHN
JENKINS, D.
KINSTON-SMITH, B.
LINDON, HON. DEAN
LOU, RENE
MAHLER, MR
MASON, CAPTAIN RAFAEL

McNAT, MR
MENZIES, BRIAN
MILLER, W.
NIVEN, WALLY
RAYBURN, REV. OWEN
SHEPHARD, SANDRA
SISTER CARITAS
STAINE, HEIME
SWAMY, DR BIDAR
SWIFT, B.
TEALE, LT-COL., 15/19H
TURTON, S. J.
USHER, RAYMOND
WAIGHT, J.
WEYER, MISS D.
WEYER, MRS D.

CANADA SPONSORS

AGRICULTURE CANADA
ASSOCIATION OF CANADIAN
UNIVERSITIES FOR NORTH-
ERN STUDIES
BANFF DESIGNS
BASSETT, DOUGLAS
BATON BROADCASTING INC.
BEATRICE CANADA LTD

BEAVERBROOK FOUNDATION
OF CANADA
BENJAMIN FILMS
BETELGEUSE BOOKS
CALM AIR CANADIAN
CAMP TRAILS
CAMPBELL'S SOUP
CANADIAN AIRLINES INTERNA-

TIONAL
CANADIAN GEOGRAPHIC
CANADIAN IMPERIAL BANK OF
COMMERCE
CANADIAN MOUNTAIN
SUPPLIES
CANADIAN NATIONAL SPORTS-
MEN'S SHOWS

CANADIAN NATURE FEDERA-
TION
CANADIAN PACIFIC TRUCKS
COLEMAN CANADA
CROWN X INC.
DEPARTMENT OF CULTURE,
GOVERNMENT OF NWT
DEPARTMENT OF ECONOMIC
DEVELOPMENT AND TOUR-
ISM, GOVERNMENT OF NWT
DEPARTMENT OF RENEWABLE
RESOURCES, GOVERNMENT
OF NWT
DHL INTERNATIONAL EXPRESS
LTD
DOWNTOWN CHURCH
WORKERS ASSOCIATION
EATON FOUNDATION, THE
EDVIRON SERVICES
EUREKA! TENTS
EVEREST MANUFACTURING
FORESHORE PROJECTS
(VANCOUVER) LTD
GEORGE WESTON LTD
GLEN WARREN PRODUCTION
GREY OWL PADDLES
IVEX INVESTMENTS
J.J. BARNICKE LTD

JACKMAN FOUNDATION, THE
JOHN LABATT LTD
JOHNSON DIVERSIFIED INC.
JONES LEISURE PRODUCTS
KEEWATIN INUIT ASSOCIATION
LAURENTIAN UNIVERSITY
MANUFACTURERS LIFE INSUR-
ANCE
McDONALDS RESTAURANTS OF
CANADA LTD
MERRILL LYNCH CANADA LTD
MINISTRY OF INDIAN AND
NORTHERN AFFAIRS
MINISTRY OF NATIONAL
DEFENCE
MOORELANDS CAMP (DOWN-
TOWN CHURCHWORKERS
ASSOCIATION)
MUSTANG INDUSTRIES
NABISCO BRANDS LTD
NALGENE TRAIL PRODUCTS
OLD TOWN
PACIFIC WESTERN AIRLINES
PATAGONIA
PRINCE OF WALES NORTHERN
HERITAGE CENTER, YELLOW-
KNIFE
PRINTING HOUSE, THE

RATHGEB FOUNDATION
RONALD A. CHRISHOLM LTD
ROYAL CANADIAN GEO-
GRAPHIC SOCIETY
ROYAL ONTARIO MUSEUM
SANDWELL, P. R.
SENECA COLLEGE
SILVA
SONAR FOUNDATION
SOUTHAM, G. T.
SPORTING LIFE
TEXACO CANADA INC.
THORNE ERNST AND WHINNEY
CHARTERED ACCOUNTANTS
TILLEY ENDURABLES
TORONTO DOMINION BANK
TORONTO SUN, THE
TORONTO TRANSIT COMMIS-
SION, THE
TRAILHEAD
TRENT UNIVERSITY
UNDERSEA RESEARCH LTD
UNDERWATER CANADA
VIA RAIL CANADA
WORLD WILDLIFE FUND
CANADA
YORK UNIVERSITY

CHILE SPONSORS

CALDERON, PABLO
CASILLAS, BRIG.-GEN. RODRIGO
SANCHEZ
COMANDANTE REGIMENTO
14 & 26
GARDASANIC, COL. LUIS
OSORIO
HILOS CADENA SA

HONG KONG AND SHANGHAI
BANKING CORP., THE
INTERNATIONAL INSPECTION
SERVICES (CHILE) SA
KUSCHEL, CARLOS IGNACIO
LESLIE, EDWIN AND JANE
LEVER CHILE SA
MALVENDA, PAMELA PEEDE

MONTES, PABLO ERRAZURIS
PEREZ, GEORGE
QUILODRAN, CARLOS BAEZA
VARGAS, MARCELLO
WACKER CHEMIE GmbH
(MUNICH)

DUBAI SPONSORS

BRITISH BANK OF THE MIDDLE
EAST
DUBAI ALUMINIUM COMPANY
(DUBAI)

JOHNSON & JOHNSON
MIDDLE EAST ECONOMIC
DIGEST

PORT AUTHORITY OF JEBEL ALI
(PAJA)
PORT RASHID AUTHORITY (PRA)

HONDURAS SPONSORS

BOCK, HERMAN
INSTITUTO HONDURENO DE

ANTROPOLOGICA E HISTORIA
KIRETT, CAPT. HORTEN

HONG KONG SPONSORS

ANN, DR T. K.
BRAY, C.
BRITISH AMERICAN TOBACCO
CO. (HONG KONG) LTD
HAMILTON, A. R.
HOARE, GOVETT & CO. LTD
HONG KONG BANK GROUP, THE

HONG KONG TELEVISION
BROADCASTS
JOHN SWIRE AND SONS LTD
LEVER BROTHERS (CHINA) LTD
MARDEN, J. L.
MATILDA HOSPITAL SEDAN
CHAIR RACE CHARITY FUND

ROYAL HONG KONG JOCKEY
CLUB CHARITIES LTD
ROYAL HONG KONG POLICE
SHAW FOUNDATION, THE
SIR DAVID TRENCH FUND

INDONESIA SPONSORS

ANKER BREWERIES
AUSTRALIAN MEDICAL
  SERVICES
BIROTIKA SEMESTA (DHL)
BLUE SWAN TOURS & TRAVEL
BURROUGHS WELLCOME
CSR PETROLEUM ASIA

COMMONWEALTH DEVELOP-
  MENT CORPORATION
DAIHATSU INDONESIA
DJANTI TIMBER CO.
GARUDA INDONESIAN AIRLINES
INTERNATIONAL SPORTS CLUB
  INDONESIA

JAKARTA LAND
JATI MALUKU TIMBER
MANDALA AIRLINES
MANDARIN ORIENTAL
MITRANAVA
NIPPON DENSO CO. LTD
TOKO SUBUR, AMBON

JAPAN SPONSORS

NIPPONDENSO CO. LTD

YAESU

JORDAN SPONSOR

HRH CROWN PRINCE HASSAN

NEW ZEALAND SPONSORS

AIR NEW ZEALAND
ALAN GIBBS
ALLIANCE FREEZING COMPANY
AMP
ANTARCTIC DIVISION DSIR
ANZ BANKING GROUP (NZ) LTD
AREC CANTERBURY BRANCH
AUCKLAND CITY COUNCIL
AUCKLAND HARBOUR BOARD
AUSTRAL STANDARD CABLES
BANK OF NEW ZEALAND
BASCANDS LTD
BEST WESTERN HOTELS/
  MOTELS
BON BRUSHES LTD
BURBERY FINANCE LTD
BURNHAM MILITARY CAMP
CABLE PRICE DOWNER LTD
CADBURY SCHWEPPES LTD
CALTEX (NZ) LTD
CANTERBURY DIVE CENTRE
CARLTON SERVICE STATION
CARTHY HOLDEN MOTORS LTD
CAXTON PRINTING WORKS LTD
CERAMCO (NZ) LTD
CEREBOS GREGGS LTD
CHAS LUNEY
CHRISTCHURCH CITY COUNCIL
CHRISTCHURCH PRISONS
CHRISTCHURCH STAR
CLYDE COLLINS TRUCK SALES
CODAN (NZ) LTD
COLLINS OLYMPIC LTD
COMBINED CO-OPERATIVE DIS-
  TRIBUTORS LTD
COUNTRYWIDE BUILDING SOCI-
  ETY
CORY WRIGHT & SALMON
DYC

DEPARTMENT OF LANDS & SUR-
  VEY
DHL COURIER SYSTEMS
DONAGHY'S INDUSTRIES LTD
DUNEDIN CITY COUNCIL
ENDEAVOR GROUP
ERNEST ADAMS LTD
ERNST & WHINNEY
FAGGS PRODUCTS LTD
FAY, RICHWITE & CO. LTD
FINLAY KITCHING & ASSOCI-
  ATES
FIORDLAND NATIONAL PARK
FIORDLAND TRAVEL
FISHER & PAYKEL LTD
FLETCHER CHALLENGE
  PROPERTIES
FLETCHER FISHING
FOODSTUFFS (NZ) LTD
GOVERNMENT HOUSE
HERTZ RENT-A-CAR
HOLEPROOF CORPORATION
HOME PRODUCTS LTD
HQ 3RD TASK FORCE NZ ARMY
HYLIN HIRE SERVICE
INTERNAL AFFAIRS (LOTTERIES
  DIVISION)
J. R. McKENZIE TRUST
JAPAN AIRLINES
JOHN HERBER LTD
JUSTICE DEPT
KABAN LTD
LANE WALKER RUDKIN LTD
LATIMER LODGE
LION BREWERIES
LION CLUB – WANAKA
LYTTLETON HARBOUR BOARD
MAINGUARD PACKAGING LTD
MASON & PORTER LTD

MASPORT
MINISTRY OF DEFENCE
MINISTRY OF WORKS AND
  DEVELOPMENT
MOBIL (NZ) LTD
MOFFATT & CO.
McCONNELL DOWELL CORP.
NEWMANS GROUP
NOEL LEEMINGS LTD
NORTHS BREAD LTD
NZ APPLE AND PEAR MARKET-
  ING BOARD
NZ BREWERIES LTD
NZ DAIRY BOARD
NZ GOVERNMENT
NZ INDUSTRIAL CASES LTD
NZ POST OFFICE
NZ SUGAR CO. LTD
NZ WILDLIFE SERVICES
NZ CORPORATION LTD
OASIS INDUSTRIES LTD
PDL INDUSTRIES LTD
PEACH PRODUCTS LTD
PHOTO PROCESS PRINTERS LTD
QUILL HUMPHREYS
RALPH BROWN
SAATCHI & SAATCHI COMPTON
  (NZ) LTD
SANITARIUM HEALTH FOOD
  LTD
SAVAGE PRINT LTD
SKELLERUP INDUSTRIES LTD
SMITHS CITY MARKET
SOUTHWARD ENGINEERING
  LTD
STATE SERVICES COMMISSION
STEEL & TUBE LTD
SUNBEAM GROUP
TAIT ELECTRONICS LTD

175

TARANAKI SAVINGS BANK
TE ANAU DOWN MOTOR INN
TELEVISION (NZ) LTD
TISCO LTD
TOURIST HOTEL CORPORATION
  – TE ANAU
TOYMENKA LTD
TRANSPAC HOLDINGS LTD
TRICITY HOUSE
TRIGON PLASTICS LTD

TRUSTEE BANK – WAIKATO
TURNER LTD
UEB
UNILEVER LTD
VIKO HOLDINGS LTD
W. M. SCOLLAY & CO. LTD
W. T. MURRAY LTD
WANG COMPUTER LTD
WATTIES LTD
WILLIAMS PROPERTY

HOLDINGS LTD
WINDSOR PRIVATE HOTEL
WORMALDS LTD
WRIGHT CARS –
  CHRISTCHURCH
WYATT & WILSON
ZEALANDIA MILLING CO. LTD

SULTANATE OF OMAN SPONSOR

HM SULTAN QABOOS BIN SAID
  BIN TAIMUR

PAKISTAN SPONSORS

ADVENTURE FOUNDATION OF
  PAKISTAN
AGA KHAN FOUNDATION

SCIENCE FOUNDATION OF
  PAKISTAN

PAPUA NEW GUINEA SPONSORS

AIR NIUGINI
BURNS PHILP (PNG) LTD
DOUGLAS, DENIS
DOUGLAS AIRWAYS LTD
DUTTON, HON. WARREN, MP
FARAMUS, GERRY
HARRISONS & CROSSFIELD
  (PNG) LTD
HUTCHINSON, DAVID

LARMER, M. J.
LOVE, H. BERESFORD, MBE
MERIDIAN MOTORS PTY LTD
NIUGINI-LLOYDS INTERNA-
  TIONAL BANK LTD
PAGINI TRANSPORT PTY LTD
RAMU SUGAR LTD
RICE INDUSTRIES PTY LTD

ROBERT LAURIE COMPANY PTY
  LTD
SOUTH PACIFIC BREWERY LTD
  (TRANSPORT)
TALAIR PTY LTD
WILMOT-SHARP, PHILIP, MBE
WOODS, JUSTICE ROBERT K.,
  CBE

ROATAN SPONSORS

AB PHAROS MARINE LTD OF
  BRENTFORD
AGUILAR, COL. MAURICIO,
  SECCION DEL PORTOCOLO,
  HONDURAN GOVT
ANDERSON, ERIC AND TERI
AUSTEN, JANE AND MIKE,
  COXENS HOLE, ROATAN
BODDEN, SAM
BODEN, CLAUDIA
BONILLA, MIGUEL A., INSTI-
  TUTE OF ANTHROPOLOGY
  AND HISTORY
BROWN, MICHAEL
COOPER, DERRY
COOPER, ROGER

CREE, GEORGE AND FRANCIS
DAWSON, FRANK G.
ESTRADA, LIC MIGUEL,
  CULTURA Y TURISMO,
  HONDURAN GOVT
FIALOS, LIC MIGUEL ANGEL
  IZAGUIRRE, CULTURA Y
  TURISMO, HONDURAN GOVT
FORLIN, DR MARIO,
  RELACIONES EXTERIORES,
  HONDURAN GOVT
GALINDO, CHERYL
GEORGE WIMPEY CHARITABLE
  TRUST, LONDON
GOUGH, REX
HASSMAN, GEORGE,

HONDURAN INSTITUTE OF
  ANTHROPOLOGY AND HISTORY
JENNINGS-BROWN, ANN
KIVETT, HORTON, LA CEIBA,
  HONDURAS
MEYER, HARVEY AND VIRGINIA
PILKINGTON, ALAN S.
PURBRICK, LT-COL. RIS, MBE,
  17TH/21ST LANCERS
TRINITY HOUSE SERVICES,
  TOWER HILL, LONDON
WHISKEY MIKE, OAKRIDGE,
  ROATAN
WHITE, H. E. BRIAN, BRITISH
  AMBASSADOR TO HONDURAS,
  TEGUCIGALPA

VENTURERS AND STAFF:
JANUARY 1986–OCTOBER 1987

COUNTRY CODES

AE	– United Arab Emirates	GU	– Guernsey	NZ	– New Zealand
AU	– Australia	HK	– Hong Kong	OM	– Sultanate of Oman
BB	– Barbados	IT	– Italy	PG	– Papua New Guinea
BH	– Bahrain	JE	– Jersey	PK	– Pakistan
BS	– Bahamas	JP	– Japan	SE	– Sweden
CA	– Canada	KE	– Kenya	SG	– Singapore
CH	– Switzerland	MY	– Malaysia	UK	– United Kingdom
CL	– Chile	NL	– Netherlands	US	– United States of
FR	– France	NP	– Nepal		America

EXPEDITION 4B – CHILE

Alvaro Acevedo Rojas (CL), Alvero Alejandro Tobar (CL), Deborah Armstrong (UK), Michael Bennett (UK), Paul Bocking (UK), Karla Borkosky (CL), Timothy Bott (UK), Gonzalo Bravo (CL), Philippe Brevet (UK), Clive Brotchie (UK), Karen Burke (UK), Andrew Burns (UK), Matthew Caldwell (BS), Magdalene Calvo (CL), Maria Calvo (CL), Jonathan Christie (UK), Bernado Cifuentes (CL), Susan Clark (UK), Catherine Clunies-Ross (AU), Antonio Colombi (IT), Will Cross (US), Anne Custance (AU), Patty Debenham (US), Stuart Dent (UK), Penelope Dickens (UK), John Dobbin (AU), Michael Draper (UK), Jim Dunleavy (US), Gary Edwards (UK), Carolina Errazuriz (CL), Earnst Errazuriz (CL), Rodrigo Eterovic (CL), Adan Farah (UK), Catherine Fearn (UK), Maria Fernandez (CL), Nicole Fischer Braun (CL), Katherine Force (UK), Paul Fox (JE), Simon Fraser (AU), Simon Frost (UK), Andres Fuenzalida (CL), Eliana Garcia (CL), Pedro Garcia (CL), Richard Garland (UK), Isabel Garrido (CL), Andreas Goijberg (CL), Pam Goijberg (CL), Timothy Goliah (UK), Marcela Gonzalez (CL), Nguk Kuan Goo (SG), Karen Graham (UK), Michael Greenwood (UK), Andrew Haddon (UK), Julie Hale (NZ), Brian Harkins (US), Anglia Harwood (UK), John Hatchard (UK), Melinda Holtam (US), Dylan Hooper (UK), Gillian Houston (UK), Patricio Illanes (CL), Claudio Isaza (CL), Christopher Jackson (UK), Kevin Jamie (NZ), Sharon Jobson (UK), Ernst Joerger (UK), Letty Johnson (US), Robin Johnson (UK), Richi Kataoka (JP), Maki Kato (JP), Julia Kennedy (CL), Peter Koyouimdjian (CL), Richard Letelier (CL), Jorge Lindsay (CL), Simon Lucas (UK), Amanda McClung (UK), Ambrose McDonough (UK), Jack McLaughlin (US), Paula Madrid (CL), Paul Maguire (UK), Paul Maine (UK), Mark Marino (NZ), Alvero Miguel (CL), Carl Miller (UK), John Moore (UK), Jolyon Moore (UK), Steve Morrison (US), Richard Northcott (AU), Simon Oakley (NZ), Anthony Oliver (UK), Andrew Olleveant (UK), Jacqueline Parias (CL), Michael Pearce (BF), Claudia Perez de Ferai (CL), Alison Powell (UK), Andrew Robshaw (UK), Mark Robson (UK), Beatrice Rose (UK), Christopher Savage (UK), Rodrigo Schiefelbein (CL), David Scott (UK), Fiona Scott (UK), Sebastian Sheppard (CL), Alexandra Silva Pizarro (CL), Maria Silva Pizarro (CL), Shona Sinisi (US),

Neil Smith (UK), Ana Maria Soza (CL), Akira Suzuki (JP), Toshinari Takayanagi (JP), Luke Tattersall (UK), Catherine Tetu (CA), Mark Thiermann (CL), Lori Thomas (US), Rona Thomson (UK), Gary Vermeer (CA), Ed Vermue (CA), Anna Walsh (UK), Fiona Warburton (UK), Kathleen Ward (UK), John Westaway (AU), Trudi Wiggins (UK), Suet Fong (Agnes) Wong (HK), Yasushi Yoshida (JP).

EXPEDITION 4B - STAFF

Justin Albert (UK), Darryl Atkinson (NZ), Vivian Bentinck (UK), Jim Best (UK), Lorna Black (UK), Garry Brown (NZ), Phillip Brown (UK), Fiona Cameron (UK), Lee Carrillo (US), Enrique Castro (US), David Collins (UK), John Cornish (UK), Paul Cornish (UK), Jennifer Cox (UK), John Daniel (UK), Mark Davis (US), Neil Deans (UK), Fiona Dolman (UK), Morag Dugan (UK), Robert Ervine (US), Eibleis Fanning (UK), Leslie Garcia (US), Martin Gardner (UK), Elaine Goodenough (UK), Joanna Groves (US), Mark Hass (AU), John Irwin (US), John Lathbury (UK), Deirdre Loader-Oliver (UK), Keith Long (US), Enrique Luis-Sanshez (US), Ceil McKinney (US), Rosamund Marshall (UK), Steven Mitchell (US), Robert Muir Wood (UK), Ramon Pares-Alvarez (US), John Pethick (UK), Pamela Phillips (UK), Geraldine Prentice (UK), Denise Reed (UK), Keith Reyes (US), David Sayer (UK), Robert Waldron (US), Nicola Weaver (UK), Tamsin Wheeler (UK), Leonard Whitten (US).

EXPEDITION 4C - *SIR WALTER RALEIGH* – PACIFIC CROSSING

Juane Ayers (US), Maria Bozolla (CL), Joseph Duffy (UK), Marie-Elise Fraulo (UK), Damian Gascoigne (UK), Lee Hastie (UK), Jennifer Hill (UK), Susan Howes (UK), Isabel Lee (HK), Philip Moran (UK), Marcelo Mota (US), Matthew Richmond (UK), Rosslyn Stevens (US), Jay Stewart (US), Byron White (US), Tony Wong (CA).

EXPEDITION 4C - STAFF

Nico Broodbakker (NL), Mary Corbett (UK), John Flenley (UK), William Foster (UK), Rick Gustausson (CA), Jonathan Hateley (UK), Brenta Henriquez (CL), Sue Ingle (UK), Roy Jarvis (UK), Michael Johnston (UK), Shane Kennedy (CA), David King (UK), Joan King (UK), John Layton (UK), Andrew Mitchell (UK), Ivan Munoz (CL), Annette Parkes (UK), Richard Parkin (UK), Nicholas Perrott (UK), Deborah Procter (UK), Karen Smith (UK), Roger Stephenson (UK), Barbara Thomson (UK), Alastair Turner (UK), Antony Walton (UK), Robert Williamson (CA), Jonathan Woodhead (UK).

EXPEDITION 4H - TAC HQ 4

Paul Bernard (UK), John Blashford-Snell (UK), Charles Daniel (UK), Cathy Davies (UK), John Davies (UK), Blanche Debenham (UK), Colin Dougan (UK), Pamela Gaffin (FR), Vanessa Hetherington (UK), Nicholas Horne (UK), Peta Lock (UK), Diane Rosenthal (US), Rupert Rucker (UK), Christopher Sainsbury (UK), Christopher Schaejbe (US), Adrian Turner (UK), Marcus Wilkinson (UK).

EXPEDITION 4I - *ZEBU*

Terence Bates (UK), John Borden (US), Jennifer Burr (UK), Mark Covell (UK), Helen Crowley (UK), Paul Doble (AU), James Graham (US), Alec Graham (US), Karen-Jaine Mills (UK), Carolyn Norris (US), James Pugh (UK), Melody Ray (US), Joanne Smith (US), Eleanor Stoffelson (CA), Gigi Waham (US), Penny Willsford (AU).

EXPEDITION 4I – CREW

Helen Bird (UK), Robert Bradley (UK), Jane Broughton (UK), Nicholas Broughton (UK), Peter Masters (UK), Shion Scudamore (UK), Philip Sefton (UK).

EXPEDITION 5A – SOLOMON ISLANDS

Astrid Balodis (AU), Nigel Daly (UK), Elizabeth Deaton (US), Masatsuga Doi (JP), Gillian Eardley (UK), Clare Farleigh (UK), James Firkins (UK), John Hansen (AU), Teru Kisuna (JP), Richard Lavis (UK), William Martin (BS), Simon Morrant (UK), Keith Morris (NZ), Judith Morrison (UK), Alison Nicholls (UK), David O'Brien (UK), Jacqueline Parks (UK), Lisa Peach (US), Fay Pendell (UK), Debbie Podger (JE), Louisa-Jane Pritchard (UK), Marcus Pugh (UK), Edward Ritchie (US), Gillian Schofield (UK), Sean Silver (UK), Shanta Sivam (UK), Jonathan Smith (UK), Sara Stephenson (AU), John Taylor (UK), Roger Tilbrook (UK), Claire Tregaskis (UK), Michio Watanabe (JP), Richard Watson (UK).

EXPEDITION 5A – STAFF

Hugh Bramwell (UK), Richard Curtis (UK), Margaret Dickson (UK), Stephan Fishwick (UK), Conrad Gorinsky (UK), Robin Hill (UK), David Knowles (BS), James Longden (UK), Trevor Newland (UK), David Parker (UK), Rowland Reeve (US), Mark Shelford (UK), Anthony Smith (UK), David Smith (UK).

EXPEDITION 5C – CHILE

Rachel Baker (UK), Janet Bell (UK), Julian Brown (UK), Christine Carter (UK), Emma Clarke (UK), Anne Cleland (CA), Craig Cohon (CA), Ruth Cross (UK), Martin Edwards (UK), Helen Ellis (UK), Malcolm Fairhall (NZ), Michael Fordham (NZ), David Gilbert (UK), Lyn Goodman (US), Jonathan Goring (UK), Phillip Gulliford (UK), Catherine Hill (UK), Elisabeth Hooper (UK), Richard Humphrey (UK), Intan Siti Zarinah Jailani (MY), Paul Jenkinson (UK), Brette Jones (US), Siobhan Jones (UK), Peter Lambert (UK), Joe Lane (CA), Sandra Laptain (UK), Michael Lay (UK), Jim Leith (NZ), Fiona MacDonald (UK), John McGlade (UK), Adrian Mumby (UK), Timothy Murray (UK), Chew Whye Ngai (MY), Richard Perkes (UK), Eugene Pila (CL), Timothy Race (UK), Andrew Ralston (UK), Ximena Rayo (CL), Bronwyn Rhynd (NZ), Mark Richard (UK), Annabel Ross (UK), Judith Sanguinetti (CL), Katherine Sharp (UK), David Short (UK), David Siggins (UK), Barbara Tate (UK), Martin Thow (NZ), Nicola Townley (UK), Dianne Tuck (UK), Gonzolo Valoute (CL), Selvem Vanniaraju (MY), Gail Walker (UK), Gail Warnock (UK), Gail Webster (UK), Sarah Whatmough (UK), Roderick White (UK), Judith Wilcox (UK), Stuart Williamson (UK), Charlotte Wood (UK), Barbara Woodward (UK), Valerie Wray (UK), Robert Young (UK).

EXPEDITION 5C – STAFF

James Bozeman (US), Thomas Brady (UK), Timothy Curtis (UK), Peter Davidson (US), Cathryn Dawson (UK), Molly Dineen (UK), Rick Gustausson (CA), Shane Kennedy (CA), Jonathan Lane (UK), Shane Lane (UK), Christopher Lewis (UK), Ceil McKinney (US), Ariel Piluso (UK), Mike Reynolds (UK), Mike Roberts (UK), Jack Rumney (UK), Dianne Russell (UK), Chi Chiu Tan (SG), John Tweedale (UK), Leonard Whitten (US), Robert Williamson (CA).

EXPEDITION 5H – TAC HQ 5

Paul Bernard (UK), Roger Chapman (UK), Cathy Davies (UK), Pamela Gaffin (FR), David Oliver (UK), Nicholas Perrott (UK), Eric Primeau (UK), Christopher Sainsbury (UK).

EXPEDITION 5I - *ZEBU*

Sally Anderson (UK), Scott Anderson (UK), Amanda Bell (UK), Richard Bewell (UK), Lance Brill (US), Hunter Burkhalter (US), Darren Eastell (UK), David Edwards (UK), Peyton Howell (US), Irene Manley (CA), Cliff Pryor (US), James Usher (UK), Erik Zakoske (HK).

EXPEDITION 5I - CREW

Helen Bird (UK), Robert Bradley (UK), Jane Broughton (UK), Nicholas Broughton (UK), Peter Masters (UK), Shion Scudamore (UK), Philip Sefton (UK).

EXPEDITION 6A - AUSTRALIA

James Acheson (UK), John Adams (UK), Ali Said Mohammed Al-Harthy (OM), Seif Nassor Said Al-Salhi (OM), Nasser Salem Al-Suleimany (OM), Caroline Arthey (UK), Edward Ayers (UK), John Batchelor (UK), Jayne Beamond (UK), Sarina Beecham (UK), David Bennett (UK), Kevin Boldy (UK), Denise Borrello (US), Julian Bowker (UK), Richard Bowman (UK), Claire Brace (UK), Scott Brooks (US), Julianne Bros (UK), Tony Brown (US), Sarah Bruce (UK), Bob Bryant (US), Colleen Burgoyne (UK), Tammy Burks (US), Caroline Caulfield-Giles (UK), Richard Cavaliero (UK), Mandy Clifford (UK), Alice Cohen (US), Andrew Collins (UK), Daayn Corish (UK), Brenda Corker (UK), Richard Corkill (UK), Paul Cowlard (UK), David Crocombe (UK), Patrick Davenport (US), Michael Davies (UK), Gary Deans (UK), Joe Dellert (US), Garth Draisey (UK), Janice Drewe (UK), Yvonne Duffield (UK), Helen Dunn (UK), Stewart Edmunds (US), Sharon Bernice Elmy (UK), Timothy Elvin (UK), Dawn Engel (US), Abdul Hamid Farid (SG), Nicholas Fenton (UK), Andrew Filer (UK), Helen Flint (UK), Ken Foster (US), David Freshwater (US), Keita Fujimoto (JP), Ken Fukui (JP), Karen Fulton (UK), David Gianotti (US), Finn Gleeson (UK), John Goodwin (US), Nigel Gray (UK), Thomas Greig (UK), Philip Grice (UK), Douglas Griffith (US), Graham Griffiths (UK), Martin Gudgeon (UK), Judith Habermann (US), Rena Harris (US), Stephen Harrison (UK), Suzanne Harwood (UK), Blake Hawley (US), Gillian Heys (UK), Richard Hollingbery (UK), Karen Hood (UK), Lorraine Hoolachan (UK), Robert Hughes (UK), Clifford Hurst (UK), Adrian James (UK), Geraldine Jennings (UK), Patrick Joyce (UK), Chizu Kanada (JP), Timothy R. Knight (UK), Ann Kruyer (UK), Michael C. Law (UK), Christine Laws (UK), Deneen Leblanc (CA), Lotte Lent (US), Adriano Leto (UK), Siu Fung Lui (HK), Dolores McCarthy (UK), Sean McCormack (US), Daniel McGuinness (UK), Clive MacKenzie (UK), Catriona MacLaurin (UK), Brian Matthews (UK), Christopher Mead (UK), Catriona Merrylees (UK), Martha Meservey (US), Janet Millard (UK), Keith Mitchell (UK), Suzanne Morison (UK), Kevin Mountford (UK), Anthony Mullaney (UK), Julie Munro (UK), Samantha Napper (UK), Ruth Naylor (UK), Benjamin Nutbourne (UK), Dominic O'Brien (UK), Brian O'Neil Martin (US), Laura O'Neill (UK), David Owsley (UK), Ralph Pannell (UK), Jane Pares (UK), Gary Park (UK), Mark Paulson (UK), Bill Payne (US), Matthew Pierson (UK), Nicholas Pigot (UK), Christopher Pinn (UK), Ruth Pintard (BS), Richard Pollard (UK), Nicholas Poulson (UK), Richard Preyer (US), Maurice Price (UK), Christopher Pugh (UK), Amy Ramsey (US), Katharine Redman (UK), Pete Reibold (US), Gillian Reynolds (UK), John Risk (UK), Alasdair Robertson (UK), Neil Robertson (UK), Paul Rowland (UK), Becky Rudd (US), Norman Russell (UK), Marc Sardy (US), Simon Schutte (UK), Francis Chu Chee Seng (SG), Carl Smale (UK), David Smalley (UK), Tracy Smethurst (UK), Beverley Smith (UK), Isobel Smith (UK), Richard Stockdale (UK), Lena Stone (US), Haruhiro Suzuki (JP), Jill Swarbrick (UK), David Swift (UK), Patrick Swift (UK), Renko Tani (JP), Timothy Tapley (UK), Sarah Thompson (UK), Gillian Thomson (UK), Bethan Treharne (UK), Craig Turner (UK), Penny-Ann Turner (UK), James Vaughn (US), Paula Verbanac (US), Richard Vinton (UK), Marion Wagner (UK), Patrick Wagstaff (UK), James Wickett (UK), Nicholas Wildman (UK), Steve Williams (CA), Gail Wiseman (UK), Joanna Wood (UK), David Wright (US), Kiyokazu Yasuda (JP).

EXPEDITION 6A – STAFF – AUSTRALIA

Duncan Adesile (UK), Craig Allardyce (AU), Mike Banham (AU), Robert Batten (AU), Peter Bindon (AU), Felicity Bowden (UK), Arthur Bryce (AU), Ralph Buckley (AU), Chris Burgin (AU), Craig Busch (US), David Cavanagh (AU), Paul Dewar (AU), Colin Dougan (UK), Steven Dunstan (AU), Paul Edgar (UK), Martin Fitzgerald (UK), John Hamilton (AU), John Haseloff (AU), Peter Herden (AU), Dave Hooper (AU), Colin Hucker (AU), Peter Jarman (AU), Gary Krynicki (US), Steven Larson (US), Jo McDonald (AU), Barry Meade (US), Vic Mellor (AU), Darron Meredith (AU), Philip Morris (US), Virginia Murray (US), Philip O'Keeffe (AU), Paul Patti (AU), Andy Philp (AU), Samuel Pitts (US), Tony Press (AU), Derek Radcliffe (AU), Peter Reece (AU), Christopher Reynolds (UK), Clive Richardson (AU), Martin Robertson (UK), Brian Russell (AU), Alison Saltrese (UK), Allen Scott (AU), Barrie Taylor (AU), Robert Taylor (UK), William Taylor (US), Dennis Thomson (AU), Eric Wardlow (US), Bob Wicks (AU), Christopher Woodall (US).

EXPEDITION 6B – PAPUA NEW GUINEA

Robert Aporo (PG), Simon Bayly (UK), Sara Blizard (UK), Jenny Bond (US), Lisa Campbell (US), Ian Cave (UK), Peter Chamberlain (UK), Togui Chris (PG), Olwen Clapham (UK), Nicola Clark (UK), Jonathan Cocke (UK), Thomas Cressey (UK), Donna Croft (UK), Mark Dacey (UK), Richard Doyle (NZ), Stephen Eagle (UK), Alison Farmer (UK), Frances Fellows (US), Neil Foster (UK), Alon Gelcer (CA), Andrew Gordon (UK), Krista Hanni (CA), Shuji Hasegawa (JP), Rosemary Hesp (AU), Nicola Hewitt (UK), Catriona Hurd (UK), Laurence James (UK), Susan Jamieson (UK), David Jones (UK), Gillian Kaye (UK), Kathryn Kelly (AU), Simon Kerslake (NZ), Simon Kiddy (UK), Thomas Kaluwebana (PG), Alastair McClung (UK), Terence McHugh (UK), Anthony Marino (NZ), Suzanne Molloy (US), Katsuhiro Nakayamao (JP), Claire Parsons (UK), Peter Pokanis (PG), Richard Potts (UK), Gretchen Sauer (US), Bob Sheridan (US), Jean Smith (UK), Pamela Smith (UK), Will Sparks (US), Ilya Stone (US), Eileen Stuart (UK), Mark Swift (UK), Sarah Thomas (UK), Joe Veleke (PG), Jerry Wenge (PG), Serena Wilson (US), Hozumi Yamada (JP).

EXPEDITION 6B – STAFF

Warwick Abbott (UK), Anthony Agar (UK), Martin Broomfield (UK), Coralie Critchley (UK), Sue Dent (UK), Janette Dunne (UK), Michael Eden (UK), Geoffrey Ford (UK), Conrad Gorinsky (UK), Moira Harrington (US), Rebecca Hughes (UK), Terry Linehan (US), Mark Miller (UK), Simon Milligan (UK), Mark O'Shea (UK), John Roberts (UK), Babette Seymour-Cooper (UK), Nigel Stuart (UK), John Swanston (UK), Peter Woodburn (UK).

EXPEDITION 6H – TAC HQ 6

Larry Barton (US), John Blashford-Snell (UK), Kathryn Crookshank (UK), Charles Daniel (UK), Nicholas Horne (UK), Michele Minnick (US), Michael Morgan (US), Ann Tweedy (UK), Peter Woodburn (UK).

EXPEDITION 6I – *ZEBU*

Josephine Asmah (UK), Christopher Beer (UK), Freyja Bruun (US), (Francis) Kate Godber (UK), John Gowen (UK), Derek Holmes (UK), Shirley King (UK), Asoka Markandu (SG), Lee Martin (US), Philippa Powell (UK), Roslyn Skinner (UK), Lola Smith (US), Tim Stevens (US), Martin Webb (UK), Lana Wedmore (US).

EXPEDITION 6I – CREW

Helen Bird (UK), Robert Bradley (UK), Jane Broughton (UK), Nicholas Broughton (UK), Tony Flagherty (AU), Peter Masters (UK), Shion Scudamore (UK).

EXPEDITION 7A - AUSTRALIA

Zahir B Ali B Zahir Al Abri (OM), Khalfan Mohammed Al Riamy (OM), Abdullah Khalfan Ali Al Rijebi (OM), Sadiq Ahmed Al Qattan (BH), Sarah Anderson (UK), Alison Angus (UK), Naoko Aoyagi (JP), Gillian Arthur (UK), Ian Atkinson (GU), Elkin Atwell (UK), Adam Babicz (UK), Raymond Bailey (UK), Stephen Barker (US), David Barnes (UK), Penelope Beeley (UK), Fred Benoit (CA), Kevin Billing (UK), Alison Bird (UK), Stuart Birrell (UK), Lucy Blue (UK), Alan Boggs (US), Julia Bottomley (UK), Brendan Al Brand (UK), Michele Brew (UK), Andrew Brookes (UK), Penny Buckingham (UK), Sandra Bushby (UK), Romayne Campbell (UK), Elizabeth Castle (UK), Sarah Cavanagh (UK), David Cazalet (UK), Ki Lung Cheng (HK), Chung Soon Cheong (SG), Sophie Cheston (UK), Paul Andreas Christoforou (UK), Jane Coatesworth (UK), Sheila Connolly (UK), Amanda Constantinou (UK), Sandra Cooke (UK), Charles Cripwell (UK), Louise Davidson (UK), Bryan Davies (AU), Graeme Davison (UK), Frederick Denman (UK), Julia Denyer (UK), Phillip Dobson (UK), Linda Dowling (UK), Mary Duke (AU), Robyn Dymock (AU), Raad El-Jassar (UK), Justin Elcombe (UK), Trish Ereaux (CA), Ahmed Hassan Faraj (BH), Ossama Fateem (BH), Sally Ann Faust (US), Roger File (UK), Susan Flood (UK), Sean Galan (US), Christopher Garrard (UK), Rachel Gibson (AU), David Gill (UK), Christopher Gledhill (UK), Timothy Gray (UK), Ian Greene (CA), David Greenwood (UK), Adrian Grist (UK), Catherine Guy (UK), Clare Haviland (UK), John Haynes (UK), Anthony Hayward (UK), David Head (AU), Claire Hedges (UK), Scott Hendry (UK), Susan Heslop (UK), Casey Hodgson (US), Neal Holmes (AU), Dominic Hoole (UK), Jill Horn (UK), Janet Hoyland (UK), Philip Hughes (UK), Adrian Immenhauser (CH), Russell Jago (AU), Peter Johnson (UK), Andrew Jones (UK), Joanne Jones (UK), Sally Jones (UK), Kazuhiko Kayada (JP), Roisin Keenan (UK), Judith Keighley (UK), John Kennedy (UK), Stephen Knight (UK), Caroline Koenig (CA), Liang Chye Koh (SG), Philippa Lack (UK), Kim Ho Lau (HK), Grace Lawrence (US), Alison Lea (UK), Andrew Leedham (UK), Daniel Lischer (CH), Deborah Lloyd (UK), Amanda Lyon (UK), Peter McAlpine (UK), Sharon McAuley (UK), Clare McClintock (UK), Grant McPherson (UK), Elizabeth McTernan (UK), Zofta Malewicz (UK), Trevor Meadows (UK), Gillian Meekison (UK), Thelma Meilenz (US), Yoshiaki Miyata (JP), Neil Morgan (UK), Sakuya Morimoto (JP), Paula Morrell (UK), Randall Morrow (US), Kerry Mount (UK), Theresa Mowbray (UK), James Munro (UK), Juliet Needell (UK), Michael Newington (UK), Ivan Nicholson (UK), Julie Nicholson (UK), AnthonyNorman (JE), Robert Nutbourne (UK), Mark O'Nions (UK), Paul Ockenden (UK), Margot Ovens (UK), Matthew Owen (UK), Barry Pearn (UK), Kevin Pepe (US), Stephen Pink (UK), Martin Poole (UK), Douglas Potter (UK), Andrew Powell (UK), Paul Pritchard (UK), Dawn Purdue (UK), Derek Quartey-Papafio (UK), Nigel Richardson (UK), Dunlap Riele (US), Graham Rowe (UK), Jonathan Rowe (UK), Lynda Russell (UK), Bridget Rycroft (UK), Darren Rydstrom (US), Michael Said (UK), Chris Sample (US), Karyn Sanders (AU), Jeff Satterwhite (US), Paolo Scalvi (IT), Elisa Scott (US), Robert Sewell (UK), Linda Sherrod (UK), Patrick Shirley (UK), Nadine Slavinski (US), Linda Smith (UK), Roxane Smith (UK), Nicholas Snell (UK), Daniel Stevens (UK), Sandra Stinchcombe (UK), Paul Stone (UK), Joanne Stratton (UK), Takako Takano (JP), Kyoko Takeuchi (JP), Sing Tung Tang (HK), Calum Taylor (UK), Nicola Thomas (UK), Andrew Thomson (UK), David Thorley (UK), Melinda Thurley (UK), Miles Tindal (UK), Jenny Toomey (UK), Michael Tschanz (US), Adam Twigg (UK), Sally Vergette (UK), Andrew Vinten (UK), Susan Volans (UK), Michael Walker (UK), Bert Warren (US), Andy Watts (US), Jayne Watts (UK), William Weatherseed (UK), David Weaver (UK), Alistair West (UK), Lynne Whitaker (UK), Andy Whitley (US), Kimberley Wilkes (UK), Amanda Williams (UK), Angela Williams (UK), James Williams (UK), Adam Willis (UK), Penny Willsford (AU), Kit Ying Wong (HK), Daniele Zanzi (IT).

EXPEDITION 7A - STAFF

Tim Abberley (UK), Richard Allan (UK), Robert Anderson (UK), K. Barry (AU), Andrew Bartholomeus (AU), Mal Beaton (AU), David Bereskin (US), Felicity Bowden (UK), James Bozeman (US), Richard Breitbach (US), Gregory Brown (US), Margaret Brownlow (AU), Carol Buist (UK), Jim Burton (AU), Edward Childs (UK), Kenneth Crow (UK), Alan Cummings (AU), Stephen Dodd (UK),

John Dowty (UK), Miles East (UK), Anthony Elliott (AU), Gary Ernst (AU), C. Fenton (AU), Martin Fitzgerald (UK), Christopher Fox (UK), Hollos Fullerton (US), Mark Geyle (AU), Elizabeth Gimmler (UK), Habiba Gitay (UK), Geoff Hawke (AU), Clare Hawking (UK), Jasmina Hilton (UK), Wayne Hosburgh (US), David Hudson (AU), Peter Hunnam (AU), Ross Hynes (AU), Peter Jenkins (AU), Jack Kinross (AU), Stefan Kobewka (UK), David Lane (UK), Mike Lueders (AU), Mick McElroy (AU), Peter McGregor (AU), Derek Minto (AU), Geoff Nimmo (AU), Steve Olive (AU), Peter Ormerod (UK), Alison Palmer (UK), D. W. Phyllis (AU), Ken Pittman (AU), Frank Pride (US), Denis Puniard (AU), Ian Robins (UK), Philip Roe (UK), Terry Scott (UK), Ian Shanks (AU), R. C. Sheath (AU), Billy Smith (US), Robert Southwood (UK), Geoff Stanton (AU), Peter Stanton (AU), Dave Steckhoven (AU), Andrew Stuart-Mills (UK), James Sullivan (US), Swoopy Summers (AU), Albert Sunday (US), Paul Trantor (AU), Percy Trezise (AU), William Voorhees (US), Linda Walters (US), Alan Whiting (AU), Ronald Worthy (UK), Janette Young (UK).

EXPEDITION 7C – TAC HQ 7

John Blashford-Snell (UK), Charles Daniel (UK), Miles East (UK), Hawk Freeman (US), Nick Horne (UK), Peta Lock (UK), Ann Tweedy (US), Lana Wedmore (US).

EXPEDITION 7I – *ZEBU*

Emily Delgado (US), Shan Fehr (UK), Richard Hadley (UK), Katie Hanton (CA), Andrew Holbrow (UK), Aaron Holloman (US), Steven Jones (UK), Christine Klar (CA), Alexandra Landrum (US), Hilary Murray (UK), Emma Pascoe (UK), Kim Rutter (NZ), David Schurz (US), Ernest Shelton (UK), David Williams (UK), Judith Wilson (UK).

EXPEDITION 7I – CREW

Robert Bradley (UK), Jane Broughton (UK), Nicholas Broughton (UK), Tony Flagherty (AU), Kevin Jordan (AU), Shion Scudamore (UK).

EXPEDITION 8A – NEW ZEALAND

Peter Abrutat (UK), Joanna Amos (UK), Robert Andrews (UK), Kaye Angus (UK), Karol Aure (US), David Baker (JE), Warwick Barbarich (NZ), Michael Belcher (NZ), James Bishop (NZ), Stephen Bobak (UK), Peter Boon (UK), Paul Brackley (UK), Jay Brown (US), Nicholas Burne-Cronshaw (UK), Janine Burns (UK), Chris Bushra (US), Jayne Butterworth (UK), Brinnan Carter (UK), David Chambers (UK), Rock Chesterman (NZ), Meng Tze Chia (SG), Stephen Chorley (UK), Andrew Clarke (UK), Peter Cooper (NZ), John Coster (UK), Christopher Coward (US), David Crawford (US), Helen Crow (UK), Steven Crowder (UK), David Croy (UK), Harris Cummings (NZ), Doug Cutter (US), Sidney Davies (AU), John Debond (CA), Jeremy Dennison (UK), Philip Denny (UK), Françoise Desoutter (US), Craig Dryden (NZ), Colin Eady (UK), Helen Egan (UK), Jane Essery (UK), Miles Farnbank (UK), Monica Favre (US), Shirley Fraser (UK), Philip Frykman (US), Alan Garbutt (NZ), Anita Glenn (UK), Katherine Goldberg (UK), Jenny Greenhough (UK), Nigel Gregory (UK), Arthur Griffiths (UK), Alison Hackford (UK), Christopher Heath (US), Sian Hemmings (UK), Louise Higginson (UK), Richard Hinkley (UK), Nicola Howard (UK), Michael Hudson (UK), Sara Humphreys (UK), Steven Hunt (UK), Laila Hyde (UK), Alan James (UK), Kristyna Janus (US), Mike Jones (UK), Belinda Jotham (UK), Kayoko Kawai (JP), Hideto Kawakita (JP), Sandra King (NZ), Joo Kim Koh (SG), Doug Kutz (US), Andre Lapointe (CA), Mark Le Sage (UK), David Leemans (UK), Fiona Lockton (UK), Fred Lulka (US), Adam Lurie (UK), Nancy MacDougall (CA), Douglas Martin (NZ), Youichi Matsui (JP), Kin Mcissac (US), Timothy Mills (UK), Stephen Mitchell (UK), Geoffrey Mulligan (UK), Angus Murray (UK), Andrew Needham (UK), Iain Nichols (UK), David O'Donoghue (NZ), Thomas Olson (US), Simon Pease (NZ), Raquel Pionkowski (US), Alan Pryor (UK), Sally Reese (UK), Louise Regan (UK), Christopher Rhodes (UK), Anthony Riazzi (US), Robert Richards (UK), Alexander Rigg (UK), Sam Rudolph (NZ), Paul Rutter (UK), John Saunders (US), Jonathan Scott (US), Timothy Sedgwick (UK), Steven Seligson (UK), Elizabeth Sewell (UK), Mike Shipman (US), Gary Smith (UK), Greg Smith (US), Kevin Smith (NZ), Jonathan Stevens (UK), Christopher Swindells (UK), Yoko Tagucki (JP), Lesley Tennant (UK), Miki Toda (JP), Hoi Cheung Tong (HK), Takuya Tsukimura (JP), Grant Utteridge (NZ), Stephen van der Voort (NZ), Robert Vince (UK), Sean Waters (NZ), Vanessa Watson (UK), David Webb (UK), C. W. Wehi (NZ), Andrew Wincup (UK), Susan Winstanley (UK), Kathy Wooten (US), Vincent Wright (UK).

EXPEDITION 8A – STAFF

Charles Burton (UK), Matthew Cook (UK), Grant Cour (NZ), T. E. C. De Kock, Kirsty Henderson (UK), Andrew Holt (UK), Ian Lattimore (NZ), Chee Ching Liew (SG), Raymond Luxford (UK), Cathy McDonald (US), Norman McPherson (NZ), Richard Pickrill (NZ), Christopher Sainsbury (UK), Basil Stanton (NZ), Robert Stephenson (UK), John Stewart (UK), Lynda Thompson (UK), Alexander Urban (AU).

EXPEDITION 8B – NEW ZEALAND

Armando Alvarez (CL), Graeme Arthur (NZ), Tony Bain (NZ), Timothy Ballantyne (NZ), Martin Barker (UK), Karen Barks (US), Catherine Barr (UK), Kerry Baskett (UK), Lynn Beasley (UK), Laurie Bertanyi (UK), David Blevins (UK), Christopher Bohnenn (NZ), Richard Boughey (UK), Steven Bradshaw (UK), Daryl Brainard (US), Catherine Broom (NZ), Brian Cairns (UK), Catherine Campbell (UK), Christine Campbell (NZ), Patrick Carberry (UK), John Carr (UK), Roy Castle (UK), Yuen-Wai Cham (UK), Tim Chiswell (NZ), Ying Chong (SG), Billy Cockerton (UK), Stephen Constance (UK), Jennifer Cossey (UK), Justin Crowther (UK), Andrew Cudby (NZ), Nicholas Curtis (UK), Andrew Cutler (NZ), Mark Dinsdale (NZ), Craig Downey (NZ), Paul Dragicevich (NZ), Claire Drummond (UK), Robert Drummond (UK), Wayne Eastwood (UK), Simon Ellis (UK), Michael Evans (NZ), Lionel Fairweather (UK), Marco Fisauli (IT), Caleb Foale (NZ), Christina Folger (US), Nicholas Forsyth (UK), Ruth Frean (UK), Gordon Friend (UK), Janet Goddard (UK), Annabel Gossett (NZ), Richard Gough (UK), Michael Gree (NZ), Alison Gregory (UK), Diane Griffiths (UK), Steven Hampshire (UK), Deborah Harcourt (NZ), Darren Hargreaves (NZ), Kristin Harlen (NZ), Mark Heitchue (US), Patricia Hewlett (NZ), Daniel Hoggarth (UK), Dennis Horsley (UK), Jacqueline Hulse (UK), Stephanie Hunter (NZ), Kouji Ida (JP), Yasuko Iwasaki (JP), Ned Jackson (CA), Warwick Jacobs (UK), Susan Jobling (UK), Carol Joss (UK), Leigh Joyce (NZ), Michael Keefe (US), Roy Keegan (UK), Judith Kerr (UK), Yukiko Kohri (JP), Angela Kydd (UK), Michael Lew (NZ), Alison Lindores (NZ), Timothy Lynch (NZ), Catriona McBean (NZ), Aron McKirron (NZ), Serena McQuade (UK), Andrew Marfell (NZ), Janine Martin (NZ), Claire Mooney (UK), John Morris (UK), Karyn Mulligan (NZ), Michael Murray (UK), Andrew Nekeare (NZ), Michael Nepia (NZ), Lai Lei Ng (US), Paul Oginsky (UK), David Orr (UK), John Osborne (UK), Karen Pascarella (US), Terry Payne (UK), Victoria Poole (UK), Colin Powell (UK), Kiersten Price (NZ), Tracy Puckett (US), Eric Ratcliff (US), Evan Reece (NZ), Paul Richard (CA), Guy Richenbach (UK), Diana Robertson (NZ), Paul Rogers (UK), Paul Rollin (NZ), Masataka Sakane (JP), Jacqueline Savage (NZ), Steven Scott (UK), Andrew Selman (UK), Dave Shea (UK), Naomi Shindle (UK), Kiran Sigmon (US), Michael Simpson (UK), Bernardo Soto (CL), Diane Spivey (UK), Geoffrey Stewart (NZ), Duncan Stoddart (UK), Tracey Strath (UK), Ralph Stutchbury (AU), Kayori Sugiura (JP), Yoshihisa Suyama (JP), Lorna Swinyard (UK), Aubrey Tai (NZ), Neil Templeton (NZ), Darrell Thomas (NZ), Jefferey Thomas (NZ), Paul Thomas (UK), Teresa Tiler (UK), Michael Tournier (NZ), John Walshe (UK), Joseph Weaver (US), Trevor West (UK), Philip Whiteley (UK), Hamish Wilson (NZ), Peter Wilson (UK), Rodney Wilson (UK), John Windley (UK), Anne Woodley (NZ), Joe Wright (US), Russell York (UK), Deborah Zanders (NZ).

EXPEDITION 8B – STAFF

John Allen (UK), Charles Burton (UK), Jennifer Cox (NZ), Ariadna Foureman (US), Geraldine Goode (UK), Belinda Jotham (UK), John Llewellyn (UK), Norman McPherson (NZ), Diana Parr (NZ), Gaye Sarma (UK), Lynda Thompson (UK), Simon Weston (UK), Nicholas Whittingham (UK).

EXPEDITION 8F – TAC HQ 8

Clive Barrow (UK), Cathy Davies (UK), Hawk Freeman (US), Ian Greene (CA), Jasmina Hilton (UK), Nicholas Horne (UK), Peta Lock (UK), Antony Walton (UK), Marcus Wilkinson (UK).

EXPEDITION 8I – *ZEBU*

Nicholas Birchall (UK), Grant Carr (NZ), Henrietta Cotterell (UK), Angus Ferguson (AU), Norm Garshowitz (CA), Jeremy Goodchild (UK), Helen Harrison (UK), Marty Hultgren (US), Monica Jain (US), Brian Lewton (UK), Matteo Malvani (IT), Livia Monami (IT), Kevin Spreng (US), Rachel West (UK), Simon Wheelans (NZ), Philippa Whitelaw (UK).

EXPEDITION 8I – CREW

Robert Bradley (UK), Jane Broughton (UK), Nicholas Broughton (UK), Tony Flagherty (AU), Kevin Jordan (AU), Peter Masters (UK), Shion Scudamore (UK).

EXPEDITION 9A – AUSTRALIA

Grant Adams (AU), Said Shateet Said Al-Musalmy (OM), Saleh Ahmed Al-Rawahy (OM), Abdullah Mohammed I Al-Riamy (OM), Abdul Al-Gader Al-Zedjaly (OM), Brian Aldridge (UK), Tracey Baker (UK), Linda Barlow (UK), Jean Barrow (UK), Anthony Barton (UK), James Brotherton (UK), James Bunce (UK), Chris Burns (US), Carlo Cavaciuti (UK), Priscilla Cedras (UK), Angela Chidlow (UK), Ian Cole (UK), Stewart Conway (UK), Stephen Crawford (UK), Keith Dobson (UK), Helen Drake (UK), Carol Duckworth (UK), Kurt Eggers (US), David Ellingham (UK), Timothy Fairbairn (UK), Malcolm Field (UK), Julie Fields (UK), Jennifer Galloway (UK), Anne Gate (UK), Helena Hartley (UK), Charlotte Hopkins (UK), Paul Howman (UK), Mark Humphreys (UK), Jacqueline Irvin (UK), Catherine Jacks (UK), Wanda Jarnecki (UK), Andrew Jones (UK), Stephen Hose (UK), Christine Joyce (UK), Tom Kilian (US), Tracy King (UK), Martin Kirke (UK), Elizabeth Knill (UK), Paul Lawless (UK), Gary Lee (UK), Shaun Lodge (UK), Curtis Lonie (US), Jonathan Lucas (UK), Fiona McBurney (UK), Dewey McTee (US), Andrea Martin (UK), Andrew Mather (UK), Alan Mezzetti (UK), Donna Minto (UK), Tracy Morton (UK), Kevin Murray (UK), Andrew Nelmes (UK), Lee Norman (UK), Paul Nugent (UK), Patricia Ortenzi (UK), Sarah Pain (UK), Simon Patton (UK), Ian Pickavance (UK), Melvyn Pickering (UK), Ruth Polhill (UK), James Redgate (UK), David Roach (UK), Graham Roberts (UK), Terence Russett (UK), Andrew Scaife (UK), Ted Schreiber (US), Stephen Shea (UK), Martin Simpson (UK), Peter Skeen (UK), Daniel Smith (CA), Kent Southard (US), Helen Stinson (UK), Matthew Taylor (UK), Brian Thorogood (UK), David Tibbles (UK), Brian Waldron (UK), Adrian Walsh (UK), Kim Walton (UK), Charles Whattoff (UK), Emma Williamson (UK).

EXPEDITION 9A – STAFF

John Allen (UK), Lorna Black (UK), Gary Byington (US), David Caesar (AU), Murray Coward (AU), Keith Crowley (UK), Cathy Davies (UK), Liam Egan (AU), James Galloway (US), Ian Greene (CA), Arthur Hill (US), Charles Ikins (US), Russell Jago (AU), Greg Melick (AU), Don Moir (AU), Ronnie Oldham (US), Errol Phillips (AU), William Rios (US), Joel Schmiedeke (US), Isobel Smith (UK), Nicholas Snell (UK), Mark Swain (AU), Gordon Taylor (AU), Michael Turkington (US).

185

EXPEDITION 9B - AUSTRALIA

Mohamed Ali Essa Al Mashani (OM), Khalifa Said Rashid Al Nassir (OM), Matthew Anthoine (UK), Ian Armstrong (UK), Saleem Atcha (UK), Janette Ayrton (UK), Helen Barton (UK), Jason Bateson (UK), Richard Bedder (UK), Karen Bennett (UK), Peter Berry (UK), Lisa Bliss (UK), Gaynor Boyd (UK), Mark Bragg (UK), Stephen Briggs (UK), Ian Brown (UK), Paul Browne (UK), Janice Butler (US), Angela Cahill (UK), Susan Capps (UK), Keith Carruthers (UK), Jeremy Connor (UK), Ian Cook (UK), Martin Cook (UK), Paul Cotterill (UK), Mark Dallen (UK), Craig Darby (UK), Robin Davies (UK), Anona Dawson (UK), Nicholas Dayton (UK), Helen Deacon (UK), Sharon Dean (UK), Katherine Dickins (UK), Jane Doran (UK), Calvin Duncan (UK), Iain Dunnett (UK), Simon Edwards (UK), Dalton Exley (UK), Graham Feather (UK), Leigh Fielding (UK), Mark Fisher (UK), Anne Fitzgerald (US), Michael Forward (UK), Paul Fraser (UK), Mary French (UK), Kohhi Fujiwara (JP), Antonio Galanti (IT), Andrew Garcia (UK), Dorianne Gould (US), William Gupton (US), Clare Hacker (UK), Steven Heron (UK), Crawford Hill (UK), Elizabeth Hodges (US), Colin Howley (UK), Judith Hurrell (UK), Lotte Irwin (UK), Timothy Johnson (UK), Toshimasa Kanada (JP), John Karnath (US), Yasmin Kassam (UK), Paul Kingscote (UK), Helen Kingston (UK), Misa Kishi (JP), Pauline Kitson (UK), Paul Kvinta (US), Richard Lawrence (UK), Russell Layton (UK), Diana Leighton (UK), Ian Lowe (UK), Michael McGrady (UK), Christopher McKenzie (UK), Andrew McLeod (UK), James McManus (UK), Morag McRoberts (UK), Claire Martin (UK), Richard Maryon (UK), Richard Mason (UK), Christopher Mayo (UK), Stephanie Meadows (UK), Thomas Meadows (UK), Antony Mellor (UK), Karen Morris (UK), Annette Mosgovoy (US), John Nabie (UK), Angus Norrish (UK), David Owen (UK), Andrew Paine (UK), Tony Parkings (UK), Julia Pearson (UK), Donald Peel (UK), Ben Penaliggon (UK), Suzanne Perris (UK), Anthony Pink (UK), Timothy Plunkett (UK), Colin Price (UK), Julie Proctor (UK), Jonathan Ridley (UK), Christopher Riley (UK), Simon Roberts (UK), David Rowbotham (CA), Rebecca Seddon (UK), Andrew Shaw (UK), Andrew Slater (UK), Marc Slater (UK), Adrian Smith (UK), Alexander Smith (UK), Mark Smith (UK), Gregg Sparks (UK), Andrew Sprod (UK), Melanie Stanton (UK), James Stretch (UK), Yumi Sunako (JP), Andrew Sutherland (US), Shinya Tago (JP), Yoshitaka Takada (JP), Kevin Taylor (UK), Simone Taylor (UK), Andrew Thompson (UK), Kevan Trott (UK), Sarah Turner (UK), Paul Tyson (UK), Jeannie Van Der Weyden (UK), Marcello Vento (IT), Lynne Waite (UK), Errol Walters (UK), Paul Webster (UK), James Weddell (UK), Duane Whitcombe (US), Shane White (UK), Paul Williams (UK), Leigh Wilshaw (UK), Mark Wilson (UK), Elizabeth Wright (UK), Philip Wroth (UK), Lesley Youlton (UK), Frank Yue (US).

EXPEDITION 9B - STAFF

Bridget Barrowclough (UK), Janet Bell (UK), Lorna Black (UK), Ray Brodie (AU), Daryl Cobb (AU), Cathy Davies (UK), Kurt Eggers (US), Anne Goodlad (UK), Charles Graf (US), Peter Gray (UK), Neil Hampson (AU), Jacqui Handley (AU), Douglas Harvey (US), Rosemary Hesp (AU), Wayne Leach (AU), Dewey McTee (US), Jim McVinna (AU), Johnny Matlock (US), Annette Merchant (US), Robert Milks (US), Gillian Newlove (UK), Douglas Nurse (UK), Teresa O'Brien (UK), Trevor Osborne (AU), Tony Pardy (AU), Ian Pickavance (UK), Diana Reinbach (UK), Diane Rosenthal (US), James Selby (UK), Bob Wicks (AU).

EXPEDITION 9F - TAC HQ 9

Clive Barrow (UK), Charles Daniel (UK), Jimmy Hazelwood (US), Antony Walton (UK), Marcus Wilkinson (UK).

EXPEDITION 9I - *ZEBU*

Michael Anderson (UK), Rose Armitage (UK), Veronika Arndt (NZ), Steven Davies (UK), Doug Draund (CA), Derek Farr (UK), Kay Fraser (UK), Becky Johnson (US), Simon Robinson (JE), Suzanna

Sherburn (UK), Catherine Stevenson (NZ), Hitoshi Tojima (JP), Ruston Toms (UK), Leonard Townsley (UK), Jeremy Trotter (US), Miwa Watanabe (JP).

EXPEDITION 9I – CREW

Jane Broughton (UK), Nicholas Broughton (UK), Tony Flagherty (AU), Kevin Jordan (AU), Peter Masters (UK), Shion Scudamore (UK).

EXPEDITION 10A – JAPAN

David Barnett (UK), Katharine Birch (UK), Judith Brown (UK), Kevin Brown (UK), Paul Capper (UK), Jillian Collim (UK), Nigel Cox (UK), Peter Doyle (UK), David Fooks (UK), Pochun Fung (HK), Susan Gibson (UK), Felicity Greenland (UK), Douglas Hacking (UK), Simon Hutchinson (UK), Yoke Wai Lee (SG), Michael Long (UK), Allan McFarland (UK), Michael O'Brien (NZ), Kathryn Paine (UK), Kelvin Powell (NZ), Euen Rellie (UK), Mark Roberts (UK), Iain Robertson (UK), George Sargent (US), James Stephenson (UK), Kevin Wilson (UK), Robert Wyatt (AU), Derek Young (US).

EXPEDITION 10A – STAFF

Evelyn Newbury (UK), Michael Shrew (US), Antony Walton (UK).

EXPEDITION 10B – JAPAN

Caroline Ashworth (UK), Sandra Baker (UK), Desmond Barry (NZ), David Briggs (UK), Karen Dickinson (UK), Louise Fothergill (UK), Robert Freeman (UK), Ben Gibson (UK), Geoffrey Godfrey (UK), John Gonzales (US), Allyson Gore (US), Dale Herndon (US), Annie Hlava (UK), Marc Jardine (UK), Julia Kimber (UK), Andrew Letcher (UK), Rognvald Livingstone (UK), Sandra Longman (UK), Fernando Lundy (BS), Christina Luraschi (UK), Roseann Marindin (UK), Simon O'Brien (UK), Sarah Pook (UK), Jason Rae (AU), Claudia Rebanks (CA), Janice Ross (UK), Joseph Schultz (US), Richard Singleton (US), Timothy Sweeting (UK), Joanne Thomas (UK), James Tomlinson (UK), John Warr (UK), Tracy Young (CA).

EXPEDITION 10B – STAFF

Donald George (US), William Young (UK).

EXPEDITION 10C – JAPAN

Anja Ball (UK), Andre Barham (UK), Wendy Brunold (UK), Jayne Budgen (UK), Kate Burford (AU), Danilo Capellini (IT), Jacqueline Catterall (UK), Margaret Chapman (UK), Nicholas Corbin (UK), Anna D'Imporzano (IT), Jeremy Daniels (UK), Simon Davies (UK), Kevin Fee (NZ), Eleanor Gray (UK), Sara Hartley (UK), Peter Heifetz (US), Claire Hodkinson (UK), Russell King (UK), Kathryn Lavender (UK), Catherine Lewis (UK), Sandra Middleton-Jones (UK), Adam Overfield (UK), John Pachuta (US), Judith Prowse (UK), Keith Ray (UK), Charles Reickhoff (US), Becky Rohrer (US), Philippa Rowley (UK), Jennifer Samways (UK), Elizabeth Scott-Park (UK), Mark Smith (UK), Par Anders Frederik Sorme (US), Fiona Stothard (UK), Simon Taylor (UK), Fritz Vogel (NZ), Joseph Whitty (CA).

EXPEDITION 10C – STAFF

Duncan Brown (UK), Wendy Gray (NZ), Anthony Le Voguer (UK), Earl Miyamoto (US).

EXPEDITION 10D - MALAYSIA

Razali Ahmad (MY), Mohammed Abdullah Al Habsy (OM), Hamoud Ali Hamoud Al Hashmi (OM), Jimmy Ambun (MY), Momoi Ambun (MY), Michael Arndt (CA), Helen Austin (UK), Andrew Baker (UK), Lynn Barlow (UK), Philip Barlow (UK), Jane Bayes (UK), James Biggins (UK), Caitlin Bodrugan (UK), Stephanie Bolukun (MY), Guido Bonvicini (IT), Mark Bousfield (AU), Bertille Boyou (MY), Nuala Bryce (UK), Moira Cameron (UK), Andrew Campbell (UK), Giulia Casamento (IT), Choong Kooi Chee (MY), N. G. Chee Guan (MY), Poh Lye Ch'ng (MY), Hoon Sua Chua (MY), Shane Clugston (AU), Tamsin Constable (UK), Andrew Cranston (UK), Roger Cutting (UK), Julie Dale (UK), Annabelle Dawson (UK), Tracy Denton (UK), Kee Aun Diong (MY), Stephen Dunsire (UK), David Eastland (UK), Joanne Elliott (UK), Kay Farley (UK), Ludovico Filotto (IT), Pamela Fletcher (MY), Anthony Fontes (UK), Michael Franklin (UK), Yvonne Frayling (UK), Charles Friel (US), Claudius George (MY), Mark Grant (UK), Caroline Grayling (UK), Patricia Griffiths (UK), Linda Hart (UK), Mark Henstridge (UK), Michael Hewitt (UK), Richard Holmes (UK), Paul Howell (UK), Sallyann Hunter (UK), Arjunaidi Idrus H. J. Yunus (MY), Kyota Iijima (JP), Jane Illingworth (UK), Louise Ingham (UK), Alice Ingram (US), Phillip Jennings (UK), Firoz Jivanjee (KE), Neil Jones (UK), Judith Karpfinger (US), Anthony King (UK), Analisa Koeman (AU), Min Fung Meussa Kong (MY), Donna Langley (UK), Francis Lanog (MY), Neal Ledger (UK), Cosmos Leparleru (KE), Rebecca Lewis (UK), Sunil Mohan Limbachia (UK), Wei Ling Lum (MY), Satha Sevam Manickam (MY), Robert Marriage (UK), William Masudal (MY), Stephanie Maxwell (UK), Shanandor Miles (MY), Harshad Mistry (UK), Patricia Mobilik (MY), David Mogg (UK), Fredoline Mojikon (MY), Anita Myers (UK), Thiaharajan Nalliah (MY), Pounggin Rombiong Nelson (MY), Gretchen O'Neil (US), Stephen Osborne (UK), Shamsaddin Osman (MY), Brian Payst (US), Catherine Pelly (UK), Francesco Picciotto (IT), Kai Yuen Poon (MY), Ragunanthanan (MY), Andrew Reid (UK), Andrea Risk (CA), Gary Roebuck (UK), Michael Roulston (UK), Helen Rowlands (UK), Sophia Russell (UK), Lorraine St Leger (UK), Frances Salter (UK), Mark Seaman (UK), Andrea Sessa (IT), Andrew Shaw (UK), Kensuke Shimura (JP), Deborah Skerrett (UK), Douglas Smart (UK), Richard Smith (UK), Patrick Staves (US), Piergiorgio Stoppa (IT), Rozlan Bin Sulaiman (MY), Rohan Talalla (MY), Philip Tan (MY), Andrew Tate (UK), Jeffrie Teh (MY), Chandran Thiagarajan (MY), Todd Thorner (US), Peter Thorner (US), Graeme Tiffany (UK), Andrew Toffolo (UK), Moira Town (UK), Bernhard Tute (UK), Nicholas Tutty (UK), Daniel Ward (UK), Lucy Webber (UK), Elaine Welsh (UK), Kathryn White (UK), John Wilkinson (UK), Desmond Wilmott (UK), Po Sang Wong (UK), Royd Wooldridge (AU), George Wright (UK).

EXPEDITION 10D - STAFF

Iskandar Abdul Rashid (MY), Anthony Agar (UK), Joanna Baker (UK), Belinda Baldock (UK), Joseph Bales (CA), Ania Maria Ball (UK), Sulaiman bin Yusuf (MY), Claire Birch (UK), Maureen Bird (UK), Alex Brydon (UK), Josephine Camus (UK), George Chesney (UK), Edward Childs (UK), Keok Chee Chin (MY), Anne Colquhoun (UK), Graham Davidson (UK), Christian De Souza (UK), Kathleen Evans (UK), Colin Fitzpatrick (UK), Ian Furness (UK), Elizabeth Gimmler (UK), Rajo Gurung (NP), David Hammond (UK), Tony Hayward (UK), Simon Headington (UK), Steven Hind (UK), Ley Kenyon (UK), Ashley Kirk-Spriggs (UK), Katherine Lawrence (UK), Chian Der Liang (MY), Narendraprasad Limbu (NP), James Loader-Oliver (UK), James Lockyer (UK), Andy Marsh (UK), Jill Myers (UK), Sara Oxley (UK), Pius Anthony Pillai (MY), Alistair Pim (UK), Choo Liang Quek (MY), Neil Roberts (UK), David Robinson (UK), David Scott (UK), Mark Shelford (UK), Brian Sichel (UK), Elizabeth Slowe (UK), Rebecca Tan (UK), Nick Thompson (UK), Kevin Tuck (UK), Anne Vernon (UK), Rebecca Vincent (UK), Maureen Warwick (UK), Alan Weight (UK), Dina Wheatcroft (UK), John Woods (UK), Yoga (MY), Nigel Zega (UK).

EXPEDITION 10E – AUSTRALIA

Nadeen Akhtar (UK), Gavin Alexander (UK), Max Arguile (UK), Katherine Aston (UK), Anne-Marie Babych (UK), Amanda Bailey (UK), Amanda Baker (UK), Jayne Barnsley (UK), Paramjit Kaur Bhogal (UK), Elizabeth Bird (UK), Stuart Bolton (UK), David Bournes (UK), Desmond Brumley (UK), Matthew Burke (US), Andrew Burton (UK), Warwick Butterfield (UK), Patrick Carey (UK), Elizabeth Clarke (UK), John Clarke (UK), Owen Clarke (UK), Philip Coates, Yvonne Cook (UK), Robert Deans (UK), Mark Denison (UK), Tejinder Dhingra (UK), Jonathan Dickinson (UK), John Dixon (UK), Andrew Dobson (UK), Nicholas Doherty (UK), Catherine Evans (UK), Tamsyn Everett (UK), Charles Forbes (UK), Simon Gaywood (UK), Sarah Gibson (UK), Kendra Gittus (UK), Jonathan Glassock (UK), Sula Gleeson (UK), Michela Gobourne (UK), Andrew Golding (UK), Christopher Hanson (UK), Beverley Haughton (UK), Clive Hayward (UK), Mark Herald (UK), Emily Hill (UK), Selvin Honeyghan (UK), Esme Hope (UK), Mandy Hope (UK), Andrea Jackson (UK), Elizabeth Johns (UK), Peter Johnston (UK), David Jones (UK), Eliot Jones (UK), Gary Jones (UK), James Kaighin (UK), Mohammed Mushtaq Kazi (UK), Lara Kellett-Smith (UK), Martin Knowles (UK), Clare Langley (UK), Sally Leeson (UK), Chin Hwee Lim (SG), Rachel Litherland (UK), Amanda Livesey (UK), Brian Long (US), Alan Loy (UK), Mark Lunn (BS), Nigel Lyman (UK), Graham McDonald (UK), Ian McLaughlin (UK), Primalyn McLean (UK), Lorna Macaulay (UK), Christopher Mackman (UK), Tahir Mahmood (UK), Paul Main (UK), Sarah Marsh (UK), Leroy Martin (US), Mary Masih (UK), Christopher Maund (UK), Denzil Merchant (UK), Andrew Miller (UK), Evan Mitchell (UK), Paul Moore (UK), Jonathan Moran (UK), Simon Mullins (UK), George Nicholson (BB), Elaine Oliver (UK), Jeanne Phuah (SG), Nigel Pickering (UK), David Postlethwaite (UK), William Prickett (UK), David Prince (UK), Lesley Pulley (UK), Isabel Rawlence (UK), Margaret Read (UK), Jennifer Reynolds (UK), Chris Riley (UK), John Ruppert (US), Thomas Ruppert (US), Robert Sanderson (UK), Neville Searchwell (UK), Adrian Sellgren (UK), Brian Seymour (UK), David Shaw (US), Douglas Shepherd (CA), Stewart Shirey (US), Richard Sibthorpe (UK), Charles Smith (UK), Michelle Smith (UK), Rachel Stables (UK), Catherine Stickler (US), John Suthers (UK), Ian Thomason (UK), Suet Ying Tsang (HK), Catherine Tyler (UK), Philip Tyson (UK), Derek Ward (UK), Julia Ward (UK), Natalie Ward (UK), Lee Wildman (UK), Yat-Chai Wong (HK), Anne Wright (UK).

EXPEDITION 10E – STAFF

John Allen (UK), Michael Ayress (UK), Anthony Barlow (US), Clive Barrow (UK), Andrew Border (AU), Gabi Bushell (UK), John Courtenay (AU), Charles Daniel (UK), Cathy Davies (UK), Juanita Dixon (US), Julia Durbin (UK), David Fell (AU), Jim Fitzgerald (AU), Andrew Garside (AU), John Geerlings (US), Mark Geyle (AU), Habiba Gitay (UK), Hank Godthelp (AU), Jerome Goodman (US), Thomas Higgs (UK), Jasmina Hilton (UK), Valerie Hunt (UK), Karen Jones (AU), Patrick Langan (UK), Susan Lloyd (UK), Ron Mallett (AU), Eric Niemi (US), Melody Nixon (AU), Penny Pepper (UK), Sean Reece (BB), Beatrice Retchford (AU), Mike Rowlands (AU), George Scaio (AU), Janette Strafford (UK), Paula Urschel (US), Exequiel Varias (US), Grant Walsh (AU), Paul Willis (AU), Sarah Wright (UK), Glenn Wyatt (US).

EXPEDITION 10I – *ZEBU*

Tim Barley (US), Graham Batten (AU), Roy Broadbent (UK), David Farmer (UK), Mike Filley (US), Christopher Hart (UK), Toshiaki Iizuka (JP), Margaret Jones (US), Stephanie Kirkman (UK), Marisol Kucharek (UK), Roger Le Gros (UK), Brett Meikle (UK), Sarah Muscroft (UK), Gordon Phippen (CA), Mary Scott (UK), Kuniko Yamamoto (JP).

EXPEDITION 10I – CREW

Jane Broughton (UK), Nicholas Broughton (UK), Tony Flagherty (AU), Kevin Jordan (AU), Peter Masters (UK), Shion Scudamore (UK).

189

EXPEDITION 11A - PAKISTAN

Catherine Abbott (AU), Iftikhar Ahmed (PK), Mumtaz Ahmed (PK), Nasser Al Akhzami (OM), Waseem Alee (PK), Zafar Ali (PK), James Allen (UK), Mohammed Amur al Azzri (OM), Ullah Asmat (PK), Caroline Austen (UK), Samantha Baggott (UK), Kathryn Bainbridge (UK), Meryl Batchelder (UK), Anne-Marie Bealing (UK), Anthony Bennett (UK), Catherine Beurle (AU), Emma Birnie (UK), Alan Blatchly (UK), Elizabeth Bragg (UK), Heather Brewster (UK), David Brown (UK), John Bulmer (JE), William Busby (UK), Lucy Carrington (UK), Andrew Christie (NZ), Jonathan Clark (UK), Kerry Clucas (US), Ann Codrington (US), Simon Dawes (UK), Aymar Du Chatenet (FR), David Edwards (US), Yvonne Elston (UK), Helena Flynn (UK), William Fox (UK), Ruth Frazer (UK), Bruno Fritsche (CH), Emma Gale (UK), Alan Giese (US), Joanna Goodburn (UK), Amanda Goodwin (UK), Patricia Gray (UK), Robert Grinsted (UK), Hilary Groom (UK), Eric Gustke (US), Kevin Hagan (UK), Charles Hanemann (US), Philippa Harbottle (UK), Susanna Hillhouse (UK), Raymond Hollingsworth (NZ), John Hoole (UK), Louise Hull (UK), Michael Jackson (UK), Omo Jakahashi (JP), Jose Jarrett (UK), Rehmat Karim (PK), Younis Kayani Suhail (PK), Ahmed Kazi Zulfiqar (PK), Polyanna Kellett (UK), Andrew Kerr (UK), Ahmed Khalid Tauqueer (PK), Basit Khan (PK), Islam Khan Azmat (PK), Ian Knight (UK), Masonori Kumagai (JP), Marie-Josée Le Blanc (CA), Susan Le Cren (NZ), Michael Lynn (US), Fiona McFall (UK), Angus McGrath (US), Fiona McKenzie (UK), Mary McManus (CA), Iqbal Majeed (PK), Doris Malenschek (IT), Parvin Marri (PK), Timothy Mather (UK), Elspeth Matheson (UK), Kristina May (UK), Ayyaz Mehboob Syed (PK), Colin Mew (UK), Helen Moore (UK), Karen Muir (UK), Yukari Murakami (JP), Abbas Naqvi Sarwar (PK), Abbas Naqvi Syed Shabbir (PK), Richard Nealon (UK), Jane Newsome (UK), Christopher Newson (UK), Beatrice Nicholls (UK), Shona Nicholls (UK), Simon Parrish (UK), Alessandra Pavolini (IT), Philip Pearson (UK), Toby Perrin (UK), Barry Porter (UK), Peter Quinlan (US), Stephen Ray (UK), Ian Risk (UK), Ali Rizvi Syed Ashraf (PK), Simon Robins (UK), Darren Rollins (BS), Jani Rollins (US), Kim Rowswell (UK), Ali Shah Syed Shaukat (PK), Nasir Sheikh Mohammad (PK), Akiko Shimura (JP), Nadeem Ahmed Siddiqui (PK), Katherine Skinner (UK), Philip Spencer (UK), David Stevenson (GU), Takeshi Suguwara (JP), Avril Thomson (UK), Lynley Twyman (NZ), Mahfooz Ursani (PK), John Watkins (UK), John Watson (UK), James Williams (US), Jonathan Williamson (US), John Willis (UK), John Winston (UK), Barbara Woodruff (UK), Kenji Yamashita (JP), Timothy Yates (UK), Irfan Zaidi Syed (PK).

EXPEDITION 11A - STAFF

Susie Barker (UK), David Bromhead (UK), Anthony Chadburn (UK), Diana Clarkson (UK), David Collins (UK), Deborah Crawshaw (UK), David Cronk (UK), Fiona Doolan (UK), Claire Godwin-Austen (UK), Rupert Grey (UK), Roberta Howlett (UK), Martin Jones (UK), Andrew Kimmerling (UK), David Mallon (UK), Lewis Owen (UK), Stephen Temperley (UK), Andrew Terry (UK), Mark Woodgate (UK).

EXPEDITION 11I - *ZEBU*

Louise Carling (UK), Jim Edwards (US), Michael Fallon (US), Christina Horvath (CA), Christopher Hutts (US), Vanessa Lane (UK), Rachael McGuin (AU), Simon Molyneux (UK), Masayuki Morita (JP), Alastair Roy (UK), Sue Safford (US), Elizabeth Smyth (UK), Michael Southern (UK), John Tucker (UK), Janet Wardle (UK), Yasuhiko Watanabe (JP).

EXPEDITION 12G - *ZEBU*

Susan Brownie (NZ), Pauline Darragh (UK), Paul Denchfield (UK), Hideo Egashira (JP), David Hepplestone (UK), Stephanie Hughes (CA), Yoshihiko Ichiya (JP), Paula Lynch (UK), Donald McCaughey (US), Paul McIlvenny (UK), Judith Morris (UK), Sonia Oldfield (UK), Frank Parrish (US), Page Ridlehuber (US), Michael Turner (UK), Barbara Vinden (UK).

EXPEDITION 12I – *ZEBU*

Ewen Balfour (UK), Gordon Davis (UK), Frances Dillon (UK), Heidi Jagodzinski (US), Nicola Jolley (UK), Janet McCay (UK), Fiona Martin (UK), Guy Power (UK), Teiko Seki (JP), Michael Sheehan (NZ), Mason Swearingen (US), Eiji Unakami (JP), David Wilson (UK).

EXPEDITIONS 12G, 12I – CREW

Jane Broughton (UK), Nicholas Broughton (UK), Tony Flagherty (AU), Keven Jordan (AU), Peter Masters (UK), Shion Scudamore (UK).

Expeditions 10F & 11E in Indonesia and Expedition 11F Australia will be covered in the third Operation Raleigh book.

IN REMEMBRANCE

Our sympathy and thoughts are extended to the families and friends of the following who lost their lives during an Operation Raleigh expedition or shortly afterwards:

Neil Carmichael (23)
Crew member from Shell on *Sir Walter Raleigh* – lost overboard during the *Pandora* project

Paul Claxton (25)
Staff photographer in Indonesia – killed in an accident on Mount Binaia

Roger Cutting (24)
Venturer on expedition 10D in Malaysia – died in an accident after the expedition.

Christian de Souza (25)
Staff member in Malaysia – died in a road accident

Ronald Guy (24)
Venturer on expedition 7A in Australia – a brain tumour was diagnosed and he died in Australia after the expedition

Alexander Hyndman (76)
Radio officer on *Sir Walter Raleigh* – passed away on holiday after the ship had returned to Hull

Louise Grandfield (26)
Venturer on expedition 1D in Turks and Caicos Islands – died in a road accident on her return home to Australia

INDEX

INDEX

195